Discover the Healing Power of Love

Are you looking for a truly satisfying love relationship? Has your relationship with your partner become less than ideal? Are you unable to express the love you feel to your partner, parents, children, and friends? Are you putting your life on hold because you're single? Discover:

- ▼ How to avoid the "four big mistakes" in love
- ▼ How to tell if you are with the right person, and if not, how to determine what kind of partner would be best for you
- ▼ How to combat "emotional numbness" and rekindle your passion for loving and living
- ▼ How to prevent relationship burnout
- ▼ How to turn the tide of an argument to end up feeling more in love

PLUS: SELF-TESTS, QUIZZES, SCRIPTS FOR SUCCESS, AND STEP-BY-STEP TECHNIQUES FOR MAKING LOVE FLOURISH AND LAST.

"UPBEAT ... INTELLIGENT ... A BACK-TO-BASICS YET UP-TO-DATE SELF-HELP MANUAL THAT ONLY A RECLUSE WOULDN'T PROFIT BY."—*Kirkus Reviews*

Also by Barbara De Angelis

ASK BARBARA
REAL MOMENTS® FOR LOVERS
REAL MOMENTS®
ARE YOU THE ONE FOR ME?
SECRETS ABOUT MEN EVERY WOMAN
SHOULD KNOW

HOW TO MAKE

L ♡ O ♡ V ♡ E

ALL THE TIME

Barbara De Angelis, Ph.D.

A DELL BOOK

Published by
Dell Publishing
a division of
Bantam Doubleday Dell Publishing Group, Inc.
1540 Broadway
New York, New York 10036

The names and circumstances of clients and other identifying characteristics in case histories have been changed to protect their privacy.

Portions of the material in Chapter 8, "The Duplication Technique"; Chapter 9, "The Love Letter Technique"; and Chapter 10, "The Power Process," are based on a teaching manual developed by Dr. John Gray and Barbara De Angelis, Ph.D., in 1982 for the Los Angeles Personal Growth Center.

ISBN: 0-440-20893-9

Printed in the United States of America

Published simultaneously in Canada

February 1991

20   19   18   17   16   15   14   13   12

OPM

I dedicate this book to the thousands of men and women who have attended my MAKING LOVE WORK seminars.

It is because of the examples you have set by healing your relationships with your husbands and wives, your children and parents, and by your willingness to make love work, that I wrote this book, in hopes that it will serve as an inspiration to others.

CONTENTS

► PART TWO ◄

Emotional First Aid— Practical Solutions for Resolving Conflict

► PART THREE ◄

Secrets About Sex

ACKNOWLEDGMENTS

I feel deeply grateful to many people who, throughout my life, have given me the love and support I needed to help make my own dreams come true:

To my family:

My father, Sidney De Angelis, for planting the seed of talent inside me and for always leading me to believe I could do and be anything I wanted;

My mother, Phyllis Garshman, for teaching me about love and the courage to start over again;

My brother, Michael, and my stepfather, Daniel Garshman, for their patience and caring;

My grandmother Esther De Angelis, for giving me my independent spirit and for always being there to help;

The memory of my grandparents David and Lillian Brunstein, for love and memories that will never die.

To the many wonderful teachers in my life:

Dr. Lawrence Rosenfeld, for starting me on my journey into the heart while I was at the University of Wisconsin;

Sondra Ray, for demonstrating the healing power of a woman and teaching me about telling the truth;

Ron Scolastico, for showing me a vision of what I am here for;

Mrs. Marie Hildebrand Bintner, for expecting excellence from me in Cheltenham High School and teaching me to expect it from myself;

Mr. Joseph Simms, for demanding that I speak and write with style and for influencing me to become a teacher by exemplifying one so delightfully;

And Mrs. Pearl Weiss, for seeing the talent and passion in an eleven-year-old girl and, through her warmth and sensitivity, encouraging me to write.

To my literary agent, Harvey Klinger, for making it all so easy and making me feel so special from the beginning.

I am also deeply grateful to the following people in Los Angeles:

Donald Marrs, for his help and guidance;

Larry Weitzman and Chuck Hurwitz, my attorneys, for seeing me through the rough times and always taking good care of me;

Karl Fleming, for caring enough to teach me and being humble enough to learn from me;

Peter Starr, for his generous support;

Wally Shirwin at KABC, for taking a chance on me;

Dr. Harold Bloomfield and Jack Canfield, for being my friends and wonderful role models;

Michael Levins and Ron Temkin, for sticking by me when I needed it the most;

Everyone from Monday Night Group, for the constant revelations and total trust.

HOW TO MAKE

L O V E

ALL THE TIME

Introduction: What This Book Will Reveal to You

Imagine yourself in the middle of making love with someone you love very much. As you lie there in each other's arms, you feel safe, warm, and totally alive, filled with a luxurious sense of certainty and confidence. You are in the right place. You are doing the right thing. You are with the right person. There is no distance between you, only one heart beating in two bodies. You are in love with your partner. You are in love with yourself. You are in love with life.

Making love is probably the greatest high you can experience with another human being. When you make love, the sense of separation between yourself and the other person dissolves, and what you experience is beyond pleasure, beyond closeness. It is the experience of oneness. Suddenly the universe makes sense. Suddenly you understand what you are doing here on this planet. Suddenly it all seems so simple.

This is what making love is all about. And it is in hopes of experiencing even a few moments of this magical state that you dream of finding your true love. The world encourages your dream with films, books, television shows, magazine articles, and advertisements, all with the same message: Life is about making love and about having lovemaking be spectacular, perfect, and unforgettable.

But there is another side of the dream: the rejection of reaching out for that person in bed and having him or her turn away; the frustration of being too busy to find the time to spend with each other; the fear of not knowing what's going on inside your lover; the pain of the shutting down and the turning off; the lying, the letting down, the leaving.

Your dream of love doesn't have to turn into a nightmare. This book is written to teach you how to make love all the time and to keep that magic of love alive. This is not just a book about sex. It is a book about mastering that quality which turns sex into making love, pleasure into ecstasy, and partnership into union. It will show you how to create that emotional high which you usually associate with sex even when you aren't having sex.

Making love can be more than an isolated act. It can be a quality of experience day by day, minute by minute, whether you are in a special relationship or not! This book will take you on an exciting journey to discover the mysteries and secrets of love. With the things you learn, I know you will be closer to making your own special dreams come true.

PART ONE

▼▼▼▼▼▼▼▼▼▼▼▼▼▼▼▼▼▼▼▼▼▼▼▼▼▼▼▼▼▼▼▼

Secrets for Making Love Work

▲▲▲▲▲▲▲▲▲▲▲▲▲▲▲▲▲▲▲▲▲▲▲▲▲▲▲▲▲▲▲▲

1 Making Love First

▶ It's Easy to Fall in Love, But . . .

The bride gazes at the groom as they stand in the chapel. "This is the most wonderful moment of my life," she thinks. "Alan is everything I've always wanted: charming, intelligent, sensitive, sexy, strong but not overbearing. All my dreams are finally coming true. Why do people say that being married is so difficult? They must have married the wrong person. I know I found the right one!"

The groom stares with pride at his glowing bride. "Janet's beautiful," he thinks to himself. "And I really feel she understands me and believes in me. It's what I've always wanted in a woman. I just can't understand all those stories about men feeling tied down and nagged when they get married. I never could feel that way about Janet. She's different."

Janet's parents sit in the front row. Janet's mother cries tears of joy. Or is there something else mixed in?

3

Perhaps Janet's mother is remembering her own wedding day, recalling that she, too, once had that radiant look. "Oh, God," she prays silently, "don't let it slip away from Janet and Alan as it did for me and my husband." Yes, some of those tears are tears of sadness, a sadness that comes from recognizing something special between two people that you once felt with a partner, and realizing that it's no longer there and that it has been gone for a long time.

At the other side of the church sit Alan's parents. But they aren't sitting together. They have been divorced for eight years. Their eyes, too, are full of tears, remembering hopes and dreams they had had on their wedding day: dreams that died over the years. They pray that their children will beat the odds and stay together; that somehow they will make their love work.

▶ Your Odds of Finding Happiness

This story could be your story, your parents' story, or a friend's story. Or perhaps you're worried that one day in the future, it will *become* your story. Well, you have good reason to worry. Approximately one out of every two marriages in the United States ends in divorce. Out of the couples who do remain married, it's certain that a good number are no longer in love, or happy together, despite the fact that they aren't divorced.

It is easy to fall in love. But it's a lot harder to *stay* in love. We all want love to work. No one plans to fall out of love. But it happens. And when it happens, it hurts.

I'll never forget the moment when I realized that I was falling out of love with my now ex-husband. It was probably the most painful and tragic moment of my life. That magical chemistry that had allowed me to see him as special and wonderful had disappeared. "Oh, my God," I thought to myself, "this can't be happen-

ing. Not to me. Not to *us*. Let it be just a mood I'm in.
Maybe I'm just tired and need a vacation."

But as the weeks and months wore on, the symptoms were unmistakable, and the diagnosis was clear: I
was in a dying relationship. And as I sat leafing through
my wedding album with hot tears rolling down my face,
gazing at the pictures of my perfect wedding day, I felt
defeated, afraid, and alone. Deep in my heart, one
question repeated itself over and over again: Where did
the love go? Where did the love go?

▶ Where Does the Love Go?

Think back to a time in your life when you had just
fallen in love with someone. (Choose someone with
whom you are no longer in love.) It seemed so easy to
love the other person, didn't it? Your lover's faults
seemed "cute." So what if he didn't always express
how he felt—it showed what a deep thinker he was. So
what if she kept you waiting for an hour while she
dressed—it showed she really cared about how she
looked. Remember how proud you were to be seen
with your partner, and how eager you were to tell
everyone about him? And sex . . . well, sex was wonderful! No, you could never get tired of this person.

What happened to that magic? When did "cute"
characteristics suddenly become irritating? How did
excitement and attraction turn into boredom and disinterest? Why did trust and respect turn into hurt and
resentment?

All of these questions really ask the same thing:
Why do we fall out of love? The mind first tells you that
it must have been the other person's fault. He or she
had "changed"! How many times have you thought to
yourself, or heard a friend say, "So-and-so was wonderful when we first met and fell in love. But now he/she's
different."

If you fall in love enough times with people who

"change" on you, your mind moves to the next stage of rationalization: that something is wrong with *you!* After all, you "pick" the wrong people over and over again. Your disappointment and frustration may turn into anger or apathy: "Relationships are a pain in the neck. I'd rather just not get involved. That way I won't get hurt."

You conclude: Love is something magical and mysterious over which you have absolutely no control. You can't trust love to last; you can't trust yourself or your partner to stay in love. And so you go from relationship to relationship hoping that somehow you'll get lucky and love will stay. Or you give up relationships and resolve to live peacefully alone. Or—and this may be the saddest choice of all—you stay in a relationship that is no longer exciting or joyful, hoping that the spark will somehow rekindle itself.

Many psychiatrists and psychologists will tell you that it's natural for a relationship to become "comfortable," and unrealistic to expect to feel intensely in love with your partner after being together for a long time. Accept the loss of romance, some experts advise, and become "companions."

When I hear this advice I become really angry. I am not willing to give up that magic of love in my life. I know it is possible to stay in love and make it work. *Just because so many fail at love doesn't mean that love is meant to fail!*

▶ Staying in Love Is Possible

Each time I have fallen in love in my life, I was elated, but underneath my elation was deep concern, and even fear. Would this love, too, evaporate? As I began working as a therapist and educator, I vowed that I was going to learn to master the art of love and relationships. I was determined to discover the secrets of staying in love—to understand what created that feeling of being "in love," and how to create that feeling every day of my life.

Today, after many years of research, as well as enlightening and often painful personal experience, I feel confident that I can make love work in my life. I am in a wonderful relationship in which the magic has continued to grow. You may be thinking, "Oh, she just got lucky and found the 'right' person." But believe me, our relationship is as fulfilling and exciting as it is because *we have worked to make it that way.*

The secret of staying in love is learning how to make love all the time.

Certainly, this concept is the reason my relationship with my partner is as powerful and passionate as it is. And learning to understand and apply it is the secret that has helped thousands of people in my seminars make love work in their lives again, including couples who have been married for thirty or forty years and have fallen in love all over again.

I know that if you work with the information in this book, you can transform your experience of love, relationships, and sexuality into ever-expanding sources of joy and fulfillment.

▼

SECRET:
> *If you never learn how to use love constructively, then love ends up using you!*

▲

When you don't know how to *use love* consciously to create the results you want, you end up making the same mistakes over and over again.

Imagine sitting down to operate a computer for the first time, when no one has taught you how to use one. After a while, you would probably be frustrated, because the computer wouldn't do what you wanted it to do. So you might say, "This computer is defective—bring me another." No one ever told you it would be difficult to operate a computer, so naturally you assume it must be the computer's fault. You try the second computer, but it doesn't do what you want it to, either. So you go on to a third, and a fourth. After a while, you either conclude that computers are no good, or that you are no good at working with computers. Both conclusions are wrong. The real problem is that you don't know how to use computers constructively.

You can master relationships the same way you would try to master a computer, perfect your game of tennis, or develop any skill. The first thing I teach people in my seminars is:

Until you are aware of what you have been doing, you have no choice but to continue doing it.

I suggest you read the remainder of this book as if you knew nothing about love and sex. I call this "beginner's awareness." Instead of assuming that you are an adult who should be an expert by now, *give yourself permission to know nothing and, therefore, to learn everything.*

► Are You Treating the Symptoms and Ignoring the Disease?

Ashley and Paul came to my seminar as a last resort before going to the divorce lawyer. They had been married for seven years, and the first few years were exciting, loving, and full of growth. Then their relationship seemed to stagnate. They became bored with each other and accumulated deep feelings of resentment and anger. They both felt the other person had let them down, because they weren't fulfilled.

Yet Ashley and Paul decided their relationship was worth saving, so they went on a campaign to fix it. They bought every book they could find on making love work and tried everything the books recommended. When Paul arrived home from work, Ashley would meet him at the door in sexy nightgowns. Paul told Ashley all of his secret sexual fantasies and they tried acting them out. They tried taking separate vacations, and they tried starting new hobbies together. They tried having sex in different positions; they tried having affairs with other partners. Nothing worked, and they ended up right back where they had started, only a lot more frustrated. "We must have a dead relationship," they told me sadly. "We love each other, but we're not *in love* anymore."

A lot of books about relationships will tell you that in order to stay in love you should do what Ashley and Paul tried to do—practice certain activities or behaviors. All of these actions are the possible *effects of already being in love*. But love is more than giving the *appearance* of love. Ashley and Paul had tried to create the *symptoms of being in love*. They weren't feeling the real thing—they were acting *as if* they were feeling it. That is why all their efforts failed.

▶ **The Seven E's of Love**

What are the positive effects of being in a truly healthy relationship, of *really* being in love? I call them the Seven E's.

The Seven E's

1. Energy . . . Truly being in love will energize you physically, mentally, and emotionally.

2. Enthusiasm . . . A healthy relationship creates a healthy and enthusiastic attitude toward life.

3. Excitement and optimism for the future . . . When you are happy and in love today, you look forward to tomorrow with excitement.

4. Esteem and self-confidence . . . A good relationship will support you in feeling high self-esteem.

5. Emotional Generosity . . . When you feel loved, it is easy to share that fullness of heart with those around you, and to become very loving and giving.

6. Ease in being oneself . . . When a relationship is supportive, you will find it easy to be yourself around your partner, your friends, and in all circumstances.

7. Emotional Relaxation . . . When you feel well loved, your whole being relaxes, filling you with a deep sense of peace of heart and mind.

The Seven E's will develop over time in a truly healthy and growing relationship. Yet love thrives only under certain conditions. *In order to stay in love, you must consciously create those conditions necessary for love to grow.* Then you will *naturally* behave in all the ways the books tell you to behave in order to stay in love.

In this book you will learn how to heal your heart and your relationships *on the inside,* not just create the symptoms of love on the outside. You'll learn how Ashley and Paul fell in love all over again and how you can do the same. You'll learn what conditions it takes to make love all the time and how to create them; and what conditions work against making love all the time and how to avoid them.

▶ Sex: The Big Cover-Up

If you think that the biggest problem in your relationships has a lot to do with sex, you are probably wrong. Don't feel too bad, though, because you are not alone. One of the most serious mistakes most people make in their relationships is attempting to isolate a part of the relationship, like sex, from the whole, thinking that when that one part is fixed, the whole relationship will be better. I call this the "cover-up" approach to dealing with problems.

▼

SECRET:
Most sexual problems are just symptoms of problems in other areas. If you try to suppress or hide the weaknesses or problems in your relationship, they will emerge in bed!

▲

Here is how one of my clients described his relationship:

"Everything is very good in my relationship with my wife. We are very close; she is a great companion, a wonderful mother to our children, and extremely intelligent. Things are very smooth in our life, and I think we are pretty happy. But there is one thing I wanted to discuss with you. You see, I'm no longer really turned on to my wife sexually. We still have sex, but it feels like we are just doing it to live up to our expectations of how many times a happily married couple should make love. And it feels pretty mechanical.

"It wasn't always like this. When we first met, we were quite passionate, and I felt very attracted to her. Things are certainly different now, but other than that, we have a wonderful marriage. I came to you because I hoped you could teach me some techniques to enjoy sex again."

My answer to this man was simple and very surprising to him:

"Your real problem lies in your relationship, and not in your bed!" Yes, I could suggest many things to create more excitement in this man's sex life, but they wouldn't work. *Sex is just a mirror of the rest of your relationship.* There is no such thing as a great relationship which just happens to have a big sexual problem.

▶ The Real Source of Lasting Sexual Excitement

As human beings, we are very skilled at fooling ourselves and others when it comes to knowing what we are feeling. But there is one area which you cannot control so easily, and that is your body. If you insist to me that you are not upset about something, and I hook you up to an instrument that measures physiological responses, your body would not lie. It would tell me that you were upset, even if you denied it.

The same thing happens during sex. *Sexual excitement is a natural reaction to certain conditions.* When those conditions are absent or inhibited, so is your natural sexual response. In this way, you're most fortunate: Sex is a great barometer for telling you how well your relationship is working, and when it needs more attention.

I'm not saying that nothing can be done to bring about sexual rejuvenation in a relationship. Some books will tell you that if you aren't turned on by your partner, you should fantasize about someone else while having sex, or try having an affair. These things may work to improve your sex life on a superficial and temporary level. But beware of the great danger in superficial sexual remedies! *As you become more and more dependent on outside stimulation (fantasy, other people, vibrators, etc.) you decrease your natural ability to feel turned on by your partner. You may feel turned on* with *your partner, but not* by *him or her.* Two people who are turned on within themselves, but not by the other person, are two people who are having sex, but not making love.

If you feel you have sexual problems in your relationship, and your sexual functions were normal, healthy, and exciting in the beginning of your relationship with your partner, then your problems most likely have little or nothing to do with sex. They are symptoms of something deeper in the relationship, such as unexpressed anger or disappointment, lack of trust, unresolved conflicts, or fear of failure. By discovering the real problems and working together with your partner to heal them, you will see your sexual "problems" diminish and eventually disappear.

Lisa and Tom were instantly attracted to one another when they met. They were thrilled that they had at last found a relationship with the right sexual chemistry. Lisa and Tom fell madly in love and soon moved in together.

One year later, Lisa and Tom had practically stopped having sex, and neither of them could figure out why. Tom felt frustrated because he had been rejected so many times by Lisa. Lisa felt afraid of Tom, and the more he complained about their nonexistent sex life, the more defensive she became. Lisa and Tom came to me for help because they loved each other very much and were desperate to change their passionless relationship.

The first thing I taught Lisa and Tom was that sex was not their problem, but a symptom of other problems they hadn't dealt with. Then I taught them everything I'll be teaching you in this book, especially how to make love all the time in their relationship, and not wait until they got into bed to do so. Three months later, Lisa and Tom were having sex again and loving it. The passion was back.

Passionate sex is a symptom of a passionate relationship. And a passionate relationship means knowing how to make love with your partner all the time, and not waiting until you get into bed to start.

In this book, I call the conditions that support making love all the time "secrets," because I feel that the knowledge of how to create the right conditions for lasting love *is* hidden from most people. When you read these "secrets," you will find they make so much sense that you may ask yourself, "Why didn't I think of that?" or "It's so simple—I wonder why I never saw it this way before." The truth is usually simple. But these simple truths about how to make love all the time are things we just aren't taught.

▶ Shouldn't You Know How to Love Already?

At this point, you may be thinking to yourself, "But I should already know all of this. I've been around. Shouldn't I know by now how to have a relationship, how to deal with love and sex?" The real question isn't whether you *should* know, but rather, *do* you know how to make love work all the time in your life?

Your pride can get you into all kinds of trouble when it comes to making relationships work, because it whispers things into your ear like, "No one can tell me anything about love," or, "Hey, don't try to tell me there's something I don't know about sex. I'm a great lover. I've never had any complaints." Pride can keep you from wanting to know more. When you stop wanting to know more, you stop growing. And when you stop growing, you stop living.

Think back to how you felt when you bought this book. Did you feel slightly embarrassed? If someone close to you gave you this book to read, did you feel hurt, wondering if he or she was saying that you weren't good enough the way you are?

If you had bought a book titled *How to Manage Your Money* or *How to Remodel Your Home,* you might feel different. In such cases you don't expect yourself to know how to manage your money just because you have it or remodel your bathroom just because you have one. But somehow, you expect that by having a few relationships in your life, you should be an expert at relationships, and you're embarrassed to admit that there is something more you'd like to know or something more you *need* to know.

▶ Who Taught You How to Love?

Stop for a minute and ask yourself these questions:

Who taught you how to drive a car?
Who taught you how to tie your shoelaces?
Who taught you how to read?
Who taught you how to have a relationship and make love work?

You probably can answer the first three questions. But I'll bet you don't have a clear-cut answer to the fourth question: Who taught you how to have a relationship and make love work? Perhaps your answer was "No one taught me." That would be part of the answer. Most likely no one sat you down and explained the secrets of successful relationships, or taught you how to communicate your feelings. Yet, when you were growing up you actually spent hours and hours studying how to have a relationship. Where? Right in your own home. You started when you were born, and your studies continued until you left home. You can think of yourself as having been an apprentice to all of the older members of your family—parents, grandparents, and older siblings.

It is inevitable that, as children, you learn by watching your parents. You learn how to open up *and* how to shut down. You watch your parents lie to one another and to you, and you learn to do the same. You watch your parents hide their feelings, and you learn to hide yours. You learn to imitate what your parents do from the moment your are born. Your mother says "Mama, mama," and when you finally imitate her and say "Mama," you get hugs and kisses and lots of other positive attention. Your father shows you how to take a few steps when you are learning to walk, and when you finally duplicate his step, he scoops you up into the air and says, "That's my boy! I'm so proud of you." The message to a child is clear: Duplicate your parents' behavior, and you will get lots of love.

▶ Do You Want Your Relationship to Be Just Like Your Parents' Relationship?

Most people answer this question with a vehement *no!* Fine. So what are you doing to make sure it doesn't turn out that way? What other input have you actually had regarding love and sex? The answer is, probably none! I find this over and over again in my seminars. Someone will come to me complaining about how awful their parents were and how they never want to turn out like them. Yet when I ask them how they plan to avoid making the same mistakes their parents made, they look at me blankly and have no answer.

Here are some examples of people who, despite themselves, grew up to relate to others just as their parents related to each other. See if you can identify with these three descriptions of childhood written by three of my clients:

PHILIP: "My father was tough and very quiet. He never told us he loved us, or even that he was proud of us. If we made a mistake, he'd give us hell. If we did well, he'd just be quiet. I don't think I ever saw him touch my mother in an affectionate way. I can't imagine them having sex together. Deep inside, I guess I know he loved me, and that he loved her. But he certainly showed it in a strange way.

"Now I am married and I don't know how the hell it happened, but I have a hard time expressing my feelings to my wife, and I hate it. I vowed I would never treat women the way he treated Mom. Yet my wife tells me she can't get through to me, that she doesn't know what I'm feeling. I watch myself, and sometimes I look just like him. I learned from him how not to feel. And part of me hates him for that."

MARILYN: "Mom was always sacrificing for everyone else. No matter what happened, she never got angry or mean. Oh, she cried a lot, but she never actually got mad. All my friends said they wished she was their mom, and I was proud of her. But, looking back, I realize she never really stood up for herself. Even when she knew Dad was cheating on her, and when he finally left, she never said a single bad word about him. When I was growing up, I thought she was an angel, but now I am angry at her for being so weak.

"The problem is, I'm just like her sometimes. I am afraid that if I sound too assertive or angry, men will call me pushy, or leave me. I tell myself over and over not to let myself be dominated by the men I have relationships with. But when push comes to shove, I become sweet, nice Marilyn, just like Mom. I don't like the part of me that is turning out just like her, always trying to be the good little girl."

JUAN: "In my house, no one ever discussed the things that were really going on. To outsiders it looked like we had a perfect family. But in fact, things were horrible. Dad was an alcoholic, but he would never admit it, and no one dared bring up his drinking. My older brother was always fighting with Dad and getting into trouble at school and with the police. But there was an unspoken rule that no one would discuss what was really going on. We lived in a world of lies.

"Now my girlfriend complains that I don't take enough interest in working things out in our relationship. She claims that I act as though nothing is wrong, and I make her feel like she is making something out of nothing. Maybe she's right. Maybe I'm still scared that if I say, 'Hey, there is something wrong here; this doesn't feel good,' I'll get punished and sent to my room, as I was when I was a kid."

If your parents unconsciously taught you certain attitudes about relationships, society sent you still another set of messages. For those of you growing up in the fifties and sixties, you probably came home from school, turned on the TV, and watched the perfect American family in their lovely home. How we all longed for perfect families like that, with parents who always had the right answers and who were always there for us! I frequently work with people in my seminars who have never forgiven their parents for not being like the perfect TV mother and father.

Growing up in the sixties and seventies presented you with a very different role model: the highly glamorized portrayal of the ideal adult life in the form of the swinging single. Happiness was freedom—freedom from commitment, freedom to do whatever one wanted. You were offered these characters as heroes. But who were your heroes of love? Where was a couple you could look to as an example of a real relationship that could inspire you?

▶ The Luxury of Love

Before you start blaming your parents, their parents, and society in general for not teaching you about love, let's gain some historical perspective on the evolution of intimate relationships. To your great-grandparents, and even your grandparents, marriage was more of a business arrangement than a romantic endeavor. A woman married so she would have someone to take care of her; a man married to have someone to bear his children and provide a home for them. Happiness and love were bonuses. Often the task of physical and financial survival took so much time and effort that staying in love, having a good sex life, and developing one's sense of self were all trivial matters compared with making enough money to bring the rest of the family to America or hoping the land would yield enough crops to get through the winter.

Our parents' generation had it a little easier in most cases. But marriage and having children were still considered the only acceptable choices. Only in the past twenty or thirty years have men and women been free to choose whether or not they wanted to have a relationship and/or marry. Widespread use of contraception, changing morality, the emerging role of women as equals in work and relationships—all of these factors influenced the transformation of relationships from an economic necessity and a social and religious obligation to one of *personal choice*.

▶ Your Freedom to Choose

In the 1980s you enter into a relationship not out of necessity or duty, but out of choice. That means that your expectations about what you get back from your relationship are much higher than your parents' expectations were. You seek intangible things from the relationship—things like intimacy, mutual belief systems, balance of power, and support in pursuing your individual sense of self.

Our ancestors were prepared and trained for their roles in marriage: Women were taught how to care for children and make a home; men were taught how to earn a living. But no one trained us in how to create intimacy, how to balance the power between yourself and your partner, or how to communicate openly about sex. Although we now have the freedom to do what we want with our relationships, we don't always have the knowlege we need to do it successfully.

Love Is Up to You

It all comes down to you. You have the freedom to choose whether or not to have a relationship. You also have the freedom to choose to learn how to have a successful relationship. If your relationships don't work the way you want them to, it's your responsibility. You can't blame your parents, your partners, or society for not teaching you. You are the only one with the power to do something about your life. Love is up to you.

▶ How to Tell If Your Relationship Is in Trouble

Allison walked into my office an emotional wreck. As she put it, one day after fifteen "perfect" years of marriage, her husband told her he was leaving her for another woman. "I am devastated," she sobbed. "Everything had been just wonderful. Fifteen perfect years, and then one day he leaves. How could this happen?"

As a relationship counselor I know that everything certainly isn't wonderful in a marriage if one day one partner decides to leave. There *are* warning signs to watch for; signs that indicate your relationship is in trouble.

The problem is that most of us (a) don't know how to recognize the warning signs or (b) ignore the warning signs and do nothing to solve the problems.

I asked Allison some of the questions in the following quiz. After she answered them, it became clear to her that her relationship had been in serious trouble for some time. Allison had made herself into a victim by choosing to ignore the warning signs that her relationship was in trouble.

THE WARNING SIGNS OF A RELATIONSHIP IN TROUBLE

This quiz is designed to help you detect some of the warning signs that may indicate trouble in your relationship. Grade yourself on each question according to *how frequently these statements apply to you.*

Very frequently . . . . 5 points

Often . . . . 3 points

Seldom . . . . 1 point

Never . . . . 0 points

Answer as honestly as you can. You may not like admitting some of this to yourself, but facing it is the first step toward changing it. And remember: *You have a much better chance of staying in love by being aware of the warning signs than you do by ignoring them!*

1. You are critical of your partner, out loud or to yourself.
2. You feel a drive to do things without your partner, a craving for your own space.
3. You find yourself looking at or being attracted to other members of the opposite sex.
4. You avoid having sex or intimacy with your partner; you don't seem to find the time or be in the right mood (headache, tired, etc.).

5. You find yourself unable to forgive certain things your partner has done in the course of the relationship, and still feel angry or upset when you think of these things.

6. You stay home a lot with your partner because neither of you makes plans for social activities out together.

7. You feel a nostalgia for the past, remembering the beginning of your relationship as a happier time, or remembering other relationships prior to this one as being more exciting.

8. You spend most of your free time with friends or activities that do not involve your partner.

9. You do not share your feelings or observations with your partner because you feel he or she won't understand or appreciate your thoughts or feelings.

10. You have some form of addiction that causes you to become numb to your feelings: drinking alcohol, using drugs or tranquilizers, over-eating, etc.

11. You and your partner don't take the initiative to plan or spend romantic time together.

12. If you have children, you and your partner spend most of your time alone together talking about the children. When you are together as a family, you pay more attention to the children than you do to each other.

13. You have a best friend with whom you share important feelings that you don't share with your partner. You feel closer to this person in many ways than you do to your partner, and feel he or she understands you in ways your partner does not.

14. You tune out what your partner says when he

or she talks to you, only half-listening to what he or she is saying.

15. You avoid being alone with your partner by working late at night, bringing work home, or overscheduling yourself so you never seem to have time for each other.

16. You are neglecting your appearance: You are overweight; you pay little attention to dressing in an attractive way for your partner; or you neglect personal hygiene.

17. You criticize your partner to friends or family and complain about the relationship.

18. You compare your partner unfavorably with other people; the others appear more attractive, more witty, more sensitive, etc.

19. You neglect to give compliments and other expressions of appreciation to your partner.

20. You fantasize sexually about other people when you are in or out of bed.

Now total up your points.

0–30 points: *Your relationship is in good shape.* To avoid future problems, work on those areas in which you had a higher score.

30–50 points: *Your relationship is in the beginning stage of difficulty.* You may not notice it yet, but in time, bigger problems will erupt. Sit down with your partner and discuss the areas in which you experienced warning signs. Work together on clearing the issues and becoming closer.

50–70 points: *Pay attention: Your relationship is in trouble.* You are well on the road either to a dead relationship or to a separation. If you want to save your relationship, tell your partner that you need to get help. Find an effective, caring therapist or marriage counselor, take a relationships seminar such as Making Love Work, work with all the tools in this book, and *do it as a team*. You need each other's help if you want your relationship to survive.

70–100 points: *EMERGENCY: Your relationship is in a crisis and needs immediate attention!* You have a chance of saving it, but only if you commit yourself body and soul to making it work. Follow the same instructions for the 50–70 point group, but do it immediately! You cannot afford to wait. You must fight off your own numbness and negativity if you want your relationship to survive. Consider this as much of an emergency as if it were a medical emergency. Only *you* can save this dying relationship.

▶ Solving the Mystery of Love

Remember Allison of the fifteen-year "wonderful" marriage? My advice to her was the same as my advice to you: *Get involved in your relationships*. Don't be a victim of them and don't be mystified by them. *Create* the relationships you want. There are reasons why you get into arguments over nothing with someone, reasons why sexual attraction disappears one day, reasons why someone suddenly gets angry with you, just as there are reasons why the engine of your car suddenly starts to smoke, or reasons why your plant's leaves turn brown.

Making love is an art and a science, just like making a meal or playing an instrument. It takes skill and practice, and daily application of those skills to make it work every day. Like all arts and sciences, making love work all the time will seem like a mystery until you have worked with it long enough to master it. Then it will be second nature.

***Love will remain a mystery until you commit
yourself to solving the mystery and learn to
master the skill of loving.***

If you are open to learning how to make love all the
time in your life, the rewards will be enormous. You
will experience new levels of feeling and trust in *all* of
your relationships, as well as in that one special relationship. You will feel more alive, more energetic, more
creative. You will feel more in love with yourself.

Love is the greatest magic there is. If you can
understand how to make love work *for* you and not
against you, then *you* become a great magician. You
are making love first in your life. And making love
becomes something that happens in every moment, not
just on Saturday night. You are making love all the
time, and what could be more wonderful than that?

2

How to Stop Pushing Love Out of Your Life

▶ **Breaking Out of Your Emotional Prison**

Terry was not my favorite type of client. He was big, mean, and tough. He was the kind of person who comes to my seminars and his attitude says, "You're going to have to prove all this to me." Yet as I watched Terry during the first day of my Making Love Work seminar, I observed that he seemed to be locked in some kind of internal battle with himself.

On Saturday, Terry raised his hand to speak. He walked to the front of the room. "I can't take this anymore," he groaned. "I hate this. I have to get out of here."

I looked at Terry and had an intuitive flash of just what he needed to do. I looked him straight in the eye and said softly, "You're scared, aren't you, Terry?"

The whole room stopped breathing for a moment. They could hardly believe that I was suggesting that this big mean guy was scared, let alone imagine how he would respond.

Suddenly Terry started to shake. "You're right," he whispered. "I am scared. But I don't know of what."

I placed my hand over Terry's heart and answered, "Yes you do, Terry. You're scared of what is inside here." I tapped his chest. "You've held it in for so long, and now all those feelings are starting to come out, and you're scared."

Terry was hardly breathing; his hands were twisting nervously behind his back. Then I noticed something very peculiar. He was clasping each wrist tightly with the other hand. The thought crossed my mind: "He looks like he is handcuffed."

Then it hit me: *Terry was an inmate in his own emotional prison.* He was emotionally handcuffed. I was challenging him to release himself from that emotional prison, and he was scared.

"Do you know you have yourself in handcuffs?" I asked gently, gesturing to his hands' locked position. "You're locked up in your own emotional prison."

I had no idea how remarkably intuitive I had been until Terry's whole face went white. He started to sob. "I just spent nearly ten years in a state penitentiary," he said. "I'm on parole now."

"But you're not a free man, are you, Terry?" I asked. "You're still doing time in that prison inside."

Terry leaned on me as he told all of us how he began misbehaving as a child in order to get attention from his mother. This led eventually to a life of crime. "I never wanted to be a bad boy," he cried over and over again. "I just wanted her to love me." Slowly, Terry's hands behind his back relaxed, until I held one of his hands, and asked him if he thought he had punished himself long enough and if he was willing to come out of his emotional prison. Terry said that he had come to the seminar hoping somehow he could break out of his emotional prison and start to love again. At that moment, everyone saw an unmistakable transformation come over him. The tough exterior melted away, revealing a powerfully loving, sensitive, sweet man. Everyone in the room fell in love with Terry in that moment as he forgave himself.

Are you an inmate in your own emotional prison, living behind thick walls that keep your love from coming out and keep others from coming too close to you? Did you sentence yourself there, thinking you would be safer inside than outside? Deep in your heart, you know that you don't have more love in your life because those walls which protect you from pain also end up keeping out happiness and love.

This chapter will help you understand how you may be pushing love out of your life by hiding behind emotional walls. It will explore how those walls get built and how to break through them so that you can start receiving all the love and support you deserve and have always dreamed of.

▶ Are You Pushing Love Out of Your Life?

Stop and think for a minute . . . Does the title of this chapter sound crazy to you: "How to Stop Pushing Love Out of Your Life"? Perhaps a part of you thinks, "You've got to be kidding. I bought this book because I want more love. The last thing I would do is push love away."

▼

SECRET:
   If you feel you are not getting all the love and support you want, you are probably pushing love out of your life.

▲

Before you begin to protest too much, ask yourself if any of the following statements could describe you.

Some of the Common Ways
You May Be Pushing Love Out of Your Life

You pretend nothing is wrong when something really is bothering you.

You feel deep love for someone, but you rarely tell them so; you may even resist showing them.

You don't ask for exactly what you want because you are afraid you'll get no for an answer.

You would like to spend more time with the people you love, but you seem too busy with work and other obligations.

When someone gives you a compliment, instead of saying thank you, you invalidate what he/she says or try not to look as if you agree with the praise.

You can easily think of people in your life whom you should write or call, but you never get around to doing it.

You feel no one knows the real you.

When someone behaves lovingly to you, you wonder what he/she really wants.

You are your own worst critic.

If you are like most people, you will be able to relate to many of the statements on this list. You may think that you are doing everything you can to bring love into your life, but you have an enemy that you don't know about: that part of you that tries to sabotage the love in your life, hides from love, or rejects love.

How Eileen Hid Who She Really Was

Eileen had been married for twenty-eight years and had several children. She was the kind of person everyone wanted to be around: happy-go-lucky, kind, generous with her time and affection, always ready to help out. When you asked Eileen how she was, she would invariably say that things were just great. She was the helpful friend whom everyone called for advice.

One day in the middle of one of my seminars, a couple who had been having difficulties in their marriage broke through some major emotional barriers and wept in each other's arms, proclaiming their love for one another. Then we noticed that tears were streaming down Eileen's usually smiling face. "Eileen, is there anything you would like some help with?" I asked. Eileen stood up. "I'm a big fraud," she confessed. "You all think I'm so happy and so together, but inside I have been dying for twenty years. My marriage is dead. We haven't had sex in ten years. I can't even talk to my husband. I try to make everything look good for the kids and for other people—and I guess for myself, too. The truth is, I am miserable."

How was Eileen pushing love out of her life? She was hiding the part of herself that she was afraid was unlovable. She thought that she had to be nice and cheerful all the time in order to get love. She never felt loved because she never let people see the true Eileen. They loved only an image of her, and she knew it. She also was pushing love out of her life by not telling her husband the truth about what she wanted in their marriage. *By never asking for what she needed, Eileen guaranteed that she would never receive the love she needed.*

The Story of "Mr. Cool"

Henry had been a policeman all his life. He was in his late fifties, and he looked it. His body was tight and tense, and his face showed no emotion or softness. Henry was tough and cool. He had to be to survive more than thirty years on the police force.

Henry came to my seminar at his wife's urging. Everyone felt intimidated by him: men, because he looked tougher than they were; women, because they knew they couldn't get through to him. His walls were too thick.

Henry sat in the back row with his arms folded across his chest. He watched and listened as men, women, and whole families broke down their emotional walls and opened up to each other. Would Henry ever allow others to see that side of him? Would he allow *himself* to see it?

I didn't have to wait long to find out. Halfway through the first day, Henry stood up and told us he had something to say. "All my life, I've been hiding behind this tough-guy image," he began. "You don't know what it's like to be in my profession." His voice was trembling. "Every day of my life I see terrible pain and suffering. But I have to be cool, because if I break down, who is going to help these people?" Henry's eyes filled with tears.

"Now I realize that I have been using that tough image to push away the people I love. I can't turn it off when I go home to my wife and children."

Henry turned to his wife. "I'm tired of pretending. Inside, I feel like a frightened little boy sometimes. I'm so scared to tell you that, honey. I'm afraid you won't love me or look up to me. But I can't stay hidden anymore. I need you to love the weak part of me, too."

His wife took him in her arms and they cried together, probably for the first time in their lives. And everyone in the seminar room was crying along with them. Henry had shown all of them a part of themselves, and they loved him for it. And for the first time, Henry felt loved for *all* of who he was, and not for the image he projected.

Henry was pushing love out of his life by acting as though he didn't need love and support from anyone.

By not letting his wife see how much he needed to fall apart sometimes, he had never felt fully accepted by her. He pushed down all his fears, and others ended up fearing *him*.

SECRET:
You push love out of your life by not telling yourself and others the truth about who you are and what you need.

---

and

SECRET:
You can never feel truly loved if you don't let others see who you really are inside.

Eileen took her first step toward discovery of these secrets by admitting to herself that she wasn't happy and that she did have some feelings of hurt and anger that she had never shared with her husband. Her next step was to tell her husband what she had been holding back for years: that she was unhappy, that she had complaints about their marriage, and that she couldn't be "Mrs. Cheerful" anymore.

Much to Eileen's surprise, her husband was actually *relieved* to hear all of this. He had always felt that something was bothering Eileen but had never felt safe enough to ask. Her husband told her he had been just as unhappy as she that the marriage was so full of tension, but had thought that Eileen was content enough. They agreed to work on rebuilding their marriage, and within a year they felt closer than they had when they first met.

Henry made a major breakthrough by showing his wife how vulnerable he really was inside. He felt such a relief—now he didn't have to put on his "Mr. Cool" act at home. Henry's wife and children made it very safe for him to open up, letting him know how much they loved *all* of him. It took Henry a while to gain trust that he could show his sensitive side and still be respected, but as the months passed, he relaxed more and his personality blossomed. He developed a sense of humor; he stopped overeating to stuff down those unacceptable feelings; and his family life became joyful and loving.

Exercise: Make a List of "Ways I Push Love Out of My Life"

Here are some things that could be on my list:

> Not writing to friends because it's been so long since I wrote them and I'm embarrassed.
>
> Not washing my hair on the days I feel unattractive, thus making myself feel more unlovable.
>
> When someone compliments me on being a brilliant therapist, I answer by saying, "It's nothing, really," for fear that if I just say thank you, they'll think I agree with them that I am brilliant and thus sound arrogant.
>
> Trying to be nice to those with whom I am angry, because I'm afraid that if I show my anger, they will like me less.

You will be amazed to discover how much control you have over the amount of love you give out and the amount of love that comes into your life. *The first step toward receiving love is learning how you aren't letting yourself feel loved and how you aren't letting others love you.*

▶ Why You Push Love Away

Why would you push love out of your life? Isn't love something wonderful and fulfilling? One word answers this question: fear. Fear of getting hurt by love, fear of making a mistake, fear of losing love, fear of emotional pain.

▼

SECRET:
You're not actually afraid of love, but of the loss of love.

▲

Love is so precious and valuable that when you lose it, of course it is going to hurt. *So you consciously or unconsciously avoid love itself in anticipation of the hurt you will feel when you eventually lose it.*

Where does the fear of love come from? You weren't born with it, that's for sure. Have you ever met a shut-down baby? Or a baby who wasn't in touch with his feelings? Ever see a baby suppress his anger? Or how about a baby who felt he needed more space? No, babies will accept as much love as you have to offer them. They trust love.

What happens to that trust? *Every time you loved and your love wasn't returned, a wall was erected around that innocent loving heart, a wall you put there hoping to protect yourself from being hurt the next time.*

Exercise: Are There Walls Around Your Heart?

To help you assess whether you have built big emotional walls around your heart, we can use a visualization. You may want to read through the exercise and then try it with your eyes closed:

> Imagine an image of your heart, loving, trusting, and open. The image might be of a beautiful

open flower, or of yourself as a child, or of beautiful colored light. Relax into the feeling of having your heart open and full of love. Remember a time, when you were young, when your heart was this way. Remember how it felt to be so loving and to trust in love. Remember how much you loved your parents and how easy life was.

Now recall the first time you were hurt by love, and you put up a wall of protection around your delicate heart. Perhaps the first wall was built when your little brother or sister was born, and you wanted attention from your mommy, but she was too busy loving someone else. Perhaps the first wall went up when Daddy left home and never returned. Feel the hurt of rejection, and observe that first wall.

Now imagine all the other walls around your heart, the walls that keep your love from flowing out and keep other love from reaching you. How many walls do you see? When was each one built? Remember what made you decide to shut down and push love away. Perhaps one wall was created when the kids down the block called you names and wouldn't play with you. Perhaps you had a crush on a little boy who sat near you in class, and when he found out you liked him, he told you he didn't like you and laughed at you. Another hurt, another wall.

As the years passed, the walls went up one by one around your heart, making it harder for you to receive love and harder for you to give it freely.

Do your walls have labels on them, like "Found out husband was having affair," or "Dad left Mom to get a divorce," or "Boss fired me," or "Rejected when asking someone out"? Are your walls very high and thick? Is there a way to pass through them? Notice which walls are older and which ones are fairly new.

Now look behind all those walls and find yourself. Picture yourself as a child, trusting and open-hearted. How does it feel to be hiding behind all those walls? Do you feel lonely? Are you afraid to come out? Does a part of you wish someone would come in and find you? If that little child could talk, what would it say?

Here are some descriptions from my seminar participants of looking at their walls for the first time:

I see myself in a beautiful garden. In the middle is a series of thick rock walls, one inside the other. In the very center is a little rock house. That's where I am. It's cold in the rock house, but I know how warm it is out in the garden. I can smell the flowers, but I don't know how to get out from behind those rock walls. I think to myself, "What am I protecting myself from? Everything looks so beautiful outside." I feel hopeless because I can't see any way out. I feel stuck and afraid.

My walls are made of steel and glass, very modern and high-tech. I can see out, and see all the people passing by and looking in. But we can't communicate or touch because of the glass and steel walls. Sometimes people stop and try to get me to come out. I try to explain that I can't come out because I am surrounded by the glass walls, but the people can't even hear me. I realize that they don't even know my walls are there, and they leave feeling hurt or rejected by me. I feel so frustrated because I see how those walls keep me from people. And I may be able to fool people sometimes into thinking I am right there for them, but I know the truth—I am really hiding behind those walls.

Everything is so very old in my visualization. My walls are overgrown with vines so that you can't see where one wall ends and another begins. Living in those vines are all kinds of little bugs and birds' nests. Everything is dusty and decrepit. No one has been here for so long, not even to trim the ivy or sweep away the old leaves. The walls have secret doorways that lead to the outside world. I used to know where those doorways were, and I would use them to venture out to share with people. Sometimes I would even let someone into my private hidden world. But I've long since forgotten how to find those doors. I feel very old and very tired.

▶ How It Feels to Live Behind Emotional Walls

You may have felt sad doing that exercise. You may even have felt some pain or pressure in your chest. It hurts when your love cannot get out and other people's love cannot get in.

You just visualized the picture from inside the walls. But what about from the outside? How does it feel to others to try to get through to your heart while constantly confronting all the barricades and barbed wire you've put there? Think back to a time in your life when you really wanted to get through to someone, but he or she wouldn't let you in. How did it feel to have your love pushed away?

I used to pride myself on being an expert in emotional barricade demolition. I would find a man who had erected enormous walls around his heart that had proved impenetrable to other women, and I would say to myself, "I'll be the one to get through to him. The others just didn't try hard enough." Then I would begin to hack my way through, using dynamite, bombs, sneaking around to find back entrances. A favorite tactic of mine was to keep my partner up late at night (when his wall guards were usually too tired to notice me slipping stealthily over the walls). I was determined to get through those barriers and find the person inside.

As I grew older, I stopped going on emotional rescue missions and found partners whose hearts were more accessible. Perhaps I had been trying to prove, as a young woman, that my love could conquer anything.

Perhaps I was just unknowingly training for my work as a therapist, because we certainly have to be experts at seeing beyond those walls and helping the other person to see also. It was a relief to retire my drill and jackhammer and allow my relationships to be easy instead of feeling like I was going to work!

Which role do you play in your relationships? Are you the one always trying to break through someone else's walls? Or are you the one who is always told, "I need you to open up more. I can't get through to your feelings"? You probably have walls around your heart of which you are completely unaware, but which push love out.

Read over these comments, and see if anyone you know could make them about *you:*

> I can never tell if she's kidding or if she's serious.
> He won't admit that he is upset, but I always know when he is.
> When she gets angry, she just shuts down, and the only way I know she is angry is that she won't talk to me.
> He is so afraid of his feelings that if I bring up anything touchy, he changes the subject right away, or pretends to listen, but I know he isn't listening at all.
> When I get angry or upset, he just stares at me with that blank look on his face, and I don't know what he is feeling. It drives me crazy!
> When she doesn't like what we're talking about, or if we are getting too close to some of her feelings, she just gets off the phone, or leaves the room, or turns over and goes to sleep—anything to escape and avoid dealing with it.

If you have ever tried to get through to someone and failed, you know how frustrating it is, how much it hurts, and how awful it makes you feel about yourself. Stop and think for a moment: Are there people in your life who are trying to love you, but you are pushing them away? What about your parents, your brothers and sisters? What about your lover? What about your friends? What about your children? Do you have walls of indifference between yourself and them?

------------------------▼------------------------

SECRET:
> *When you push love out, it not only hurts you, but it hurts others as well.*

------------------------▲------------------------

Nothing frustrates me more in my work with couples than to see one partner trying desperately to get through to the other, while the other partner pushes the love away. *This is one of the major reasons relationships don't last: One or both partners won't let the other in emotionally.*

Sue and Adam sat in my office. Sue had insisted on marriage counseling; Adam had come against his will. Sue was heartbroken that the marriage wasn't working. Adam thought things would be fine if Sue just stopped complaining so much. Now, after two months, things were at a standstill. Adam had had a turbulent childhood without much love or safety and was scared to death of being hurt again if he showed how vulnerable he was. But now he was at a crossroads. If he didn't take a chance and decide to risk loving again, he would lose everything important to him: his wife and children.

I asked Sue to tell Adam how much it hurt her when she couldn't reach him and how much she and the children needed his love and affection. Sue sat there weeping, reaching her hands out to Adam: "Please, honey," she pleaded, "I know you are afraid, but I need you to let me in, to show me you need me, too. I can't go on this way. I love you, but I need your love back."

Adam sat with his arms folded tightly across his chest. "Well, I love you, Susan," he replied. "But I still think that you shouldn't need to hear it all the time." Adam knew what Sue wanted to hear. He just wasn't willing to give it to her, maybe because he had never received it himself.

"Don't you see, Adam," I said, leaning forward and touching his arm, "Sue has been trying to get inside your heart for five years now. She can't go on any longer. Wake up! If you don't let her in, you are going to lose her and the kids, and you will live your life alone and without love. Please take that step!"

Adam just sat there. Some powerful dark force had him frozen. He heard what I said; he knew it was true. Still, he couldn't reach out to his wife. Sue left Adam a few months later and has since remarried.

▶ What Are Your Excuses for Being Unloving?

I felt sad for Adam, but I didn't feel sorry for him. All of us have been hurt. None of us has had the perfect childhood. And yes, loving is scary, and a risk. But that is no excuse for being unloving toward others. I have seen too many people use their childhoods or past mishaps in love as an excuse to be cold and hurtful toward others. And I have seen just as many people with painful backgrounds use that experience to live their lives as a different example, to learn from past mistakes and become loving, giving human beings.

Stop using your past as an excuse for how you are today.

Exercise: Whom Are You Pushing Away?

Here is a four-step exercise to help you see how you may be pushing people away, and what excuses you make to justify not letting them in.

STEP ONE: Make a list of the important people in your life, including family members, spouse, parents, friends.

STEP TWO: Answer each of the four questions below in relation to each of the people on your list.

1. What would _____ say about how I push him/ her away?

2. When I do that, how does _____ feel?

3. What _____ wants from me is:

4. My "excuses" for not giving _____ what he/ she wants are:

Here is a sample answer to the questions:

From Jeff: married; forty-six years old

1. What would my wife Jane say about how I push her away?
   I keep secrets from her.
   I don't plan intimate or special times together.
   I don't always tell her what I am feeling, especially my fears.
   I compare her with other women.
   I don't include her in making plans for our future.
   I sometimes pay more attention to our daughters than to her.

2. When I do that, how does Jane feel?
   Alone
   Criticized
   Not supported or appreciated

Taken for granted
Frightened about our future

3. What Jane wants from me is:
   For me to share more parts of myself
   For me to take more of the sexual initiative
   For me to plan special romantic times together
   For me to be more patient with her
   For me to compliment her more

4. My excuses for not giving Jane what she wants are:
   I'm too busy with work.
   She is too demanding.
   My father wasn't very affectionate, and so it is hard
     for me to be.
   She doesn't really need this much attention.
   I'm not sure how to be more loving.

STEP THREE: After you have finished this exercise,
read it over. Ask yourself these questions:

1. Would many of the people close to me have the
   same complaints about how I push them away?

2. How difficult would it really be for me to do more of
   the things that would make my loved ones
   happy?

3. Have I been making my excuses more important
   than loving those I care for?

STEP FOUR: Make the decision to let down some of
your emotional walls. Start by sharing this exercise
with your partner and your family. Ask them to comment on how accurate you were in understanding their
feelings. Let them know you want to experience more
love and closeness and ask for their help.

▶ The Mind Protects and the Heart Connects

I've created a saying that will help you understand more about those walls around your heart: *The mind protects and the heart connects.* The mind tells you, "Watch out, you could get hurt again." The heart connects, because it is through love and sharing that you connect with the world around you and to the personal world inside of you.

It's natural for you to avoid anything that is associated with pain and hurt. Every time you have been hurt by love, your tendency and willingness to love has decreased. Love becomes associated with rejection, sacrifice, obligation, dependence, struggle, and loss of identity. The mind acts like a guard at the door of your heart. The only problem is that when your mind finally gives you the message that it is safe to open up and love, your heart may not open quite so easily. If the heart's door is used to being closed, it may just stay stuck even when you want it to open.

▼

SECRET:
It's not love that hurts—it's when you stop loving that hurts.

▲

When you are loving, you feel alive, happy, and warm inside. Even if the other person isn't receiving your love, if *you* continue loving, you reap love's benefits. Remember when you were a teenager and you had a crush on someone who didn't even know it? Remember how excited and alive just loving that person made you feel? It had nothing to do with whether he or she was loving you back. *It just felt good to be loving.*

The problem is that when people do something you don't like, it becomes difficult for you to continue loving them, and so you *stop* loving them. It's *then* that you feel hurt. *The deepest hurt in your life comes when you withdraw your love from others.*

If you think that your parents have hurt you in your life, think again. The real hurt you feel about your parents is that, because of things they have done, things which *you* disapproved of, you have at times stopped loving them. And it hurts not to love the people who brought you into the world. If you think your lovers have hurt you and that that's what has been painful about your relationships, think again. The real hurt came when you decided you couldn't love anymore. Of course, it hurts when people don't return your love or do things that are cruel. But *it hurts* more *when you then stop loving them.*

Love connects you to the power within you. That's why it feels so good to be in love. When you stop loving others, you weaken your connection to your inner power and your ability to love yourself. You always win by loving, because that experience of loving is nourishing you and empowering you.

▶ It Hurts You When You Stop Loving

Leonard's mother died when he was eleven years old. Her death left Leonard's father with Leonard and his little sister to bring up on his own. Leonard's father reacted to his wife's death by shutting down his emotions. "I can't afford to fall apart now," Leonard's dad thought to himself. "Not when the kids depend on me for everything." So Leonard was brought up strictly, without much show of affection, although Leonard and his father did do many things together in a buddy-buddy sort of way.

When his mother died, Leonard, like his father, also shut down emotionally. He was afraid to risk caring for anyone again. So Leonard cut himself off from his father and refused to let himself feel anything for him. Time passed, and Leonard left home. He seemed to have a hard time forming relationships with women and experienced a lot of inner resistance to getting a career started. Leonard would call his father a few times a year to say hello, but other than that, they didn't have much contact.

Leonard came to me wondering why he had such a difficult time with making any sort of commitment, both to people and to a career. "I seem to have such a low opinion of myself," Leonard confessed. "I feel so alone."

I asked Leonard to close his eyes and go back to the time of his mother's death. At first, Leonard felt nothing, just as he had felt nothing for years since. Then he suddenly got in touch with that little boy still inside of him. And that little boy was in pain. "Mommy, why did you leave me alone? I needed you, and you went away."

"And what about your daddy?" I asked gently.

"I will never let this happen again," Leonard's "little boy" self answered. "From now on, I don't care about anyone."

"If you don't care about your father, then who is your family?" I asked Leonard.

"I guess I feel I don't have a family," he answered, and then he began to weep. Suddenly, it was all becoming clear to him. Leonard had cut himself off from his roots, from his sense of belonging. In the process he had doomed himself to a life of feeling alone. By pushing his father's love away, Leonard was doing more harm to himself than anyone else could by rejecting him or abandoning him. *Leonard had been abandoning himself all his life*.

Leonard could hardly wait to call his father and tell him he loved him. His father responded with so much happiness that Leonard decided to go home and visit that weekend. When he returned, he called to thank me and tell me he felt whole for the first time in his life. He and his father would never be completely open and demonstrative with one another, but they had a relationship again, and Leonard had his roots back.

▶ Which Do You Choose: Connection or Separation?

The result of pushing love out and living behind those walls can be summed up in one word: separation.

Separation

Separation is an emotional state in which the energy or feeling between yourself and a person or experience is not flowing freely, and there is a certain detachment or barrier to the relationship between yourself and something or someone else. Most of us are experts at separation.

I feel that the habit of emotionally separating is the major psychological problem most people experience in their lives. It is the cause of much of the pain people inflict on themselves and others. For many people, emotional separation is a chronic condition. Taken to an extreme, the state of separation expresses itself in the frightening political situation that exists between most countries of the world.

▼

Are You Choosing Separation?

Here are a few signs to be aware of:

You notice yourself criticizing and judging someone.

You feel as though you don't care what someone thinks about you or what happens.

You are with other people, but you feel lonely anyway.

You feel that no one really understands what you're thinking or feeling.

You are making love with someone and thinking about something else.

You pretend to be nice to someone, but inside you are furious, or just plain bored.

A friend or lover wants to clear things up with you, and you refuse to talk about it.

You feel isolated, as if you are from a different planet, and there is no one here who understands you.

▲

These are some symptoms of being in the state I call emotional separation. You are behind your walls. You may feel lifeless, depressed, apathetic, skeptical, negative, and hopeless, as if nothing really matters.

Here are some common examples of separation. See if you can relate to them.

You walk into a party. Immediately, you start to feel as if you can't relate to anyone there. Even though you haven't said a word to anyone, you don't like the people. You start making negative mental judgments about people you see: That woman is wearing too much makeup; that man sounds obnoxious; look at that woman falling all over that man—how pushy. You feel bored, disappointed, and then depressed. You either leave right away or stay there feeling cut off, alienated, and miserable.

You're out on a date with someone you really care for, having a wonderful time and feeling close to him/her. In the middle of a conversation, the other person criticizes a film that you saw and liked. Your friend disliked the film intensely. Suddenly you feel strangely sad, and find yourself feeling far away from your partner. You become very quiet. You feel as if somehow the other person has pushed you away or done something to hurt you. You wish you could just go home. As your date continues to talk, you wonder why you can never find partners you really like.

You are having sex with someone, and everything is proceeding wonderfully. Suddenly your partner begins doing something you don't particularly enjoy. You notice your mind starting to wander. You begin to dislike the way your partner smells, and you find yourself getting irritated at the things he or she is saying and doing. Soon you feel disgusted with the whole thing and can't wait for the experience to be over. You feel irked and lonely.

In all three of these examples you have chosen to separate yourself emotionally from the person or the experience you came in contact with. The result is a sense of tension, depression, and a feeling of not belonging or being out of sync. *Other people will perceive your separation as aloofness or an uncaring attitude.* They may decide that you're hard, stuck-up, defensive, and difficult to please. When you separate, you create hurt, resentment, and frustration in the people around you.

Connection Makes the Difference

The opposite of separation is connection. *Learning to master connection is one of the keys to making love all the time in your life.* I define connection as an unrestricted flow of energy between yourself and a person or experience; a consciously perceived and accepted relatedness. Connection creates a feeling of aliveness, energy, creativity, self-esteem, fulfillment, and love. It is the essential ingredient in loving.

Let's look again at the three examples above, and see how you could experience them from the point of view of choosing connection:

You walk into a party, and immediately you feel you can't relate to anyone there. You notice yourself starting to separate emotionally, but it doesn't feel good to you. You decide to get more connected. You walk up to someone else who is standing alone and say, "Hi. I was feeling kind of left out, so I thought I'd come over and say hello. I don't know anyone here." The other person is grateful that someone else feels the way he did. You immediately feel connected because you are sharing a common experience.

You're out on a date with someone you really care for, and you are having a wonderful time. In the middle of a conversation, your date criticizes a film you saw and liked, and you notice yourself feeling sad and drifting away. You don't want to separate, so you say, "Before we go on, I have to tell you that I feel really hurt by what you said about the film. You know, I'm afraid to tell you this, but I liked that film very much, and I feel that if you didn't like it, you will think I'm stupid for liking it, or that I'll feel you don't like me or my taste." Your partner says he had no idea that you'd take what he said personally, and asks you what other films you have enjoyed. You find you do share some common tastes, and the dinner continues with the two of you feeling even closer because of the honest communication.

You are having sex with someone, and everything is proceeding wonderfully. Suddenly your partner begins doing something you don't particularly enjoy. You notice your mind begins to wander. You really dislike making love when your mind is somewhere else, so you decide to avoid separating. You change your position so that you're engaged in an activity that you know you both enjoy. In a minute, you feel relaxed and very connected again. Later on, you mention to your partner that you felt a little uncomfortable with that one incident, and offer suggestions of how you could have enjoyed it more.

In these three examples, you chose to connect rather than to separate. Finding strategies for connection is one of the most powerful ways you can stop pushing love out of your life.

SECRET:
Choosing to separate yourself from others is the biggest way you push love out of your life!

If you take all the energy you put into separating from others and from your own feelings and use that energy to connect with others and yourself, you will tap into a tremendous personal power that can impel you toward creating deep and lasting fulfillment in your life.

Don't expect to be able to master connection overnight. You are an expert at separating, so you have to build up your ability to choose and maintain connection. Later on in this book I will give you specific techniques for mastering connection in all the situations, whether it be learning to connect to your own feelings or learning to stay connected to those you love.

The first step is to *start noticing when you are not connected*. Be aware of the signs of separation that I mentioned earlier in this section, and ask yourself if you are choosing to feel emotionally separate rather than connected. Once you notice that you are not connected, you can make the choice to reconnect. This is making the choice to love. And in this moment you are "making" love!

▶ Need Is Not a Dirty Word

What is your reaction to the word "need"? If I asked you to associate "need" with another word, you may have chosen one of the following:

Weak	Obligation	Lack of confidence
Fear	Pain	Deficiency
Dependence	Control	Giving away power
Attachment	Incompleteness	Insecurity

Most people associate "need" with one or more of the above words, and most of these words have a negative meaning. It's okay to *want* something, this philosophy teaches, but not to *need* it. "Need implies that you are not complete and whole in yourself. It's not okay to need love, approval, affection, emotional support, and appreciation. You should be self-sufficient and able to supply all those things to yourself."

This philosophy is *one of the most damaging influences present in relationships today.* Having needs goes hand in hand with being human. When you turn your back on your needs, you turn your back on a very human and vulnerable part of yourself.

Suppressing your needs is one of the fastest ways to build those walls around your heart. Every time you say, "I don't need you. I don't need anyone," that wall gets thicker and thicker. Acknowledging your needs gives purpose to your relationships. It allows your partner, your children, your parents, or your friends to feel valued and appreciated. There is nothing worse for your self-esteem than to feel that no one needs you.

How does it feel not to be needed? Pretty awful. Here are some comments from my seminar graduates about how it feels when someone makes a point of letting them know they aren't needed:

When Bill tells me he doesn't need me and that he doesn't want me to need him, I feel like just giving up. It is as if he could be with any woman. I don't feel special or important. I feel like I am just filling in the category of "woman" in his life. I cry just thinking about it.

Tricia is so determined not to need me that I feel as though she never gets close to me. I don't feel she's giving our relationship a chance. She is always trying not to care too much, and that makes me feel like saying, "Why the hell should I try to open up and care for her when she could take me or leave me?"

Bruce keeps telling me he wants me to feel free, to have my own space. Whenever I tell him I would like more time together or more closeness, he accuses me of being "needy." I hate that! I am so afraid to admit to him that I do need him. Then he'll leave for sure. When he hears the word "need," he runs so fast you'd think his life was in danger. The truth is that I want a man who needs me, too.

▼

SECRET:
When you don't tell the truth about your needs to yourself and to others, you are pushing love out of your life.

▲

Exercise: How to Develop "Need Awareness"

Remember Henry, the police officer? Henry's life had become empty because he wasn't willing to admit or show his need for love. As a result, Henry's wife didn't have much self-worth because she didn't feel needed by him. I gave Henry and his wife the following exercise to help them develop *need awareness*. They would sit down together and takes turns saying the following phrase, filling in the blank each time: "I need you in my life because _____." Their answers would be something like this:

"I need you in my life because you make me feel a sense of belonging."

"I need you in my life because when you drive, we never get lost, and when I drive, I never get there!"

"I need you in my life to tell me I am doing a good job and that my hard work is worth something."

"I need you in my life to hug and hold me at night."

As you can see, some of the needs are very practical, while some are more emotional. Do this exercise with your partner or with your children, and you will find a deep sense of appreciation and caring growing between you as you realize how much you need others and how much you are needed!

Another way to develop "need awareness" is to make a list of the people you care for in your life. Under each name list *why* you need that person. The list might contain small things like "I need Gloria because she gives me a ride to work each day," or more significant things like "I need my mother because she lets me still feel like a little girl sometimes."

The final step is to *tell* each of these people why you need them, and express your gratitude for their presence in your life. Often we wait until those we love have passed away or have left us before we recognize how much we love and need them. By then it is too late to tell them.

The time to tell the people you love how much you love and need them is now, while they are still around to appreciate it.

Celebrate your needs—they make you human and allow you to feel alive!

▶ Your Needs Help You Feel Passion for Life

One surprising and powerful truth about need that I discovered is that *it's impossible to feel passionate about someone if you don't feel that you somehow need that person.* That's why most relationships are more passionate in the beginning, and why the passion dies as time passes: The couple loses sight of their need for one another once that need is being fulfilled daily.

Jeffrey was a client who demonstrated the relationship between need and passion in his life. Jeffrey hadn't been involved in any relationship for two years. Living alone, he began to feel acutely his need to share love with another person. Every night that he slept alone, every Sunday as he went jogging by himself, he was aware of that feeling inside that cried out, "I need someone to care about, and someone who cares about me." Eventually Jeffrey met Elaine. They fell madly in love. Their sex life was romantic and passionate. Jeffrey was very conscious of how much Elaine was filling a need in his life, and so his need for her allowed him to feel deep passion.

As the months passed, and Jeffrey became more attached to Elaine, he began to suppress and deny his feelings of need for her, unconsciously, of course. Why? Because Jeffrey was afraid of losing Elaine, afraid of losing the love he needed, and ultimately afraid of the pain of losing her. As he suppressed his need, his passionate desire for Elaine diminished dramatically. I worked with Jeffrey until he felt safe admitting how much he needed Elaine in his life. One night, as they were doing the need awareness exercise described earlier, Jeffrey began to cry. He revealed again to Elaine how much she meant to him, as he hadn't done since he first met her. That night Jeffrey and Elaine had the most passionate lovemaking they'd ever experienced. Jeffrey had discovered one of the secrets of making love all the time:

▼

SECRET:
Pushing needs out of your life kills your ability to feel passion.

▲

Suppression of their natural needs for one another is *one of the major causes of the eventual disintegration of a couple's sex life*. The more you allow yourself to feel and express your natural needs, the more potential for passion and fulfillment you will experience in your relationships.

When I teach my seminar, Making Love Work, I can always spot those people who desperately need love and are most afraid of not receiving it. *Invariably, the greater the deprivation of love a person feels, the greater the person's appearance of not caring or needing anything*. These people go out of their way to let me know, as they arrive at the seminar, that they don't need to be there, that they don't really care about having a relationship, that they are just curious or are there to do a friend a favor. The more they do this, the more certain I am that, buried deep inside, there is a very vulnerable heart that needs lots of love, and simply doesn't feel it can ever get it.

▶ The Difference Between Need and Dependence

You probably aren't afraid to admit that you need air. Why? Because you know that there is an abundance of air. So there is no chance of your being deprived of it. Have you ever heard someone say, "I want air, but I don't need air"? Or how about, "Needing air deprives me of my independence"? Of course not. And yet when it comes to needing love and relationships, we hear these statements all the time. Why?

Because you don't feel there is an abundance of love available to you. And it's not safe to need something of which there might be a shortage.

The problem is not that you need love, but that you depend on others to create love in your life. You must depend on yourself to create loving relationships. Need and dependence are not the same thing. I need love in my life, and I need my partner in my life very much, but I don't depend on him to create my happiness for me. Only I can do that. Therefore, I am responsible for fulfilling all of my needs. This understanding eliminates the fear that, if I say I need someone, I am giving my power away to them, and that I will be hurt if they do not fulfill me. I *do* need someone, but if that person doesn't fulfill my basic needs, I am responsible for finding someone else who will.

▼

SECRET:
Needing *others* is *not* a mistake. Giving up your responsibility for satisfying your needs *is* a mistake.

▲

Need and responsibility must go hand in hand. If you can't get your needs met from one source, you are responsible for locating another. In this way, you are always self-sufficient and self-reliant.

▼

SECRET:
You *need* others, but you *depend* on yourself.

▲

Lori and Pat
"Pat has been a bachelor for fifteen years," Lori told me. "He is used to being independent, and not needing anything or anyone."

"That's understandable," I responded. "Give him time."

"But you don't know how bad it is, Doctor," Lori exclaimed. "When we were making love last week, I felt so wonderful, and I said to him, 'Oh, darling, I love you so much. I need you so much.' And Pat looked at me and said, 'I love you, too, Lori, but I don't *need* you.' I went crazy. How could he say that in the middle of lovemaking?"

"Did you talk about it?" I asked.

"Yes," said Lori, "for hours! Pat explained that to need me meant giving his power away to me. I insisted that I needed him, yet I didn't feel I was giving him my power. I know he needs me. What can I do?"

Once I explained the difference between need and dependence to Lori, she could hardly wait to tell Pat.

The next day Lori telephoned me. "It was wonderful!" she bubbled. "Pat and I discussed the difference between need and dependence. I wasn't sure if he understood or not, and I was a little disappointed because he didn't seem very responsive. Then last night, we were in bed and began making love. Right in the middle of everything, Pat said, 'Darling, I love you . . . and I need you . . .' And then he quickly added, 'But I don't depend on you!' We laughed, and felt so close. Thank you!"

Has anyone ever called you "needy," or have you ever felt someone in your life was "too needy"? What you really mean when you call people needy is that they seem to be dependent on you for their happiness.

Real personal strength doesn't come from *not* having needs, but from

(a) having and admitting your needs
(b) being committed to fulfilling them
(c) figuring out *how* to fulfill them

It's not people's needs that bother you—it's their ab-
dication of their responsibility to fulfill their needs that
you resent so much. Again, it's a simple case of con-
fusing need and dependence.

▶ Needs Are Like Magnets to Attract What You Want

Someone in my seminar once asked me the difference between a "want" and a "need." "There is a
very easy way to understand the difference," I answered. I looked around the room and asked, "How
many people in here *want* to use the bathroom right
now?" About three people out of fifty raised their
hands. "Fine," I said. "The difference between want
and need is that if any of you *needed* to use the
bathroom right now, you would be out of here in two
seconds!"

Need is a powerful motivator. If I want money, I
will have a certain energy level that is devoted to ob-
taining that money. But if I *need* money because I will
be kicked out of my apartment tomorrow if I don't pay
my rent, I am much more highly motivated to go out
and get that money. If I need to go to the bathroom,
you can bet I will find one. If, in the same way, I am
aware that I need love or need a relationship, I will be
putting out a lot of energy toward finding one. I believe
that need is like a magnet that can attract what you
want *if* you deal with it properly.

Edward was a perfect example of someone who
felt that needing a woman meant that he was weak. He
stood up at my seminar and said that whenever I
mentioned the word "need," he became very angry. To
him, the word meant weakness, lack of personal
power, and that he was incomplete without someone
else.

"Edward," I asked, "are you in a relationship?"

"No," Edward replied.

"Would you like to be?"

"Yes, I would," he answered.

"Why do you think you aren't in a relationship?" I questioned.

Edward gave a list of reasons which included the fact that he was very busy at work, that he had very high standards, and that everyone was away for the summer.

"Edward, do you *need* a relationship?" I asked.

"No, absolutely not," Edward insisted.

"Well," I said, "that's why you don't have a relationship, Edward, because you don't feel you need it."

At first, Edward did not understand. I explained the difference between need and dependence. Edward started to soften. Finally he said, "Well, the truth is, deep in my heart, I guess I do feel I need love. I do need a woman in my life." The whole room applauded wildly—especially the women! It was a lot easier to love Edward when he was telling the truth about what he needed than when he was pretending he didn't care. "You'll see, Edward," I said. "Now that you feel your need, it will act like a magnet, and you will attract someone into your life."

Edward's need must have had a pretty powerful force attached to it, because one woman in the seminar was so moved by his admission that she found herself attracted to him immediately. She realized that she, too, had been pushing need out of her life. She got together with Edward at one of the seminar breaks and they spent the rest of the seminar together. They fell in love and have been together ever since.

▶ How to Demolish Those Walls Around Your Heart

Whether your emotional walls are created by suppressing your need for others or by hiding how much you really care, they have the same effect: *They isolate you from the one thing that would make their existence unnecessary: the healing power of love.* When you live behind protective emotional walls, you sacrifice a very important freedom: *the freedom to love whenever you want to.* Your life is governed by fear of rejection, fear of loss, fear of loneliness.

All those walls that separate you from others also separate you from your own self, and naturally make loving and liking yourself much more difficult. Probably the greatest sacrifice you make by pushing love out of your life is the sacrifice of living a life of full feeling. I believe that most of the depression, boredom, and malcontent people experience in their lives has its source in the suppression of feeling. One big value of staying open to all of your feelings is that:

What you can feel, you can heal.

Through the absence of feeling, you isolate yourself from others and from yourself. You become numb and find yourself trapped all alone with your thoughts, trying to figure everything out. It is through feeling that life becomes spontaneous and exciting. Without feeling, the inner self has no chance to come out and playfully express its genius and brilliance.

▶ The More You Feel, the More Alive You Become

If you look to the lives of many creative geniuses, you will see that theirs were lives of passion and intense feeling. It is through feeling that the great artists, writers, and musicians were able to bring out their inner vision for all to appreciate. You, too, have an inner beauty that demands expression. It is through letting love emerge that you can feel safe to let even more of yourself emerge: to create, to take a chance, to try something new.

Begin to reconnect with yourself by telling yourself the truth about *all* of your feelings. As you read through the different sections of this book, you'll notice yourself experiencing many emotions. Give yourself permission to be aware of all of them. Some may be quite painful or scary because they are so strong. But *you* are stronger than your fear, and facing it is the first step toward conquering it.

Remember, you are always the winner when you choose to love. You always win when you choose to open up to your feelings rather than shut them out. The more you feel, the more of you there will be for others to love.

This is my final secret for this chapter about how to stop pushing love out of your life:

▼

SECRET:
Love is safe when you know how to use it.

▲

Like all powerful forces in the universe, love can be used to hurt or to heal. You can learn to use love to create indescribable joy for yourself and those you share yourself with. At first, it may not be easy. You may have spent years and years pushing love out of your life. And it may seem easier to stay shut down than to risk opening up your heart again. But remember:

EACH TIME YOU STOP LOVING, A PART OF YOU DIES.

EACH TIME YOU CHOOSE TO LOVE AGAIN, TO REACH OUT, TO RECONNECT, AND TO FEEL, YOU COME ALIVE.

Take the chance . . . and your rewards will be worth it!

3

The Real Reasons Why Love Stops Working

Have your ever been in a relationship that started out with love and ended with hate?

Have you ever been passionately attracted to someone only to find yourself bored and disinterested with him or her as time passed?

Have you ever loved and trusted someone in the beginning only to feel betrayed and bitter in the end?

One of the most devastating emotions I've ever experienced is that sense of confusion I've felt while watching one of my relationships fall apart before my eyes and *not knowing what to do about it or why it was happening.* At these times I would think to myself, "I am going crazy. What is happening? What were we even fighting about? I feel so hopeless. Love is impossible. I am doomed to be sad and alone forever."

In this section, I hope to clear up your confusion about what makes relationships go from good to bad, from love to hate, from passion to indifference. *Rela-*

tionships don't just turn sour one day; rather, they *deteriorate over time*. If you know what signs to look for, you can avoid the distintegration of your relationships and the destruction of love.

▶ What You're Really Fighting About

A relationship between two people is an interplay of two energy fields: The mental, emotional, and physical energies of one person interact with those same energies of the partner. In the course of all relationships, obstacles to the smooth flow and melting together of these two different sets of energies arise. We call those obstacles "problems." Problems keep two people from feeling a clear flow of energy or connection between them. And when there is a problem, fighting and heartbreak usually aren't far behind.

What are some of the common issues you fight about in relationships?

Sex	Money	Household duties
Relatives	Time	Communication
Jealousy	Bringing up the children	Power

When a problem arises in a relationship, you stop feeling good with your partner, and the relationship stops being fun in that moment. Your mind says, "Hey, you're not feeling good, and it's all because of this problem. Now, you have two choices: You can pretend the problem doesn't exist and hope it will disappear, or you can try to solve the problem, and when it's solved, you will feel happy again."

I used to take the second approach. I tried to become a master problem solver in my relationships. I thought that if my partner and I solved all of our problems and came to agreements about everything, we would have a successful and happy relationship. We would spend hours, sometimes even days, talking about our problems: agreeing and disagreeing on each point, taking notes, and drawing up lists and graphs until we had worked out a solution. It was like the Geneva peace talks!

One day my partner and I noticed something very strange. We had just spent three hours solving a problem. We kissed and made up, expecting to feel in love again. For about fifteen minutes we felt relieved and happy. Then my mate brought up another explosive issue, and we started arguing all over again. I decided to agree with his point of view. For a few minutes we felt good again, and then he brought up still another issue. No matter how much I agreed with him, he still felt like fighting with me. It was then that we realized *we weren't fighting about the issues; we were fighting because of something else.*

Perhaps you've noticed this same phenomenon in your relationships. You make up after an argument, yet within a short time you're fighting all over again. It's enough to make you want to give up on relationships once and for all!

There is an explanation for this frustrating pattern, and it's one of my secrets for understanding love:

▼

SECRET:
You are never fighting for the reason you think. You are fighting because you are not feeling loved, supported, or understood by another person.

▲

Two people will get into an argument if there is a weakness in their emotional connection and the flow of love between them. Coming to an agreement about the issue in question won't resolve the real source of the problem: emotional distance and separation. This explains why you sometimes fight over an issue, while at other times you let the same issue go without an argument. The following story about Sue and Ray illustrates this point vividly.

Let's follow Sue and Ray through a potentially explosive situation in their relationship. We'll look at two different instances of the same incident.

Example One: No Stored-up Emotional Tension

This week Sue and Ray are getting all the love they feel they need from each other. They've agreed to meet for a romantic evening out together. Sue returns from work first and is getting dressed when Ray comes home. Here is how their conversation goes:

> SUE: Hi, honey, I'll be ready in fifteen minutes.
>
> RAY: That's right, we did decide to go out tonight, didn't we?
>
> SUE: You don't sound very excited. What's wrong?
>
> RAY: To be honest, Sue, I am just exhausted. I was in meetings today for three hours, and didn't even finish all I needed to do.
>
> SUE: I'm sorry your day was so hard, honey. You do look pretty drained.
>
> RAY: I feel drained, and I guess the idea of going out isn't really appealing. Are you terribly disappointed?
>
> SUE: Well, yes, I was looking forward to it, but I know how it feels to have one of those days. Why don't we just stay home and have a cozy evening together? I hate seeing you so tired, and I worry about you when you work so hard. We'll go out another time.
>
> RAY: *(Giving Sue a hug)* Thanks for being so sweet about it, Sue. A cozy evening together sounds like just what I need. Let's move our date to next Tuesday, okay?

Sue's reaction to her exhausted husband seems logical, doesn't it? She is worried about the man she loves and wants to do what's best for him.

Now let's look at the same incident, but change the circumstances a bit. This time, we'll pick another week, when Sue and Ray *aren't feeling as emotionally connected to one another.* Maybe Sue is secretly annoyed that Ray paid more attention to his friends than to her at a party a few nights before. Maybe she feels he isn't doing his share around the house. In some way, *she feels she is not getting all the love and appreciation she needs.*

Example Two: Stored-up Emotional Tension

> SUE: Hi, honey. I'll be ready to leave in fifteen minutes.
>
> RAY: That's right, we did decide to go out tonight, didn't we?
>
> SUE: *(Getting annoyed)* What, you didn't even remember? Thanks a lot for making me feel special.
>
> RAY: Well, it's just that I had a terrible day and feel pretty wiped out.
>
> SUE: I work full-time, too, Ray, but you don't hear me complaining about it. I made a special effort to get home early to change and get ready.
>
> RAY: Well, Miss Perfect, I'm glad you aren't tired, but I am, and I can't go out and have a good time when I feel this way.
>
> SUE: *(Raising her voice)* This always happens! You end up sabotaging our evenings alone together with some dumb excuse. I'm always the one who has to make the effort to do something special for us.
>
> RAY: Look, Sue, the last thing I want to hear now is you nagging me about our relationship. Let's just drop it.
>
> SUE: Don't call me a nag! *You're* the one who ruined our evening.
>
> RAY: *I* ruined it? You have it all wrong—you

are so damned demanding, and when you don't get your way, you throw a big tantrum, like a spoiled bitch.

SUE: How dare you call me a bitch! I don't even want to see you tonight, so go have a nice evening alone! *(Sue walks out and slams the door.)*

What is the difference between these two incidents? In the first example, Sue and Ray had a strong emotional connection which allowed Sue to feel concern for Ray because she herself felt loved. In the second example, Sue had been feeling some Emotional Tension (E.T.) and a separation from Ray, although she was unconscious of it. *The incident acted as a catalyst to give Sue an excuse to express her angry feelings about being neglected.*

▶ The Difference Between Disagreement and Disapproval

The contrast between Sue's reactions can be summed up in two words: *disagreement* and *disapproval*. Disagreement occurs on the mental or rational level. You may disagree with your partner's choice of a tie. Or you may disagree with his being too tired to go out after work.

Disapproval, on the other hand, occurs on the emotional level. Disagreement turns into disapproval when you start to withdraw emotionally from your partner. Disapproval implies: "You did something I disagree with; therefore, I can't love you as much as before. So I am pulling away for now." You *disagree* with your partner's choice of a tie, and then *disapprove* of him for making that choice, and you turn off your love for him.

It's your disapproval of others that turns simple disagreements into big issues.

How Disagreement Turns Into Disapproval

Ray chooses a certain tie to go with a sport jacket. Just as he is finishing tying his tie, Sue walks into the room. Sue thinks that Ray's tie clashes with the colors in his jacket.

Theoretically, Sue shouldn't feel less love for Ray because of his tie color. They simply have a difference of opinion. But if there is some emotional tension stored up between Sue and Ray, she will not only *disagree* with his tie choice but will notice herself actually feeling less love for Ray at that moment. She has started to *disapprove:* to shut down; to feel turned off; to put up a wall.

If you notice yourself constantly disapproving of your partner, it's a sign that there is a tremendous amount of underlying tension in your relationship.

This explains why in the beginning of a relationship, couples rarely argue or fight. Their emotional connection is strong, and very little tension has built up in the relationship. The funny little habits your partner has are "cute" in the beginning. Only months or years later, when the emotional connection is shaky, do you feel that the qualities that used to be "cute" are driving you crazy!

You can notice yourself changing from a *disagreeing* lover (healthy) to a *disapproving* lover (not healthy) when you catch yourself assigning negative qualities to your partner's character: He is tacky; he lacks class; he is inconsiderate; she is overemotional; she is not understanding. When you move from evaluating the *problem* to evaluating the *person,* you are disapproving, and not just disagreeing.

▶ Little Issues Hide Big Issues

Jill and Herb came to me complaining that all they did was fight. Jill felt that Herb picked on her all the time, and Herb felt nagged by Jill. They each had a long list of complaints about the other and were on the verge of separating. I asked them to write down their grievances:

Entries on Jill's List About Herb	*Entries on Herb's List About Jill*
Doesn't shave on Sunday	Nags him about paying the bills
Drinks beer after dinner	Doesn't let him forget he lost money in the stock market last year
Curses in front of the children	
Forgets to turn the alarm back on for her in the morning	Treats him like a little boy in front of the children
	Expects him to work on the house on his day off

I listened to Jill and Herb argue over every little point. I knew we could have sat there forever and never resolved anything. Finally I asked, "Jill, does Herb love you?"

The question shocked her. "Well, I guess he does," she answered quietly.

"Does he tell you he loves you?" I asked.

Jill's mouth began to quiver. "Well, no," she replied, "not much."

>ME: Would you like Herb to express more love to you?
>JILL: Well, Herb isn't that kind of person.
>ME: Yes, but would you like him to be?

JILL: Yes. *(Starting to cry)*

ME: Herb, do you feel appreciated by Jill?

HERB: Well, she certainly has a lot of complaints about me.

ME: Sounds to me like you don't always feel appreciated by her.

HERB: I guess you're right.

ME: Would you like to feel closer to Jill—more loved by her?

HERB: Yes, that would be nice.

Within a few more minutes I had Jill and Herb talking about the real problem in their relationship: *Neither of them felt loved enough. All their little issues were "safe" ways to express their resentments and hurts without really dealing with the important issue— not enough love.* Jill and Herb had only just begun their work, but at least they knew where to start: *not* by making agreements about the bills and the alarm clock (although it's okay to communicate about these things, too), but by expressing their need for love and attention from one another.

The major cause of conflict between two people is a lack of strong, positive emotional connection. So my formula for dealing with conflict is:

---

1. **Put the issue aside.**

2. **Reestablish your connection with your partner by dissolving the Emotional Tension.**

3. **Then go back and deal with the issue.**

Later on in this section, I will give you powerful, step-by-step formulas for resolving conflicts and feeling more in love.

▶ Love—The Big Magnifying Glass

Have you ever felt your partner overreacted to something you said?

Do you suspect you might be making a big deal out of a small issue?

Have people ever told you, "You always take things I say the wrong way"?

Do you have trouble forgiving, even after an argument is over?

If you answered yes to any of these questions, you will appreciate the information in this section. Because sometimes in a relationship, even when things are going well, tension and conflicts arise that don't even seem to have a cause in present time. In order to fully understand why relationships can be so dramatic, let me explain my "magnifying glass principle."

Each of you carries around a big bag of feelings. Some of these feelings are very old, left over from when you were a child. For example, you might be carrying around some anger at your father for not giving you the love you needed as a child. Other feelings are more recent, such as anger at your husband for not noticing your new dress last week. These emotions are different pieces of the puzzle that makes up your uniqueness.

Love is like a powerful lens scanning all of your emotional walls for any emotions lurking inside that need to be expressed and released. Being loved by someone gives you a feeling of safety and security. Confident in that safety, you can venture out from inside yourself and connect with your lover. But on the way out, you will encounter those walls you've placed around your heart for protection.

The closer you become with a partner, the more your unexpressed and repressed feelings will surface.

Did something ever happen to you that was so bad it made you go numb—until you saw a friend or relative, and instantly burst into tears and embraced each other? That feeling of being loved makes it safe enough for you to let out the feelings inside. (This is why I prefer working with people in a seminar setting rather than privately. The safety produced by the increasing love in the room is an ideal atmosphere for emotional healing.)

Earlier I pointed out that if you aren't getting the love you want, you may separate from your partner, and this causes arguments. Taking this concept one step further, we see that *when you are reminded of the hurt of not having been loved in the past, you might also separate from your partner and tend to overreact to things that happen to you.* Most of us carry around old, unresolved emotions that surface when something happens to remind us of the original event.

This phenomenon occurs in our relationships all the time. If you once loved and experienced pain and fear, the next time you love—even if the new relationship is wonderful—those old feelings of pain and fear will tend to surface for the purpose of healing and release. This is another reason why we tend to overreact, dramatize, and fight over "nothing" in relationships: Old emotions are surfacing, and you are using the relationship as an opportunity to get rid of those emotions at last.

▶ Why Are You Overreacting?

Jack and Felicia, married for ten years, are driving to meet some friends for dinner. They begin discussing a friend whose husband recently left her. Felicia feels a lot of sympathy for their friend, who has been desolate since her husband left. Half-teasingly, she says to Jack: "You'll never leave me, will you, honey?"

"Well," Jack answers, "I know you wouldn't fall apart even if I did—you're much stronger than your friend is."

Immediately, Felicia gets knots in her stomach. She remembers her father leaving her mother, and how much it hurt her. She jumps to the worst conclusion: Since Jack didn't immediately assure her that he wouldn't leave her, that means he thinks it could happen. Is he preparing her? How long has he been unhappy with her? Felicia gulps and says, "You're scaring me; please don't say things to hurt me."

Jack feels criticized and put down, and responds, "Don't be so sensitive. You are so insecure sometimes."

"Oh, no," Felicia gasps to herself. "He thinks I am insecure. He probably thinks I am too weak for him." She starts to cry.

"Now, why are you crying?" Jack snaps, recalling how his mother never trusted his father, and how much this hurt him. "Can't I ever talk to you about anything?"

Felicia and Jack sit in the car, not speaking. Felicia is afraid Jack will leave her, and Jack feels shut down and angry that his wife isn't much fun to be with.

This incident is a perfect example of how love brings up old repressed feelings. Neither Jack nor Felicia communicated clearly, and this was a minor problem. But their poor communication was *magnified* by old feelings each had inside.

▶ Love on the Rocks

For many couples, months and years of scenes like the above drama will cause them to end the relationship. The closer they get, the more old feelings will emerge and the more rocky the relationship will look. They will find things to blame their feelings on: She doesn't want enough sex, he comes home too late. But what is really happening is that the everyday tensions are magnified a hundredfold by old repressed feelings.

If a couple continues to repress the old feelings, not knowing how to resolve them, they may numb themselves to *all* feeling in an attempt to keep peace in the relationship. Finally, unable to take it any longer, they will bail out of the relationship and eventually find someone new. Of course, when enough love and safety build up in the new relationship, the same cycle will begin all over again. Many people will continue switching partners as soon as old uncomfortable emotions surface in a relationship, thinking that they are with the wrong person. *But more often, the mistake is* not *your partner, but your inability to release and resolve the surfacing old repressed feelings.*

We can do one of two things when we feel some old repressed feelings surfacing. *Option one:* Shut down all feelings in an attempt to repress those old uncomfortable feelings. *Option two:* Express the repressed feelings when they surface. Each of these choices can cause some problems.

Option One: Shutting Down All Feelings

PROBLEM: As soon as you suppress your uncomfortable or undesirable feelings you will end up suppressing your love for your partner as well.

You cannot selectively suppress feelings. The only way to suppress a feeling is to suppress your ability to feel. When you decide to feel again, those same old suppressed feelings will pop up again.

You can leave one uncomfortable relationship and feel relieved because you aren't feeling anymore, but when you fall in love again and decide to start feeling, all those old ghosts will be back to haunt you.

Option Two: Express the Repressed Feelings When They Surface

PROBLEM: This option usually results in your overreacting. The intensity of your emotions will probably be out of proportion to the incident that is calling them forth. So if your husband comes home late one day, and you cry, he will interpret your behavior as *overreacting,* even though your old feelings of abandonment are surfacing.

This is the way most "normal" relationships work: You seesaw between option one, to feel nothing, and option two, to feel and express too much. It's no wonder you sometimes feel like you are going crazy in your relationship!

▶ Doing Emotional Housecleaning

Every relationship will have its ups and downs, its conflicts and problems. And as we've seen, *every conflict is really an opportunity to grow closer and experience more love.*

REMEMBER: WHEN YOU ARE FIGHTING, IT'S FOR ONE OF TWO REASONS:

1. **You aren't getting the love and appreciation you want, and emotional separation has built up.**

2. **Old repressed feelings are surfacing and magnifying the present situation into something more awful than it actually is.**

Some people avoid conflict as if their lives depended on it. Actually the reverse is true: Your aliveness and growth depend on dealing successfully with conflict and using it as a springboard for self-discovery.

An intimate relationship is a guaranteed way to do some emotional housecleaning! I'll be giving you practical tools and techniques for resolving conflicts and appropriately expressing those old repressed feelings later on. With the right tools, that process of clearing out the old hurts, resentments, and fears can be one of the most exciting adventures of your life!

4

How Something So Good Can Turn Out So Bad

The Story of Richard and Lynn—Suburban Philadelphia, 1971

Lynn checked herself in the mirror one last time. "You look good," she said to herself. After working all day as a hospital administrator and doing errands on the way home, she still had pushed herself to create a delicious dinner for Richard, shampoo her hair, and get dressed for the party they'd been invited to at the Bermans' house that night. "You are pretty terrific," she said out loud. She blushed to think of how much she sounded like the model wife. Well, her life was wonderful. Richard was a great husband, and she was lucky to have him.

Lynn looked over the table once more to make sure the candles were lit. Everything looked lovely. It was seven o'clock. "Richard should be home any minute now," she thought.

One hour later, she heard the key turn in the door as she was trying to doctor up the chicken, which was overcooked. "Why couldn't he at least have called?"

she grumbled to herself. "Now, Lynn, don't go getting all upset over nothing. After all, he didn't commit a crime; he was just late. Don't make a fool of yourself and ruin the whole evening by making a scene."

Richard sat down to dinner and noticed that Lynn seemed a little tense. "Why can't she loosen up?" he thought to himself. "Maybe I should tell her how pressured I feel when she puts on such a big show at dinner like this, like I am supposed to be in a great mood. Hell, I had an awful day. Guess I'd better not say anything. It will just ruin her night."

Lynn watched Richard eat, and was glad she hadn't brought up the lateness. At least now they wouldn't fight en route to the party. Lynn really hated fighting.

It was very crowded in the Bermans' that night. Lynn turned around to say hello to a friend, and when she turned back, Richard was gone. "Typical," she thought, slightly annoyed. "He's off to be the life of the party." Richard had a habit of not including her in conversations. "Oh, well," she thought, "at least he isn't an alcoholic like Janet's husband."

Richard slipped through the crowd to talk to a business associate. "I wish Lynn would take more interest in my work," he thought to himself. "She's always so caught up with her job and the kid and her friends; I seem to come last." As he watched her across the room, he smiled. "Hey, Rich," he said to himself, "don't be so hard on her. After all, you both agreed she'd keep on working after the baby was born. What do you expect?"

Lynn noticed Richard talking with Doris. Like Richard, Doris was a terrific tennis player. Doris always seemed to light up when she saw Richard. "Hey, there you go again being jealous," Lynn admonished herself. "You know how much Richard hates that side of you. Lighten up. Have another drink."

That night, as they got into bed, Lynn noticed that

Richard hadn't put on his pajamas. That meant one thing—he wanted sex. "God, I'm beat," Lynn thought. "But he does have a beautiful body. I hate saying no—we might really get into a fight." Their lovemaking was the usual. Some kissing and a few caresses, and then Richard entering Lynn and moving forcefully until he climaxed. Richard pecked Lynn on the cheek and said, "Good night, honey. You're the perfect wife," and was soon asleep.

Lynn felt a gnawing sense that something was wrong, but she couldn't figure out what it was. "Maybe I should have told Richard I was irritated at the party," she thought. "No, that would have been stupid," she decided. "After all, he is a great provider, he loves me and the baby, and we get along really well. I can't forget how lucky I am. Some of my best friends aren't even married yet. It's best to just forget about these little picky things that bother me. Yes"—she smiled and burrowed under the covers—"I have a lot to be grateful for."

Some people might conclude that Lynn and Richard have a pretty good relationship. They have learned to live with their differences, to deal with their problems and get along harmoniously. Well, this analysis couldn't be further from the truth. Lynn and Richard were married in 1971 and twelve years later they are going to end up divorced.

The Attorney's Office, 1983

Lynn sat tapping her foot and stared at her watch for the sixth time in ten minutes. "Relax, Lynn," her attorney said, "Richard will show up."

"Oh, sure," Lynn replied. "As usual, I'm kept waiting. I've spent twelve years waiting for that inconsiderate jerk."

The door opened and Richard and his attorney walked in. "Sorry we're late." Richard smiled apologetically.

"So what's new?" Lynn snapped.

"See," Richard pleaded to his lawyer, "she's starting in on me already!"

"Okay, everyone, let's just relax, sit down, and discuss this like adults," Lynn's attorney began. "As you know, we are here to try to settle this divorce without going to court, which will save you both tremendous costs."

"Sure," Richard said, "I think we can settle these differences in a friendly way."

"Oh, cut it out, Richard," Lynn snapped again. "We don't need to see your Mr. Nice Guy act. I lived with that for years, so don't waste our time."

"Lynn," Richard answered coldly, "just because I am a much less nervous and irritable person than you are doesn't mean I am putting on an act. Some people are even-tempered, but of course you wouldn't understand that, would you?"

"You call me irritable?" Lynn retorted. "Well, who wouldn't be irritable living with someone who was oblivious to everyone but himself. You never noticed me, or how much I tried to please you." Lynn started to cry.

"That's because you were so damned busy you never noticed me. And when you did, you looked for every opportunity to criticize me. I want a woman who appreciates me, not one who is trying to rehabilitate me and make me into someone else. Someone who shows me some kindness and affection—in bed, for instance." Richard ended his speech.

"Don't be crude, Richard," Lynn threatened, "there are other people here, you know."

"Crude," Richard repeated, his face getting redder and redder, "crude—that's just what sex is to you, isn't it? That's why you moved into the other bedroom seven years ago. That's why you never seemed as interested in sex as I was, because you think it's crude. Well, you're just frigid!"

"How dare you call me frigid!" Lynn shrieked. "I was working full-time and being a mother. I was tired. Besides, you were the one always drooling over anything in skirts, every party we went to, and that slut you used to play tennis with . . ."

Richard interrupted, "I never laid a hand on anyone but you, but maybe I should have."

And as Richard and Lynn continued to attack each other, all the years of stored-up resentment started to pour out. Their attorneys exchanged glances and very discreet smiles—yes, this was going to be a very long case.

When Richard and Lynn fell in love, they had every opportunity to have a happy life and make their relationship work. But they made one fatal mistake: They didn't tell each other the Complete Truth.

There is a big difference between telling the Complete Truth and being honest. We often feel we are being honest when, in fact, we are expressing only *part* of what we think or feel. We leave out the parts that we fear may not be well received, or ignore the parts we don't want to face ourselves. We aren't really lying. We're just telling the part of the truth that is easy to tell.

One of the most important ways to make love work for you in your relationships is learning how to communicate the Complete Truth.

The first step is to figure out what you are feeling in the first place! Only then can you tell the Complete Truth about it.

▶ Are You a Master of Emotional Disguise?

If you are like most people, you are probably an expert at hiding your feelings. You hide the truth not only from others but from yourself as well. After a while, you may even forget how you really feel inside, and when people ask you, "What's wrong?" or "What do you want?" you answer, "I don't know." You might want to tell them how you feel, but you've become so good at hiding from your feelings that you've forgotten where you put them!

The following quiz will help you understand the ways in which you may be hiding the truth about your feelings from yourself and others. Add up your score as you give yourself points for how frequently these statements apply to you:

Often .... 3 points

Sometimes .... 2 points

Rarely or never .... 1 point

1. When I am angry about something, I find myself smiling as I describe it or laughing and making light of it.

2. If I am upset with someone, I avoid rather than confront that person.

3. When a person hurts my feelings, I respond by becoming sarcastic.

4. I have a difficult time telling people I love how I feel about them.

5. If people ask me if I am upset with them, I don't let them know how angry or hurt I am, and tell them not to worry about it.

6. When I know I've made a mistake, I have a hard time saying I am sorry, and might instead point out how the other person has made mistakes.

7. When I feel upset, I: (score each answer separately)
   a. Smoke more
   b. Drink more

   c. Eat more
   d. Take more drugs
   e. Sleep more

8. When I am intimidated by someone, I act cold and distant.

9. If I have been treated unfairly, I retreat into my emotions and cry rather than confront the person with my anger.

10. It takes a lot of effort for someone to get me to express strongly how I feel if my feeling isn't a positive one.

Now, add up your points:

14–20 points: *Congratulations!* You are doing well at telling the truth about your feelings. You may want to do some work on the questions on which you scored a 2.

20–30 points: *It's time to do some work on communicating your emotions.* Too often, you're hiding how you feel from yourself and others. Practice the techniques in this book and commit yourself to being more honest.

30–42 points: *You are a master of emotional disguise.* Most of your energy is spent hiding your feelings, protecting yourself, and fooling others. Inside, you are very frightened and need a lot of love and acceptance. Until you learn to share the truth of your feelings with yourself and with others, it will be difficult for you to have harmonious, fulfilling relationships—your partner will have a hard time knowing what you are feeling. Use this book as your textbook for learning how to express those feelings buried inside. Good luck! You can do it!

▶ Your Emotional Map

I have spent my years as a therapist and seminar leader trying to solve the mystery of our emotions, and I'm very excited to have created what I call the Emotional Map.

The Emotional Map is a simple yet powerful formula to help you understand your own feelings and the feelings of others, and to assist you in moving out of any unpleasant emotions, such as anger, hurt, or fear, and back to a state of love. According to the Emotional Map, whenever you feel upset or emotionally off balance, you are experiencing five levels of feeling at the same time. These levels are:

FIVE LEVELS OF FEELING

1. **ANGER,** blame, and resentment
2. **HURT,** sadness, and disappointment
3. **FEAR** and insecurity
4. **REMORSE,** regret, and responsibility
5. **LOVE,** intention, understanding, and forgiveness

When something upsets you, you usually experience one predominant emotion, such as anger, hurt, fear, or remorse. But like the earth's surface, our emotions build one on top of the other, in *layers*. At the core of all the layers is the essence of human emotion: love and the need for connection and intimacy.

Anger, blame, and resentment are your first line of defense to protect yourself by scaring off your attackers. Underneath it lie hurt, sadness, and disappointment—much more vulnerable emotions. The hurt covers up the even more vulnerable feelings of fear and insecurity. The layer just before the core of love is remorse, regret, and responsibility, which are painful feelings of failure in love. Underneath all the anger, hurt, fear, and remorse is love. *The other emotions are simply a reaction we go through when something interferes with our ability to feel loved or loving.*

Whenever you feel angry or hurt or any other disturbing emotion, you are temporarily "out of love." If you think about the central core of love being like "home," feeling angry or afraid is like being away from your center, "away from home."

> ***Emotional Tension can be resolved only by experiencing and expressing each of the four layers of emotion that cover up love.***

When you express only some of the emotions you feel from a conflict or upset in your life, the conflict never gets fully resolved, and the Emotional Tension from the conflict can't be released. You can't get down to *love*. What happens to that Emotional Tension? You repress it and carry it from relationship to relationship. In this and the following chapters, I'll teach you how to use your Emotional Map to create much happier, tension-free relationships.

▶ How to Express the Complete Truth

Now that you understand the Emotional Map, you can begin to see why you may have experienced communication problems in your relationships:

▼

SECRET:
> *Most communication problems stem from communicating only part of the truth, not the Complete Truth.*

▲

When you are upset, and attempt to tell your partner how you are feeling, you probably focus on the most obvious, "outermost" layer of your emotions—your anger or hurt. Your partner does the same thing. Your messages to one another sound unloving and thus are very difficult to listen to.

Let's look at a simple example of how this works. Marcia and her husband, George, have just returned from a trip to Japan. At a welcome-home party given in their honor, Marcia is telling a group of friends about a tour that she and George took. George interrupts Marcia several times, correcting her version of the story. "How dare he do this!" Marcia fumes to herself. When the party is over, she confronts him with her feelings: "How could you be so critical of me? I felt furious with you. You ruined my whole evening!"

Is Marcia communicating the truth to George? Yes. She is angry and resentful. Yet her anger is only part of the truth: It is the tip of her iceberg of emotions.

How will George respond to Marcia's anger? Probably with anger of his own:

> MARCIA: How could you be so critical of me? I'm furious with you.
> GEORGE: I wasn't being critical, I was just correcting you.
> MARCIA: Well, you were rude.
> GEORGE: Rude? You are really overreacting now. Calm down.
> MARCIA: I am overreacting! You are just so cold sometimes.
> GEORGE: Oh, you are impossible to please!

And on to round two!

Now let's look at the Complete Truth about Marcia's feelings:

> **Anger:** We've already heard Marcia's anger.
> **Hurt and sadness:** Why does Marcia feel so

angry at George? Because what he did hurt her, and she feels sad about how she was treated. It hurts when someone who loves us doesn't approve of us.

Fear: Underneath her hurt is some fear and insecurity: "I'm afraid George is getting tired of me. I'm afraid I can't express myself well in front of people. I'm afraid George and I will keep fighting."

Remorse and responsibility: Underneath Marcia's fear is some remorse and a sense of responsibility—not guilt in the sense of being bad, but a feeling that the situation is causing problems for herself and the person she loves, and remorse about anything she did to cause that. "I'm sorry I didn't tell the story accurately." "I'm sorry I get nervous speaking in front of people." "I'm sorry we're fighting."

Love and intention: Underneath all these other emotions is Marcia's intention—what Marcia really wants. She doesn't want to fight. She doesn't want to be right. She feels: "I want to make you proud of me, George. I want to learn to be as good a storyteller as you. I want us to get along."

And at the core of her feelings is love. If Marcia didn't love George so much, she wouldn't really care what he thought about her. Because she loves him, she also feels sad when she doesn't please him, becomes *afraid* of losing him, is *hurt* when he criticizes her, and gets *angry* when they don't get along.

Here is how Marcia could have expressed the Complete Truth: "George, I want to tell you how I am feeling right now, because it is preventing me from feeling close to you, and I want to feel close again. Just listen to everything I have to say before you make any judgment. *I am really angry* at you for being so critical of me when I was telling the story. I think it was rude and it embarrassed me in front of my friends. *It hurts* me that you don't like the way I express myself. *I'm afraid* that maybe you aren't proud of the way I express myself and that my intellect bores you. I'm afraid that you are tired of me, and that that's why you were so critical. I'm afraid this will turn into a big fight and *I'm sorry* I got nervous telling that story. I'm sorry we are fighting. *I want* you to be proud of me, George. I want us to feel really safe with each other. *I love* you so much, and being happy together is the most important thing in the world to me. What you think of me really matters and that's why I got so upset."

This, then, is the Complete Truth. The reason Marcia felt so angry at George was because she loves him so much. (Expressing the Complete Truth puts the whole conversation into perspective.) Marcia can move through *all* of her feelings, get the real message across to her husband, and, above all, *she can avoid letting anger push down her powerful love for her partner.*

▼

SECRET:
   Underneath all unpleasant emotions is love and the desire for connection.

▲

If you are angry at your wife for frequently not wanting sex, beneath all that anger is *your love for her* and *your wish that you could be more intimate and passionate together.* If you are angry at your husband for not pursuing his goals at work, underneath your anger is *your love for him* and *your desire for him to make all his dreams come true.* If you are angry at your boss for treating you poorly, underneath your anger is *your caring for your job* and *your desire for your boss to like and respect you, and for you both to get along.*

Here are some examples to show how someone might tell the Complete Truth about several upsetting incidents we all encounter in life. Notice how the initial feeling is quite different from the real feelings underneath.

Incident: **Your husband criticizes your appearance and compares you with another woman.**

Your initial feeling:

Anger and resentment

Feelings underneath:

It really *hurts* me when you don't think I'm attractive.

It makes me *sad* when you compare me with someone else.

I'm *afraid* you're getting tired of me.

I'm *afraid* if I don't lose weight you'll stop loving me.

I'm *sorry* I don't make you proud of me.

I'm *sorry* I haven't been taking good care of myself lately.

I *want* to look beautiful for you.

I *love* you, and your opinion of me is important.

Incident: **Your wife complains about your not being able to afford a vacation.**

Your initial feeling:

Anger and resentment

Feelings underneath:

It *hurts* to feel that I'm not a good provider.

It makes me *sad* that we both work and still can't afford the things we want.

I'm *afraid* I'll never be as successful as you want me to be.

I'm *afraid* I'm not smart enough to make more money.

I'm *sorry* we can't go on that big trip.

I'm *sorry* I can't give you everything you deserve.

I *want* to make more money so we can travel together everywhere.

I *love* you so much and only want to give you the best.

Incident: **Your partner complains that the house is a mess and you are disorganized.**

Your initial feeling:
Hurt and depression

Feelings underneath:
I'm *angry* at you for not doing your share of the housework.

I *hate* it when you act as if I'm supposed to be the perfect housewife when I work full-time just as you do.

I really *hurts* me when you don't appreciate how much I do for you.

I'm *afraid* you'll never treat me as an equal.

I'm *afraid* we'll never get our life together organized.

I'm *sorry* I don't ask you for more help cleaning and just expect you to remember.

I'm *sorry* I don't let you know how overwhelmed I feel sometimes.

I *want* to work on communicating my expectations better.

I *want* us to make some schedules for sharing our housework.

I *love* you and do love to take care of you and our home.

I *understand* you're still getting used to being a "liberated" man.

Incident: **Your wife isn't in the mood to make love.**

Your initial feeling:
Anger and rejection

Feelings underneath:
It really *hurts* me when you don't want to make love with me.

It *hurts* when I open up to you in bed and you push me away.

I'm *afraid* you have lost interest in me.

I'm *afraid* our sex life will never be passionate again.

I'm *sorry* I don't always take enough time to turn you on.

I *want* us to be romantically in love and have a wonderful sex life.

I *love* you, honey, and I'm attracted to you.

Incident: **Your son has a party and leaves the house in a mess.**

Your initial feeling:
Anger and blame

Feelings underneath:

I'm *angry* at you for being so inconsiderate.

It *hurts* me when you act as though you don't care.

It *hurts* me when you are selfish and don't think about my feelings.

I'm *afraid* I spoiled you.

I'm *afraid* I didn't do a good job of being a parent.

I'm *sorry* I didn't let you know how important it was that you clean everything up.

I *want* you to feel more a part of the family and member of the household.

I *love* you and need to know you really care about me and my feelings.

The techniques I'll be teaching you in later chapters will help you to express your Complete Truth. But just understanding your Emotional Map will help you identify your feelings more clearly when you are upset. When you do decide to communicate the Complete Truth, just follow your Emotional Map through the layers back home to the feeling of love, making sure to include emotions from each of the levels. I promise you will feel better, and so will the other person!

▶ What to Do When You Get Stuck

Have you ever felt stuck in being angry, and even though you didn't want to feel angry anymore, you couldn't seem to snap out of it?

Have you ever felt so sad and depressed that it seemed as though nothing could chase away the black cloud of doom around you?

Have you ever felt so frozen with fear and insecurity about something that no matter how much you told yourself you were overreacting, you couldn't stop?

These are some examples of what happens when you don't express all your levels of feeling. You may think you are angry, but actually you are hurt; you think you are depressed, but actually you are frightened. Without expressing the full range of your feelings, you will never dissolve the Emotional Tension, and so you get stuck in one particular feeling.

Look over the Emotional Map and ask yourself: Which of these emotions do I have a difficult time expressing? Chances are that you have been "trained" not to feel certain emotions, so you "get stuck" in others. If you are a male, you may have been taught that it was not okay for you to show feelings of vulnerability such as hurt or fear.

The one emotion many men were given permission to express was anger: If someone hits you, hit back; don't sit there and cry.

A SECRET ABOUT MEN FOR WOMEN:

When men experience a strong emotional reaction, they often express the Emotional Tension through the only outlet they have been taught is acceptable: anger and blame.

If a man doesn't feel safe expressing vulnerability, he might stay stuck in anger until he gets even, or he might just shut down entirely and appear unreachable. Remember, when you are hurt—when you feel love is being taken away—it's very difficult to admit that vulnerability. *Often you pretend you don't care, when the truth is you are very hurt.*

Staying angry is one of the ways we resist feeling our hurt. (Of course, this applies to women as well as men, although women have less negative conditioning about showing their vulnerability.)

Do you get angry more often than you would like to? Chances are that you are more hurt than angry, and you've been using your hot temper to avoid feeling your hurt and fear. Ask yourself what hurts you and what you fear or feel insecure about in each incident. Give yourself permission to cry more often and to find the child inside you that needs a lot of love. When you give yourself permission to express your hurt, fear, and remorse, you will experience a tremendous emotional and physical release and will find yourself much less angry and irritable.

Do you have a partner who gets angry very frequently? If you suspect that your partner covers up his or her vulnerable feelings with anger, you can help by:

• Not responding to your partner's anger with your anger.

- Asking your partner if you have hurt him, or if he is afraid. (By doing this you are giving your partner permission to express those feelings.)
- Expressing what you think your partner's more vulnerable feelings might be, even if he isn't aware of how he is feeling. *Example:* "Honey, it must have really hurt you when I told you I thought your fishing trip sounded stupid. You are probably afraid I'll never support you and your fishing outings and that we'll always argue about it."
- Imagining your partner as a little hurt child who doesn't know how to ask for comfort or reassurance. This will help you not to *react* to the anger, but instead to *respond* with love.

Do you have a hard time expressing your anger? Some people have the opposite problem of getting stuck in anger: They can't or won't express any feelings of hostility. Often women have been conditioned to believe that it's not "nice" to get angry, and they substitute vulnerability for anger. It is acceptable for women to cry and feel frightened. They may even get stuck in sadness to the point of feeling an extremely exaggerated sense of insecurity. *The crying becomes a cover-up for rage.* There are men, as well, who have been taught to suppress their anger, and retreat into self-deprecation instead.

Another way you may cover up your anger is by becoming very critical and sarcastic. Often people who don't feel safe getting angry will constantly criticize and bicker with their partner. In this way they avoid the frightening experience of feeling the full force of their anger and confronting their partner with its true cause.

The Result of Suppressing Your Anger
One result of constantly repressing your anger is depression.

Depression is not intense sadness. It is suppressed anger that has been redirected at yourself.

If you are unable to resolve your angry feelings in constructive ways, you store those angry feelings inside you. Since it takes a lot of energy to suppress anger, you may find yourself feeling tired, lifeless, hopeless, and depressed. You are using up vital energy to keep that anger from showing.

If you suffer from depression and are sure the cause isn't physical, ask yourself if you suppress your anger. Give yourself permission to express your anger along with the other layers of feeling.

- Make a list of all the people you are or have been angry at.
- Use the techniques described in Part Two to release the anger that is weighing you down.
- Ask your partner or family members for permission to express the Complete Truth, including your angry feelings when they come up.

Do you have a partner who has a hard time expressing anger? If your partner rarely expresses anger but cries a lot, becomes withdrawn and distant, or seems depressed or critical, you can help by:

- Giving your partner permission to get angry and express the Complete Truth by using the Emotional Map.
- Asking your partner when he is crying or distant if he is angry at you and encouraging him to be honest.
- Expressing what you think her angry feelings might be even if she isn't aware of how she is feeling. *Example:* "Helen, it must have really made you angry tonight when I didn't include you in the conversation with my friends from work, and paid attention to them through the

whole dinner. You probably feel I was totally ̣insensitive."

One of the most common ways you may hide from your own anger is to surround yourself with lovers and friends who hide from theirs. A couple who is frightened of facing their angry feelings often gravitate toward one another in relationships, and neither gives the other "permission" to feel and resolve the anger. The result is a lot of repression, and a relationship lacking honesty and passion.

If you find yourself with a partner who shares your own fear of anger, sit down and talk about it. Express *why* you are hesitant to face your angry emotions, and what you're both afraid might happen if you did. Work together using the tools and techniques in this book to heal your fear of anger.

▶ Why You Don't Tell the Truth

There are three main reasons why you don't allow yourself to feel and express the Complete Truth about your emotions:

1. Fear of disapproval
2. Fear of hurting someone else
3. Fear of punishment

Fear of Disapproval

Depending on our background and experience, each of us labels certain emotions as being "good" or "bad," "right" or "wrong." If little Suzie starts to cry because Mommy and Daddy are leaving on a trip, Mommy says, "Now, Suzie, there's nothing to cry about—let's see a pretty smile for Daddy." Suzie concludes two things: (1) In order to get Mommy and Daddy's love, I have to smile and stop crying; therefore, (2) crying must be bad and a sign of weakness.

As you grew older, you formed a self-image designed to inspire others to love you. *Whenever you started to experience a feeling that threatened your ability to be loved, you repressed that feeling.*

Is Fear of Disapproval Running Your Life?

The fear of receiving disapproval for telling the truth about your feelings can be powerful enough to run your whole life. The most dramatic example I've ever seen of this occurred with a man I'll call Bill. Bill was a very soft-spoken, gentle guy, always smiling and trying to appear friendly. Bill was in a marriage that felt dead both to him and to his wife. As he sat through my seminar, he started to get in touch with the faintest feelings of anger inside him, and the more he felt the stirrings of anger, the more frightened he became.

It seemed that when Bill was a young boy, he had seen his father get angry once, and the next day his father had a heart attack and died. Bill associated anger with sickness and death.

Bill told me that he had something he wanted to tell the truth about. I knew he wanted to admit that he was angry with his wife for not giving him the love he needed and for not communicating with him.

Bill stood up but was speechless. Everyone in the room could see that he was waging a huge inner battle. His face got paler and paler, and just as he whispered, "I'm angry at my wife," he fainted. Everyone in the room gasped. Bill quickly revived, and I calmed everyone down and pointed out to them that this is what happens when we suppress our feelings. Bill was so fearful of his anger that he ruined his marriage and his chances for happiness as an adult by never asking for what he wanted. He had stuffed his anger down, numbing himself in the process.

IS FEAR OF DISAPPROVAL RUNNING YOUR LIFE?

Here are some of the ways that fear of disapproval can run your life. Give yourself one point for each statement that seems to describe you.

1. I frequently go along with what other people want or suggest rather than make my own choices.

2. I often notice myself disagreeing with what others say but keep my opinions to myself.

3. I have a difficult time in leadership positions telling other people what to do.

4. I become extremely nervous if I have to give people negative feedback and often let them think everything is fine when it isn't.

5. When asked to make a decision, I frequently am noncommittal because I'm afraid to make the wrong choice.

6. I find out what other people like or how they feel and agree with them rather than offer my own innovative thoughts.

7. I disapprove of or criticize others first if I am afraid they might disapprove of me.

8. I hide my fear of other people and their judgments of me by being apathetic, or acting like I don't care.

9. I avoid people who intimidate me or with whom I feel some tension.

10. When I lend people money, I have a difficult time asking them to return what they borrowed.

11. I frequently don't ask for what I want sexually from a partner and have had few satisfying sexual experiences.

12. I have a difficult time saying no to people when they ask for favors or want something from me that I don't want to give.

Now add up your score.

0–4 points: You have a normal amount of fear of disapproval. Continue to work on being yourself.

4–8 points: You are letting your fear of what people think of you stop you from being the unique person you are. It's time for a change.

8–12 points: *Emergency!* You are letting your fears of disapproval run your life. Take action to change this habit now!

Fear of Hurting Others

Let's imagine that when you were fifteen, your boyfriend told you he didn't like the way you kissed, and you felt terribly hurt and rejected. Ten years later, you are making love with your husband and you feel he is rushing you. You want to tell him to slow down, but you're afraid you will hurt his feelings. You have an *unconscious memory that telling the truth hurts.*

Fear of Punishment

The third reason you are hesitant to tell the truth in relationships is out of fear of getting "punished" or penalized for doing so. You may have acquired this conditioning when you were a child. Often, the times you told the truth were the times you got in the most trouble, so you decide that it is safest not to tell the truth.

▶ What Happens When You Don't Tell the Truth

Love dies in an atmosphere of dishonesty. *You can't push down unpleasant feelings—the anger, hurt, fear—without pushing down the positive feelings as well. Not communicating the truth in your relationship is sure to kill the passion.* Passion comes from feeling intensely. When you suppress the truth, you are destroying your ability to feel. And when you stop feeling, you stop loving.

Most of all, *you* know when you aren't telling the Complete Truth in life: You lack the inner sense of peace; you feel something is out of balance; and your own sense of self-esteem droops. You are out of sync with your personal integrity. There's only one way to get back to a place of personal integrity—practice telling the Complete Truth, first to yourself and then to others. You will love the effect it has on all of your relationships.

5

Avoiding the Four Biggest Mistakes in Love

▶ The Four R's—Warning Signs of a Troubled Relationship

Relationships don't just fall apart overnight. There are warning signs to look for, signs that your levels of Emotional Tension are rising and that the relationship is in trouble.

I call these warning signs the *Four R's*. The Four R's encompass the four stages of tension in a relationship. You pass through these stages frequently, and if you don't learn how to avoid them, *the four R's will turn into the four stages of the death of your relationship.*

The Four R's are:

Resistance　Resentment　Rejection　Repression

Resistance

It is normal to experience some resistance in your relationships with other human beings, especially those very close to you. Resistance occurs when you notice yourself taking exception to something another person is doing, saying, or feeling. You feel annoyed, critical, a little separate from them.

EXAMPLE: You are in bed with your partner, ready to go to sleep. He starts to stimulate you, in hopes of making love. You notice yourself feeling resistance to him, a feeling like "Oh, no, I wish he'd be more gentle or start off by kissing me. It bothers me when he rushes like this."

EXAMPLE: Your wife is talking with her best friend and jokes about how you never help with the children. You notice yourself feeling resistance to what she says and being a little annoyed.

Most people handle signs of resistance by ignoring them and pretending nothing is wrong. You probably have thoughts like: "Don't get so upset over nothing," or "You're being too picky; no one's perfect," or "Just forget about it. Why rock the boat?" This is your first mistake. Ignoring feelings of resistance is the first step toward moving right through the Four R's.

"If you don't reveal your feelings of resistance and resolve them with your partner, these little resistances build up and turn into the second R: resentment.

Resentment

Resentment is a more developed state of resistance. Now you no longer feel merely annoyed by something your partner does—*you can't stand it!* While resistance caused annoyance, resentment causes anger. You feel angry, critical, hostile, frustrated, unloving. At that moment you have begun to separate from your partner and retreat behind your emotional walls.

EXAMPLE: You experience night after night of sex without your partner's being patient or gentle enough, and you don't express your feelings of annoyance to him. The night comes when you no longer simply *resist* his techniques of lovemaking—you really *resent* it. You feel: "I hate the way he paws at me. I hate how insensitive he is."

EXAMPLE: You have listened to your wife put you down over and over again about not helping with the children without telling her your feelings of resistance. Finally, you begin to feel fed up—you *resent* her attitude: "I hate how damned critical she is of me. She doesn't appreciate how hard I work all day for her, and then she goads me for not helping with the children."

If you don't tell the truth about your feelings of resentment and resolve them with your partner, the resentment builds up and turns into the third R: rejection.

Rejection

Rejection means separation: emotional, physical, or both. This stage of the Four R's occurs when so much resistance and resentment have built up that it is impossible for you to be comfortable staying emotionally connected to the other person, and so you separate yourself from him or her. Rejection may occur in two ways:

1. *Active rejection:* Your partner is aware of how angry you are because you are:

Threatening to leave

Refusing to cooperate or do what your partner wants

Complaining about your partner to others

Verbally abusing your partner

Refusing your partner's sexual advances

Spending as much time as possible away from your
partner

Leaving the room and refusing to talk about issues
during a fight

2. *Passive rejection:* Your partner *may be unaware*
of how angry you really are because you are:

Fantasizing about other sexual partners

Having an affair

Not responding sexually when your partner makes
love to you

Losing sexual desire "for no apparent reason"

Becoming a workaholic; having no time for your
partner

Tuning your partner out when he/she speaks to
you

Disagreeing with every point of view your partner
takes

Secretly longing for your "freedom"—to leave the
relationship and be on your own

Sex and Rejection

In this third state of the Four R's, your sex life will
deteriorate, if not disappear entirely. *You can't feel
turned on to someone at whom you are so angry, so
you turn off.* You may just feel a lack of attraction or
diminished sexual desire. You may tell yourself you
don't have an interest in sex anymore. Or you may
actually feel repelled or disgusted at the thought of
having sex with your partner.

If you stay together in the stage of rejection, your
relationship will be either very rocky, or very dull. This
depends on whether you are engaged in active rejection or passive rejection.

Many couples do not survive this stage. The breakup is usually very painful and filled with anger and bitterness.

If you don't tell the truth about your feelings of rejection and resolve them with your partner, the tension builds up and turns into the next level of separation: repression.

Repression

Repression is a state of emotional numbness. You enter this stage when you are tired of resisting, resenting, and rejecting. You successfully repress all of your negative emotions, numbing yourself to them in order to be comfortable.

You may repress your feelings consciously or unconsciously. Often in the state of repression, you tell yourself such things as:

"It's just not worth fighting over anymore."

"It doesn't really matter, anyway."

"We have to learn to get along for the sake of the children."

"I'm too tired to deal with this anymore."

"Everyone has these problems, so let's just forget it."

"We have to look good because of the kids [the church, my job, our neighbors], so let's just act civilized to one another."

If you are in stage four, your emotional numbness will spill over into the rest of your life. You lose your passion and aliveness. You may feel very even, flat, or bored. Often you experience fatigue and low energy. You may have successfully repressed the pain, but you have repressed joy and excitement as well.

Repression is the most dangerous of the Four R's, because in this stage you can fool yourself into believing that your relationship is fine, when in fact it's in grave danger. I often work with couples who are so repressed that they truly believe they do not have any problems. Of course, they have little or no sex life, no passion, and no dreams left. They may say they have "worked through" their problems. What they mean is that they have repressed their feelings and can now live comfortably, if not passionately, together.

A couple in stage four may *appear* to be content. You might notice that they never fight or argue and that they are very polite to one another. You may even envy their relationship—until one day you hear that they have separated or divorced. You think to yourself, "I can't understand it. They seemed so happy." "Seemed" is the right choice of words. They were repressing all of their unpleasant emotions and ended up killing the relationship.

Living in stage four is also physically unhealthy. When we push down our deepest hopes, dreams, and desires, we create tremendous strain, which takes its toll on our physical well-being.

I believe that one of the most serious problems in society today is that *many people are walking around in a state of permanent emotional repression*. When simply repressing their feelings becomes difficult, they turn to alcohol, drugs, food, tranquilizers, overwork, and other unhealthy methods to help them stay numb.

One of the reasons I became so dedicated to teaching my seminars was that I knew that people needed to learn how to deal with emotional tension in relationships and how to identify and express their emotions in positive ways. I have seen thousands of people come to my weekend workshops in dead relationships, deep in repression, and walk out two days later feeling more alive, passionate, and in love than they have in years.

The Four R's apply to all your relationships—not just with a lover, but with your parents, your children, your boss, your friends, and even yourself.

How Richard and Lynn Healed the Four R's

Remember the story at the beginning of Chapter 4 about Richard and Lynn? Richard and Lynn started out very much in love but they went right through the Four R's and ended up in an attorney's office twelve years later. What went wrong for them?

Like most young couples, Richard and Lynn had beautiful dreams of living happily ever after. But they never discussed how they would handle their emotional tension. No one had ever taught them how to deal with feelings or resolve conflict. So when conflict arose, they simply went through the Four R's. They ignored the issues, pretended everything was fine, and systematically destroyed their love and trust for each other.

What were the issues Lynn and Richard didn't deal with?

For Lynn:

Richard's chronic lateness
Richard's need to be the center of attention
Lynn's feelings of being left out
Richard's flirting and Lynn's jealousy
The mechanical quality of their lovemaking
Lynn's feelings of being unappreciated

For Richard:

Lynn's need to have everything "perfect"
Lynn's insensitivity to how hard Richard worked
Lynn's absorption in her job and the children and her disinterest in Richard's work
Lynn's habit of being outwardly nice to Richard and then criticizing him sharply
Lynn's passive attitude toward sex

The first thing I did with Lynn and Richard was to take them back in their memory to the time when they fell in love and got married. They had been so busy fighting in the past few years that they had forgotten they had ever loved one another. I asked them to bring their wedding album into my office. Together, we looked at the pictures. Both Lynn and Richard began to cry when they saw their young, hopeful faces. They cried for the dream that had died and for the part of them that had died when they closed their hearts to each other.

Now that they both felt more vulnerable, I explained the Four R's to Richard and Lynn, pointing out how years of little resistances had driven them to reject each other. I knew it would take time, but if Richard and Lynn were willing to learn to express the Complete Truth to each other rather than just blame, they had a chance of healing the pain they had caused each other and creating a new beginning.

I worked closely with them, teaching them how to tell the Complete Truth about their feelings. They were both amazed to discover emotions in each other they had no idea existed: Richard never realized how much Lynn had been motivated by her desire to please him—he had thought she was just a perfectionist. He also never knew (because she never told him) how much she loved sex, but needed more foreplay and variety. As for not paying enough attention to Richard, Lynn had always believed that she could make Richard happy by being a "Superwoman," working full-time and raising a family. She never realized how much he missed being "number one."

Lynn was surprised to learn that Richard desperately needed her approval and that he had been devastated each time she criticized him, or even gave him suggestions. Now, after twelve years, she was finding out there was a very needy little boy behind his walls.

Richard admitted that his lateness was due to the fact that he had a hard time saying no to people, and constantly overextended himself. This was something Lynn never knew because Richard was afraid to deal with it himself. Lynn listened to Richard talk about his feelings and found that this man needed a tremendous amount of attention, but that he had been afraid to ask Lynn for the affection and validation he desperately desired. The more they shared the Complete Truth, the more they realized how truly compatible they were, and how many of their needs were identical.

Lynn and Richard's story had a very happy ending. They decided to remain separate, start dating, and continue to work on themselves and their relationship. They took several of my seminars in order to break down some of the emotional walls they had put around their hearts. And they continued practicing the techniques I teach in this book. After nine months, they went away on a long vacation that they both insisted was better than their honeymoon had been. When they returned home, Richard moved back into the house with Lynn. Since, then, their marriage has flourished. They have been reunited for three years now, and are more in love than they had ever been before.

There are millions of Richards and Lynns out there. Perhaps you are one of them. If so, I hope you will be inspired by their story. It's not too late. Using everything I've shared with you, you can heal the wounds in your relationship and make it what you have always dreamed of.

▶ How the Four R's Affect You Every Day

Moving through the Four R's can take years or months, but it can also happen in a few minutes. Suppose I'm at a party and my partner comments on how beautiful another woman looks. Watch me go right through the Four R's:

"Why did he say that? That wasn't very considerate [*resistance*]. I hate when he does that to me. Sometimes he is so insensitive [*resentment*]. I don't even want to look at him now. If he thinks I'll make love with him tonight, he can forget it [*rejection*]. Oh, well, I'm not going to ruin my evening just because of one thing he said. After all, nothing really happened. It's no big deal [*repression*]."

Now I'm all smiles again. But if enough moments occur in which I go from feeling resistance to repression in sixty seconds flat, I will stop feeling in love with my partner and will not feel attracted to him.

▶ Dating and the Four R's

Karen was very depressed and confused when she walked into my office. "I feel like such a failure with men," she stated. "I seem to blow every date I have."

"Tell me about your latest date," I said.

"Well, David asked me out. I really liked him when I first met him. I was excited to get to know him. We spent the day at the beach, and we were supposed to go out to dinner that night. By the end of the day, though, I was feeling really turned off to him, and so I said I was tired and wanted to go home. Then he called me Tuesday to see if I wanted to go out again, and I found myself refusing him. I felt awful afterward, and I just don't understand why I keep doing it."

"Okay, Karen," I said, "let's start again at the beginning, and I want you to tell me everything you were feeling during your date and how much of it you actually communicated to him."

"Well," Karen said, "I was having lots of fun at the beach, but then David started saying things like 'Do you like to sail? We could go sailing sometime.' I felt he was being a little premature making all these plans for us on our first date."

"Did you tell him that?" I asked.

"No, I guess I didn't," Karen replied. "Then he kept talking about fun things we could do and I got more and more annoyed at him. We went back to his place to get ready for dinner, and I was feeling really irritable when all of a sudden he said, 'Wouldn't it be fun to take a shower together with our beach clothes on?' I felt embarrassed because that felt intimate to me, but I didn't want to hurt his feelings, so I went ahead and did it, anyway. After that I just wanted to get out of there and be alone, so I left. And when he called me on Tuesday, I acted like a real bitch to him."

As you can see, Karen's date turned from delight into disaster because she didn't communicate the Complete Truth to David. She started out feeling *resistance* to his making so many plans for them and not telling him how pressured that made her feel. Her resistance turned into *resentment* that he was being so pushy. Naturally, David didn't know he was being pushy because Karen didn't say anything. Instead of saying she felt embarrassed when he mentioned the shower, she pushed down the feeling and her resentment turned into *rejection*. By Tuesday, she felt nothing for David. She had thoroughly *repressed* any attraction for him, and she believed she didn't care for him at all.

If Karen had told David the truth, asking him to go a little slower with her, the chances are that he would have slowed down, she would have felt better, and he certainly would have felt better knowing he was no longer turning her off. I gave Karen the assignment to call David up and explain the whole incident, telling him the Complete Truth. It turned out that he had had no idea of what was going on and had concluded that she was a little crazy. After the call, they both felt so connected that they decided to go out again, and they have been dating ever since.

▶ How to Avoid the Four R's

There is only one solution for preventing your relationships from moving through the Four R's:

> *The moment you notice some Emotional Tension between you and your partner, tell the Complete Truth about how you feel, using your Emotional Map and the techniques you will find in later chapters.*

If you tell the truth about feelings the moment either of you notices them, you will nip resentment and rejection in the bud. It's a lot easier to resolve a small conflict than a big one that's been brewing a long time.

Don't wait!
Don't overlook small issues!
Don't think that what you are feeling is too insignificant!

After all, would you rather fight over something *significant?*

▶ Emotional Clearing Formula

Here is a step-by-step procedure you can use whenever you notice yourself feeling upset, tense, or resistant:

STEP ONE: Acknowledge to yourself that you are emotionally uncomfortable, and that you want to do something about it.

STEP TWO: Ask yourself: If I were upset, what would it be about? List every possibility until one "clicks"—creates the most tension when you think about it. *That's* what's really bothering you.

STEP THREE: Using your Emotional Map, explore the

Complete Truth about your feelings regarding the issue. You also can do this in written form using the "Love Letter Technique" explained in Chapter 9.

STEP FOUR: Based on having explored the Complete Truth about the issue, ask yourself: What is it that I really want in this situation?

STEP FIVE: Express the Complete Truth, as well as what you want, to the person with whom you are upset, making sure to emphasize the love and caring that's at the root of your upset.

▶ Your Feelings Are a Gift

Most people try to *control* their feelings —treating their emotions like unruly children that need discipline. But your ability to feel is a *gift*, not a curse. Just as your nerves report physical sensations to help keep you safe physically, so your feelings tune you in to what you need for emotional health.

What Your Feelings Are Trying to Tell You

When you experience anger: "You don't like something that is happening to you. You've got to take steps to change this."

When you experience hurt or sadness: "You aren't getting something you need or want. You must ask for it or go out and get it."

When you experience fear: "You are cautious of failure, loss, or pain. You need to figure out if these things are really to be feared."

When you experience remorse or regret: "In some way, you are responsible for causing an undesirable result or circumstance for yourself or another. Are you truly at fault? What can you do to correct what has happened?"

Instead of trying to control your feelings, learn to listen to them and resolve them.

Steps to Successful Response to Your Feelings

1. Try to understand the message your feelings are sending you.

2. Dissolve the tension your unresolved feelings are causing in your mind and body by expressing the Complete Truth about them to whoever is involved.

3. Make sure to complete the process by getting back in touch with your feelings of love, harmony, and understanding.

▶ Negative Side Effects of Repressing Your Feelings

1. You may become numb and therefore unable to experience positive emotions such as love and passion.

2. You may overreact to people or events in your present life because of stored-up feelings from the past.

3. Through physical symptoms and disease, your body may express tension from holding on to repressed feelings.

Are You Becoming Numb?

Do you feel apathetic about most things?
Do you often feel bored with life and living?
Are you disinterested in learning new things or
   having new experiences?
Do you sometimes feel dead and empty inside?
Is it difficult for you to feel passion with and for
   your partner?

If you answered yes to several of these questions,
you probably have become emotionally numb due to
repressing your feelings. You aren't alone. Many people live their whole lives as passionless witnesses to
the process of living, missing out on the many joys life
has to offer.

> *Repressing your negative feelings gradually
> numbs your ability to feel—period.*

If you think you might be emotionally numb, here
are some steps you can take to begin feeling again:

Healing Emotional Numbness

- *Admit to yourself* that you are more emotionally numb than you want to be.

- *Make a list of people you feel angry or upset
  with,* past and present. Commit yourself to
  clearing up those relationships by expressing
  the Complete Truth about your emotions until
  you feel loving again.

- *Make a list of old grudges you still carry.* Explore your part in the conflict, and communicate with as many of the people involved as

possible, using the Complete Truth, until you no longer feel like a victim.

- *Make a list of dreams you have given up on and goals you have never completed.* Begin taking steps toward unearthing those buried dreams and making them come true.

- *Make a list of incomplete communications—* feelings you've been holding in; things you've been meaning to discuss with family or friends. Begin completing your communications by sharing the Complete Truth with all involved.

- *Take a careful and honest look at your intimate relationship* based on all you learn from this book. If your relationship doesn't have as much love and passion as you'd like it to have, sit down with your partner and create a plan for working together on revitalizing your relationship.

Work with the exercises in this book, reach out to the people you care for, and fight through your numbness to all the wonderful feelings and experiences waiting for you on the other side.

▶ Are You Overreacting?

Do you tend to lose your temper over small things?
Do you cry frequently over everyday tensions and events?
Do you get very irritated at long lines, waits in restaurants, and other people's mistakes?
Do you feel others are always picking on you or putting you down?

If you answered yes to several of these questions,

you probably overreact to people or circumstances in your life due to stored-up feelings.

Stored-up Emotional Tension pollutes your experience of your emotions in present time.

For instance, if you feel stored-up anger at your father, you may find yourself getting angry at all authority figures: your boss, the police, the government. If you feel unresolved hurt and sadness from a divorce, you may find yourself becoming melancholy and depressed when tiny things go wrong. If you have suppressed guilt feelings from a time when you did something to hurt someone, you might always feel people are out to get you, or feel criticized and attacked if your partner says the slightest critical thing to you.

How Michael Felt Controlled by Women

Michael grew up in a family in which his mother was a dominant, aggressive figure. Michael grew to hate hearing his mother find fault with his father—and everyone else—and tell him what to do. Michael learned that, in order to survive, he had to suppress his anger at his mother, since she became even more controlling whenever he expressed himself. Michael left home at seventeen, went to college, and became a successful attorney. He married a very warm, affectionate woman named Dara. Where his mother had been harsh, Dara was soft. Where his mother had been judgmental, Dara was supportive. It seemed the perfect match.

Then the trouble started. Michael and Dara began fighting frequently. According to Dara, she would make a suggestion about a case Michael was working on, or comment on something he had said at a party, and Michael would blow up. "Don't tell me what to do!" he'd bellow. "All women are the same, they just want to control me." Dara was shocked. This wasn't the loving, gentle man she had met and married.

When Michael and Dara came to me for counseling, it was easy to see what was happening: Michael had years of rage at his mother stored inside of him; rage he had successfully suppressed in order to survive at home. But now, that old anger toward his controlling mother was causing him to overreact in his relationship to his wife. Every time she would attempt any kind of assertive behavior, or even give helpful advice, Michael would interpret her actions as an attempt to control him.

I taught Michael some of the techniques I'll be teaching you in Part Two. The more he used his Emotional Map to heal the hurt little boy inside of him, the less he overreacted to Dara.

Are You Beating Up Your Body?

When you suppress your emotions, psychological tension results. Something is trying to come out and you are pushing it back in. Since your mind and body are intimately connected, the psychological tension will be reflected in your body. If you persist in ignoring the emotional tension, your body may try to "help" you release the tension you've created.

I'm sure you have found yourself getting angry at someone, trying to control your feelings, and suddenly developing a splitting headache or upset stomach. Your body is giving you a message. It says, "Hey! Pay attention. There is something you need to look at and resolve!"

In recent years, medical and psychological research has established that certain personality types who have a difficult time expressing emotion or resolving anger are more prone to cancer and heart disease. One study showed that a group of women who expressed their anger and hurt over having breast cancer and refused to become "good" patients (i.e., controlling their emotions and passively accepting treatment) had a statistically much higher survival rate than a group of women who had a hard time expressing any negative feelings at all!

You may also be using addictions to numb yourself to physical or emotional pain. Millions of people in the United States abuse their bodies with drugs, alcohol, cigarettes, and overeating. All of these habits have one thing in common: They temporarily numb you to pain or discomfort.

I don't even talk about addictions in my weekend seminars, but through using the techniques I teach and learning to express feelings rather than repress them, many people find that their need for numbing addictive substances simply disappears. If you are a prisoner of an addiction, this book can be an important first step for you in understanding why and how you use these habits to help you push down your feelings.

▶ Love Can Help You Heal Repressed Feelings

Love is the greatest healer on earth. When you are in an intimate relationship with another person, all of your old repressed feelings will emerge: the childhood pain; the anger at having been hurt in love; the fear of failure and rejection. You have found someone with whom you feel safe enough to act out some of those old emotions, hoping that that person won't run in the other direction, but will work with you, as you will with him or her, to help you heal the old hurts and break down the emotional walls.

Healing your heart is part of what intimate relationships are about. The process doesn't take a month or a year, but continues over the life of your relationship with your partner. The more safety you feel with the person you love, the safer you will feel to bring up old unhealed traumas.

SECRET:

Each time you achieve a new level of love and close-ness in your relationship, a new level of repressed feelings may surface, ready to be healed by that new love.

This is why it sometimes seems that *the closer you and your partner get, the more tension or misunderstandings occur between you.* But don't despair! By working with your new understanding of the Four R's, your Emotional Map, and the importance of communicating the Complete Truth, you can begin to use and appreciate your relationships for the gift that they are.

▶ Is Therapy for You?

Whether or not you are in an intimate relationship, working with a counselor or therapist can be another effective way to resolve much emotion you have been suppressing. People often ask me for advice on choosing a therapist. I recommend the following guidelines:

1. Make sure your relationship with your therapist creates the warmth and caring you need to feel safe enough to do the healing you want to do. I've heard too many clients tell me horror stories about seeing a therapist once a week for a year or more who they never felt really cared about them and from whom they experienced very little warmth. They talked, and the therapist listened. There are many wonderful, caring professionals who can provide you with a very safe environment in which you can grow.

2. Make sure your therapist isn't suppressing his or her emotions either, but can easily share and express feelings. Therapists are people, too and many of us are still learning to get rid of our own emotional walls. Find someone who seems to be relating to you from his or her heart as well as his intellect.

3. Be sure that your therapist can guide you not only in healing past traumas but in how to behave in the present. It's not enough to "analyze" your past—you need to unlearn behaviors that don't work for you, and learn ones that do.

4. If your therapy doesn't seem to be going anywhere after five to ten sessions—that is, if you don't notice any new insight, lessening of Emotional Tension, or improvement in your relationship—then tell the truth to your therapist about your feelings. Perhaps this will change things and your therapist will speed up the pace of the therapy. I am a firm believer in short-term therapy for most "normal" people, and a few sessions with a good therapist should produce positive effects in your life right away. If nothing changes after you discuss this with your therapist, consider trying another therapist. This does not mean there is anything wrong with the one you are with. It may mean you would grow more quickly with someone else. But don't leave without letting him or her know why.

5. Finally, only you can heal yourself. A therapist is not a healer, but at best, a loving guide who can help you travel through your own emotional jungles in safety. Don't expect miracles. But with persistent work and an open heart you can get the results you want and deserve.

▶ What You Feel, You Can Heal

My final secret for this chapter expands on an idea I brought up at the end of Chapter 2:

▼

SECRET:
What you can feel and fully express, you can heal.

▲

When you (1) feel your emotions fully and (2) tell the Complete Truth about them, you will be able to heal unresolved Emotional Tension. And you will be free to love more fully. At first, telling the Complete Truth in your relationships will be difficult. It's a little like starting an exercise program. You'd rather do anything than run those two miles or do that half hour of aerobics. Telling the Complete Truth means asking for what you want rather than pretending nothing is the matter; talking about your feelings with your partner rather than slamming a door or watching TV while silently fuming; letting someone know your feelings were hurt rather than deciding you don't care about them anyway.

Remember: *Love thrives on truth.* And learning to communicate with truth is your only hope for keeping the magic of love alive year after year in your relationship. In the following chapters I'll teach you practical techniques for communicating the truth safely and effectively. The truth will set you free. And that freedom will help you fall in love and stay in love.

6 | Whose Fault Is It, Anyway?

▶ The Secret Connection

Have you ever wondered . . .

Why nice, even-tempered people often attract partners with bad tempers?

Why the more upset a woman gets, the more detached and cold a man becomes?

Why, when a woman feels hurt and begins to cry, her partner can't bring himself to comfort her, and may even become angry with her?

Why a very independent and strong woman suddenly becomes insecure and needy when she starts a relationship with a man?

Why the more a woman insists nothing is bothering her, the angrier her partner will become?

Why the more a man reassures his wife that he has everything under control, the more worried and panicky she gets?

The answer to all of these questions lies in understanding the secret connection in our relationships. Once you understand how the secret connection works, you will see why relationships succeed or fail, and what makes them sometimes seem so crazy. This secret connection is called the Seesaw Effect.

I'll explain the Seesaw Effect to you by using an analogy.

Imagine two containers of liquid, like two storage tanks standing upright. These two tanks represent two people in a relationship. We'll make them husband and wife and name them John and Mary. Connecting the two tanks is a pipe. The connecting pipe is like the sensitivity that a husband and wife feel toward each other. Let's call this the connection. When you are married or living together; when you are family members; when you work very closely with someone; and, most important, when you have a sexual relationship with someone, you develop that connection.

The more connected you are to another person, the more intensely you share and experience his or her feelings. Have you ever known your partner was upset about something, even when he denied it? Has one of your children ever perceived a mood you were in before you even realized how you were feeling? It is the emotional connection between you that allows you to "know" what others are feeling.

So now we have two "tanks" and a connecting pipe. What is inside these tanks? They contain the emotions of John and Mary. The pipe "connects" their emotions, so that John and Mary can feel each other's feelings.

▶ How the Seesaw Effect Works

Let's watch what happens between John's and Mary's "emotional tanks":

1. John says something one day to Mary. Mary feels anger. (Imagine anger as a liquid, bubbling up in Mary's tank.)

2. Mary's conditioning tells her, "It's not okay to get angry. John won't like it."

3. So without even realizing it, Mary begins to repress her anger, to push it down. (Imagine Mary pushing that liquid in her tank down.)

4. When Mary pushes down her anger, it is forced through the connecting tube to John's emotional tank. (Imagine anger beginning to bubble up in John's emotional tank.)

5. All of a sudden, John starts to feel angry and irritable with Mary. John unconsciously feels Mary's anger as she suppresses it, but he experiences it as his *own* anger.

6. The more Mary insists that nothing is wrong, the angrier John feels.

7. The more upset John gets, the more Mary tries to calm him down. She attempts to push down his anger just as she pushed down her own.

Mary and John's conversation goes something like this:

> JOHN: Mary, I can't take that extra weekend off as we had planned. We are just jammed at the office.
>
> MARY: *(Pushing down her anger)* Oh, that's okay. I guess I'll just cancel our vacation.
>
> JOHN: *(Irritated that she sounds like a victim)* Well, you don't have to sound so miserable about it.
>
> MARY: Look, it's no problem. Please don't upset yourself over nothing.
>
> JOHN: Well, stop looking at me as though I'd

just ruined your life. I hate it when you get so depressed.

MARY: Honey, just calm down.

JOHN: *(Yelling)* What do you mean, calm down?

MARY: John, you don't have to yell. I can hear you.

JOHN: *(Getting angrier and angrier)* You are impossible to talk to; you just sit there looking morose; what's the use . . .

MARY: There is really no reason to argue like this, honey. Let's be reasonable.

JOHN: *(Losing his temper)* I'll yell if I want to! You are driving me crazy, do you know that?

The more Mary suppresses her anger, the angrier John gets, until there is a big explosion. And Mary will say to herself, "I just can't understand why John always loses his temper and screams at me . . . I guess men just can't control their anger."

The secret of the Seesaw Effect is:

The emotions your partner suppresses, you may express. And, of course, the reverse: The emotions you suppress, your partner may express.

When You Deny Your Anger, Your Partner Will Get Angry at You

Michael and his wife, Joan, came to my seminar and told this story:

"I've never really been an explosive person," Michael explained, "but when Joan and I moved in together, a strange thing began to happen. I began snapping at her when we talked, and raising my voice. In fact, the nicer she was, the angrier I became."

"I felt as if I were living with a monster," Joan added. "I would think: 'What am I doing to deserve this?'"

"What would happen to me was a mystery," Michael continued. "I would feel very happy and loving at work and couldn't wait to see Joan. I would walk into the house, start to talk with her, and feel myself getting angry and snappy with her. So I would leave the room. Ten minutes later I would come back feeling great—that is, until I saw her, and I'd get angry again. I began to think maybe it had something to do with *her* feelings."

"When Michael asked me if *I* was angry about something, I denied it," said Joan. "I was brought up not to get angry, or even to feel anger. Finally, with his prompting, I did think of one incident between us that had bothered me just a little. What happened next was amazing. It was as if I gave myself permission to get angry. I felt full of rage, and angry words poured out of my mouth, more than I imagined I had ever felt."

"I felt as though a huge weight had been lifted off of me," Michael said. "Once Joan expressed her anger, I didn't always have to do it for her."

Michael and Joan are not very different from many couples in which one partner controls his or her anger and the other feels it and expresses the anger.

▶ The "Good" Parent and the "Bad" Parent

Think about your parents for a moment. Was one of them the "good parent": gentle, never really raised his/her voice or punished you, and seemed to be taken for granted or mistreated by the other? And was one of your parents the "bad parent": lost his/her temper, was irritable, yelled, and did the disciplining?

With your understanding of the Seesaw Effect, think about your parents again: Perhaps your "nice parent" was suppressing a lot of anger and resentment, and the "angry" parent was expressing that anger in an attempt to dissolve some of the Emotional Tension!

Why Trying to Calm Someone Down Doesn't Work

Did you notice in the previous example that the more Joan tried to calm Michael down, the angrier he got? Joan was trying to get him to repress his anger just as she had pushed it down in herself. Even the hand gesture that accompanies the phrase "calm down" is one of pushing down: pushing down the feeling.

The more you suppress your own anger, the more you will resist hearing your partner's anger, and the angrier your partner will become. So the second part of the Seesaw Effect is:

▼

SECRET:
You will resist those emotions in your partner that you suppress in yourself.

▲

▶ How the Seesaw Effect Can Make a Woman Seem "Overemotional"

Women: Have you ever wondered why, when you are with certain men, you begin to feel so insecure and hypersensitive? Have you ever felt as though you were going crazy in a relationship and becoming a completely different person from when you are on your own?

Men: Have you ever wondered why apparently strong, sensible women seem to "fall apart" around you? Have you ever felt that the more reasonable you become, the more unreasonable a woman gets?

One reason for this phenomenon is the Seesaw Effect.

Beth came to me for counseling about her relationship with her husband. Beth was a very attractive, poised woman in her thirties who was married to a well-known psychiatrist. She told me she needed to see me to determine if I thought she was a manic-depressive. Beth began telling me about her relationship with her husband. "My husband is just perfect," she said. "He is a wonderful psychiatrist. He never gets upset. Whenever a problem comes up, he never loses his cool. And he handles his clients so well, never getting disturbed by anything they say or do. I wish I could be more like him. That's really my problem," she admitted. "I always feel so embarrassed because I lose control of my emotions, and David sits there so calm and in control.

"Last week, for instance," Beth continued, "we were at a party and I was feeling very sad and started to cry. My aunt had passed away two weeks before, and we were very close. David came over to me as I sat in the corner and said, 'Darling, I think you are getting hysterical and losing control. There is nothing to cry over—the past is the past. You are embarrassing us. Now, if you don't get a grip on yourself, I'll have to give you something to calm you down.' That made me cry even harder," Beth explained.

Shocked by everything I was hearing, I gently asked, "What does David think about all this you're telling me?"

"Oh, he is the one who told me I may be manic-depressive," Beth answered.

As I listened to this poor woman's story, I felt tremendous rage. This was a perfect example of the Seesaw Effect in action. David's powerful suppression of feeling had caused his wife to express all of his suppressed emotions. The calmer he got, the more hysterical she became. The more she mirrored back to him his own feelings of anxiety, fear, insecurity, and anger, the more he resisted her, resorting to giving her tranquilizers to "calm her down." He was unable to face her expressing the emotions he worked so hard to bury in himself.

The interesting aspect of this story is that as Beth

sat there telling me about her relationship, she was working very hard to stay calm and suppress all her emotions. She was trying to be like David. And as she suppressed her anger at her husband, I sat there feeling furious at him, expressing it for her!

In my work with women, I'm sorry to say how frequently I see this pattern: a husband who is controlling, emotionally detached, and who never reveals any vulnerability or fallibility to his wife; and a wife who is driven to overemotionalism and even to questioning her sanity because of the dynamics of the Seesaw Effect.

As a woman and a therapist, I feel tremendous compassion for the millions of women in this country who choose to take or are put on Valium and other tranquilizing medication as a "solution" for handling their "unacceptable" emotions. You must give yourself permission to communicate about all your feelings, using the techniques I share in this book. If you do feel you are "going crazy," try seeking the advice of a female professional, and not just your husband or a male doctor, in order to receive feedback from both the male and female perspectives.

There are relationships in which these roles are reversed and it is the woman who suppresses all her feelings, while the man becomes overemotional. This is more unusual because of how men and women are conditioned—women still are given more permission to express emotion than men—although, fortunately, this is beginning to change.

▶ From Depression to Expression

Beth had never had permission to get angry; only to cry. Since her husband hated it when she cried, however, she just suppressed all of her feelings and went right through the Four R's to repression. The result: a feeling of depression—anger directed at the self.

Of course, Beth was not just a victim. She allowed herself to be controlled by her husband. Yet it was even more difficult for her to own her power in this case, considering how our society sanctifies the opinions of doctors. "Of course, David is right," she had thought. "He is a trained professional." David needed to give himself permission not to have to be perfect and to express some of the inevitable concerns and vulnerabilities that anyone in the helping professions feels.

► Children and the Seesaw Effect

The Seesaw Effect occurs not only in intimate relationships but in family relationships as well. We can redefine the principle and say, *The emotions that parents suppress, their children may express.*

Children, even infants, are very sensitive to the emotions of those around them, and until children are taught to hide their feelings, they freely reveal their observations and reactions with an honesty adults often lack.

Parents often feel that they should hide their feelings or hide the truth from their children in order to protect them. But I disagree. If you suppress or hide your feelings from your children, they will feel your emotions, anyway, and will only become confused by the mixed messages they are receiving: You tell them nothing is wrong, yet they perceive that you are unhappy. The result: Your children may start feeling that they are responsible for your anger, unhappiness, sadness, or depression.

This was the case with Christine and her daughter Casey. Christine came to me complaining that her three-year-old was always whining, complaining, and throwing tantrums. I asked Christine if she was the complaining type herself. "No, quite the opposite," she answered proudly. "My husband says I am so strong and good-natured. I guess I learned from my mother to grin and bear it."

I suggested to Christine that as a young working mother and wife, she probably had some resentments and angry feelings inside and that she could be suppressing them. Her daughter, acting as a mirror, might be expressing them for her. Children who throw frequent temper tantrums and often whine and cry may be expressing the frustrations and anger their parents are suppressing. We agreed that the next time Casey started whining, Christine would sit down and start whining herself, complaining about everything she felt burdened her.

Christine didn't have to wait long. That night, Casey started her routine: Why did she have to go to bed so early? Why couldn't she stay up? She hated nursery school, and so on. So Christine sat down on the floor and began, "Oh, why do I have to do all these stupid dishes now? I worked so hard all day, and now I have to be a maid. Sometimes I am so tired. It's hard being a mommy sometimes."

As Christine whined away, Casey stopped and stared at her mommy with amazement. Then, after a moment or two, she came up, kissed Christine on the cheek and said, "Good night, Mommy," went into her room, and went quietly to bed. Christine was overjoyed! She saw that expressing her suppressed feelings really worked. It gave Casey instant relief, and naturally, Christine felt better, too.

Children who are hostile, angry, and rebellious often are expressing suppressed anger occurring in the family. Brothers and sisters who fight all the time may also be expressing the family's suppressed feelings. That is why it's so important for a family to work together in solving problems, whether the problem involves one individual or the whole family. If each person in a household took responsibility for telling the Complete Truth about his or her feelings, home would be a much more peaceful, harmonious place.

▶ The Multiple Tank Effect

If you ever have been in a relationship with two lovers at once, you know how complicated it can get. Now that you understand the Seesaw Effect, you can see extramarital affairs or open relationships can cause not only emotional pain but tremendous confusion as well.

Let's suppose there are three people in a relationship: Jack and Jill, who are married, and Harvey, who is having a secret affair with Jill. Now we have three emotional tanks connected. Jack is affected not only by his wife, Jill, and her emotions, but by Harvey's emotions as well. If Harvey suppresses his anger, it goes via Jill to her husband Jack's tank. Jack may then feel very angry, without knowing why. He may be feeling not only his wife's angry emotions but the emotions of his wife's secret lover as well!

If you *really* want to get confused, imagine that Harvey, the secret lover, is married to a woman named Helen. Now there are four emotional tanks connected. See how complicated it can get?

Intimate relationships between two people are difficult enough to make work. Adding a third or fourth person results in complete chaos and emotional confusion. I feel quite strongly that open relationships and affairs don't work in the long run, and one of the reasons is that they confuse the emotional balance between partners. This is why I tell people that *there is no such thing as a secret affair.*

You may be having an affair with someone, and your partner may not know about it, but that person's energies and emotions are interacting with yours and affecting you. Therefore, they are also affecting your legitimate partner. Your partner may be unaware of why he or she is feeling strange or uncomfortable, but he or she will feel it nevertheless. The solution to the problems in any relationship is *not* to fill in the gaps with an additional relationship, but to heal the wounds between you and your partner and find the magic again, and if that is not possible, to end the relationship and start over.

The Multiple Tank Effect also occurs in families. This explains why going home to a family dinner or just talking to your parents or relatives on the phone can be so traumatic: You are all connected with interlocking tanks. Either you are all expressing what others are suppressing or the connecting pipes have broken from too much pressure and no one is feeling anything. Often it feels as though you are either on a battleground or in a graveyard, and neither is a very pleasant feeling.

Learning to resolve and release your Emotional Tension on a daily basis is one way you can contribute to creating peace on the planet. At least you are not adding to the ever-growing stockpile of suppression and negativity that exists around us.

▶ Breaking the Emotional Connection

"Falling out of love" doesn't just happen overnight. It is what happens when two people break the emotional connection that exists between them. How does that emotional connection get broken? Let's return to our analogy of the emotional tanks one last time. Imagine that both partners in a relationship are suppressing their feelings. Neither is telling the Complete Truth. When both are "pushing down" on their emotions, all the pressure goes onto the connecting pipe. Eventually it bursts.

When the emotional connection is broken, all the magic and passion are gone from the relationship. You may feel as though you "love" your partner, but that you aren't "in love" anymore. Something substantial is missing, and what's missing is the involvement and intensity that come from feeling that emotional connection.

At this point, couples can live "comfortably" together if they still want to. This is possible because they no longer feel tremendous Emotional Tension. The Seesaw Effect doesn't affect them anymore! But along with the tension, they will have lost the love, the aliveness, and the opportunity to grow from the relationship.

Can a couple who has broken off their connection get back to an intimate, loving relationship? Yes, it is possible. It takes a lot of hard work, however, with complete commitment from both partners to make love work.

I suggest that you avoid getting to the stage where you have broken your emotional connection by:

- Understanding the Seesaw Effect
- Learning to recognize it when it occurs
- Practicing the techniques in the next section so that you can regularly dissolve the tension before it builds up and erodes your emotional connection

▶ What You Can Do to Minimize the Seesaw Effect

You can't escape the Seesaw Effect. It's a dynamic of human interaction which is a part of any relationship. However, as we've seen, you can learn a lot about yourself and others by paying attention to the emotions your partner and others mirror back to you.

You can minimize the emotional damage caused by the Seesaw Effect by following these guidelines:

- Start expressing your emotions (by telling the Complete Truth) instead of suppressing them.
- When you notice yourself resisting your partner or someone close to you as he/she expresses his/her feelings, stop and ask yourself: "Is he [she] expressing something I don't want to experience or look at in myself?"
- Anytime you notice Emotional Tension building up between you and another person, especially an intimate partner, and your feelings are intensifying by the minute . . . Stop! Then: Practice some of the techniques in the chapters that follow.

▼▼▼▼▼▼▼▼▼▼▼▼▼▼▼▼▼▼▼▼▼▼▼▼▼▼▼▼▼▼▼▼

PART TWO

Emotional First Aid— Practical Solutions for Resolving Conflict

▲▲▲▲▲▲▲▲▲▲▲▲▲▲▲▲▲▲▲▲▲▲▲▲▲▲▲▲▲▲▲▲

7

How to Use the Techniques That Make Love Work

This section contains the most powerful techniques I know of for making love all the time—techniques to help you resolve Emotional Tension in yourself and in your relationships. Using them, you will be able to make love work on a daily basis.

I have taught these techniques to thousands of people over the past few years and have seen couples and whole families use them to transform their relationships from ones of anger and hopelessness to ones of passion and joy. I've seen individuals change from feeling powerless and depressed to feeling powerful and alive.

I use these techniques all the time in my own life to keep myself clear of Emotional Tension, to help me stay in touch with my feelings and with my partner, and to keep the magic of love alive in our relationship. *These techniques work!* I know from experience.

▶ Emotional First Aid for Your Relationships

We have learned to pay attention to our bodies when they let us know they need help. But when it comes to relationships, most of us are terribly neglectful, ignoring the tension and unpleasant feelings and hoping they will just go away. They *don't* go away— they just worsen, until what was once a minor issue becomes a major crisis.

Don't wait until your little problems turn into big problems to pay attention to them.
Give your relationships the emotional first aid they need as soon as you notice signs of Emotional Tension.

Don't wait until your next argument to try these techniques. It's a lot harder to resolve a month's worth of tension than an hour's worth. So look for the signs of Emotional Tension and separation, and use these techniques right away.

▶ Developing an Emotional Green Thumb

If you walked into my mother's home, you would marvel at how healthy and resplendent her plants are. Every time I visit, I never fail to be impressed by those plants. And each time, I say to myself, "I wish my plants looked like this." There's only one problem: My mother gives those plants daily care. The moment she notices a leaf that's a little brown, she pulls it off so it doesn't spoil the rest of the plant; at the first sign of any problem, she administers first aid to the plants, and that's why they look so healthy.

I, on the other hand, will walk past a plant in my house, notice a browning leaf, and tell myself, "When I have time, I really should trim off those dying leaves and see why the plant is so dry." A week or two passes, and again I'll notice the problem plant and say to myself, "I really should take care of that plant." A few months of this kind of procrastination, and one day I notice that the whole plant looks pretty dead. By then, it is too late to revive it.

If you treat your relationships as I treated my plants, you will wake up one day and find that they, too, are dead or dying.

I finally got smart and hired a plant service to take care of my plants, since I have such a busy schedule of teaching and traveling that I can't care for them properly by myself. But you can't hire a service to take care of your relationship—to come in once a week and make sure you have loved each other enough and kept your hearts open. It's up to you!

The three techniques I'll describe are:

The Duplication Technique
The Love Letter Technique
The Power Process

Each of these techniques can be used in two ways:

1. You and your partner (as well as family and children) can use them together.
2. You can use the techniques by yourself.

The techniques are quite simple and don't take much time to do. *The best way to learn how to do these techniques is to try them out, not simply to read about them.*

I tried to anticipate every question you might have when practicing these techniques with a partner or by yourself. But don't wait to put these techniques to use until you think you'll do them perfectly. Start practicing them in your relationship today!

8 | The Duplication Technique

▶ Why Arguing and Complaining Make Things Worse

Have you ever engaged in a shouting match with your partner until you were too tired to argue anymore?

Have you ever said to a partner during an argument terrible and hurtful things which you later regretted?

Have you ever had a fight with your partner and ended up fighting about something completely different from what you started fighting about?

Have you ever tried expressing your displeasure to your partner about something small, only to have him react very defensively and blow up at you?

Have you ever felt upset with someone and tried to express your feelings, only to have your feelings come out "wrong," until even *you* are confused about what you are really feeling?

All of us at times have felt frustrated, frightened, and hopeless in our attempts to talk with our partners about what's bothering us. Before I teach you the Emotional First-Aid Techniques, I want to give you a close-up view of a typical fight between a husband and wife, and show you what is wrong with the way they are trying to communicate and why it will never work.

THE CHARACTERS: Bob and Susan, a married couple.

THE INCIDENT: Bob and Susan have arranged to meet at home after work at 7:00 P.M. for a special night out. Bob doesn't arrive home until 8:00.

BOB: *(Walking in the door)* Okay, honey, I'm home. Are you all ready to go?

SUSAN: What do you mean, am I ready? I've been waiting for an hour!

BOB: Well, I'm home now, so let's get going.

SUSAN: Don't tell me what to do—you didn't even bother calling to tell me you would be late. You're so inconsiderate!

BOB: Stop being so insecure, Susan. You're always trying to control my time and keep tabs on me.

Bob and Susan's argument continues to escalate, as they drop "emotional bombs" on each other—statements designed to infuriate the other person. Bob says things like, "What did you think I was doing, having an affair?" "How do you think it feels to come home to a hysterical woman after a hard day at the office?" and "You know what? You'll never love anyone as much as you love your father."

Susan's "emotional bombs" are statements like, "How come you always take longer with your female clients?" "You are so unreliable—I just can't trust you at all!" "Don't you dare call me hysterical—just because you are so damn cold and unfeeling," and "No wonder your mother left your father—you're just like him."

Why Arguing Doesn't Work

1. *You don't express the Complete Truth about your feelings, but instead get caught up in expressing only anger and blame.* Bob and Susan obviously feel strongly about how their evening is turning out. If you read their dialogue, however, they both express only the first level of the Emotional Map: anger and blame. They get stuck on the anger and never get down to the love!

2. *You react to the angry things your partner is saying, rather than really listening to the message your partner is trying to convey.* Bob was trying to explain why he was late; Susan was trying to tell Bob how anxious she had been while waiting for him. But they both stopped listening and started reacting, until they ended up throwing insults back and forth. Their true messages got buried underneath the emotional bombs they hurled at one another.

3. *You use the argument as an opportunity to dump all your suppressed anger and resentment on your partner, bringing in past grievances instead of dealing with the present issue.* Bob and Susan start out arguing about the evening and end up arguing about his mother and her father—is it any wonder that they aren't going to resolve their conflict? They both use the argument as a dumping ground for unresolved tensions from the past, thus making it impossible to come to any kind of reconciliation in present time.

4. *You don't give yourself an opportunity to explore the Complete Truth about your own feelings, and therefore, you don't express the real message to the other person.* Bob and Susan got so caught up in throwing their anger back and forth that neither of

them took the time to explore the Complete Truth about how they were really feeling. Their real messages to each other got lost *even to themselves.*

In this next section you'll learn what Bob and Susan *really* wanted to say to each other and how they could have done so without having it erupt into a bitter argument.

▶ The Duplication Technique

The Duplication Technique can be used with your partner or with a friend or family member. It is a wonderful method for:

- Expressing the Complete Truth about an issue
- Understanding what your partner (or other person) is really trying to tell you
- Figuring out what you are really feeling
- Feeling understood by the other person

When you notice tension building between yourself and your partner:

1. Stop arguing!
2. Take turns expressing the Complete Truth about your feelings to each other.
3. Take turns duplicating, or mirroring, what the other person says after each statement.

▶ How the Duplication Technique Works

The Duplication Technique is based on this principle:

> ***When someone duplicates your feelings, it dissolves Emotional Tension and creates connection.***

We all act out this principle many times during our day: When it is raining and you feel irritated by the weather, and someone says to you, "Boy, isn't it terrible outside?" you feel better. That person is duplicating your own frustration about the weather, and hearing someone echo your complaint dissolves some of your tension, and also creates a feeling of connection between you.

When you come home after a tiring, frustrating day and tell your partner about it, and he says, "That's awful. You must have been so upset. You did all the work and didn't get any credit," your partner is duplicating your anger and frustration about what happened to you. Hearing him do this helps dissolve some of your tension and creates a warm feeling of intimacy and connection between you.

When your son falls down and hurts his knee and comes home crying, and you hold him and say, "Boy, that must have hurt, didn't it? I bet it was scary to fall off that slide like that," you are duplicating his fear, and he will feel less tense and very connected to you.

▶ How to Practice the Duplication Technique with a Partner

Step One: Stop fighting and decide to practice the technique.

As soon as you notice some tension building between you and your partner, stop, and suggest you practice the Duplication Technique.

Agreeing to practice duplication is harder than it seems. If you are feeling irritated with your partner, the last thing you want to do is throw back his/her complaints about you. In the beginning, you won't want to practice duplication. But don't let that stop you. *The more you don't want to do it, the more you need to do it!*

Step Two: Decide who goes first.

Whoever feels more motivated to resolve the tension can agree to go first. It really doesn't matter, because both of you will get a turn. *Never fight about who goes first,* and don't try to figure out who "needs" to go first. You can even flip a coin to decide.

Step Three: Let the first person take his/her turn.

Let's say you have agreed to go first. All you need to do is follow your Emotional Map and express the Complete Truth about how you feel, starting with your anger and blame, and moving through hurt, fear, and remorse, down to love. (See chart below.)

Emotional Map of the Complete Truth

Level One: Anger and blame
Level Two: Hurt and sadness
Level Three: Fear and insecurity
Level Four: Remorse and responsibility
Level Five: Love, understanding, appreciation

After each line or two, pause, and give your partner a chance to duplicate, or mirror, what you just said. As he repeats your feelings, you will feel relieved because you are expressing the Complete Truth, and your partner is beginning to fully understand what you are trying to say.

Don't stop until you are expressing the love and intention.

Mistakes to Avoid

1. *Don't criticize your partner for the way he repeats what you say.* You will have much more emotion

in your voice than he will at first. That's okay—just keep going, and as he sees the vulnerability underneath your anger, his voice will fill with more emotion because he is feeling more of your love.

2. *Don't stop if you get stuck.* Let's say you are expressing your anger and can't seem to feel the fear underneath. Just close your eyes, take a deep breath, and say to yourself: "I'm afraid that . . ." and fill in the blank in your mind. Before long, you will be an expert at expressing the Complete Truth.

Step Four: Let the second person take his/her turn.

Now it is your partner's turn to express his/her feelings and for you to duplicate them.

In the beginning, you will probably feel uncomfortable repeating your partner's feelings about you. But don't stop! As you hear your partner move through his Emotional Map down toward the love, you will feel more and more connected to him, tension will begin to dissolve, and it will feel easier to say what he is feeling. You don't have to *agree* with what he says; only acknowledge that he feels it. By the time your partner expresses the remorse and love sections of the Complete Truth, you will actually enjoy repeating his phrases!

Note: If it doesn't become easier to repeat your partner's feelings and either of you starts feeling very angry, stop! Your conflict has developed beyond the point of mild Emotional Tension, and duplication will not work. In this case, you need to use the Love Letter Technique described in the next chapter.

Step Five: Discuss what you learned about each other and the issue.

When you have both expressed the Complete Truth and have been duplicated by each other, you should understand what was really bothering you, as well as feel more in love with each other. Now take this time to let your partner know that you do understand how he must have been feeling by summing up what you heard him say. Ask yourselves:

> What have we learned from this?
> How can we prevent this kind of situation from happening in the future?
> Do we need to make some new agreements to help us avoid a further conflict about this?

By now, you and your partner will not only have resolved the conflict, but you will probably feel closer than before you began arguing, and you will have learned more about each other and the relationship!

This is the conscious way to deal with conflict, so that conflict becomes a gift, not a detriment, to your relationship.

▶ A Sample of the Duplication Technique

Let's look at the Duplication Technique in action: We'll use Bob and Susan, arguing over Bob arriving home one hour late for their night out. You have already seen what happens when they argue the old way. Here is what would happen if Bob and Susan decided to practice the Duplication Technique:

Step One: They stop fighting, and one of them suggests practicing duplication.

Step Two: They decide that since Susan was angry first, she will go first.

Step Three: Susan's turn.

Susan will express the Complete Truth about her feelings, starting with her anger and continuing until she reaches the love.

After each line or two, she will pause and Bob will duplicate, or repeat, what she said.

Is Susan aware of all the levels of the Complete Truth when she starts? *No!* That's the whole purpose of the Duplication Technique: It allows her to get in touch with *all* her feelings and express them appropriately to Bob.

Here's how their conversation starts off using the Duplication Technique:

> SUSAN: I'm so *angry* at you for coming home late!
>
> BOB: *(Duplicating her lines)* I'm so angry at you for coming home late!
>
> SUSAN: You're such an *insensitive jerk* for not even calling me.
>
> BOB: You're such an insensitive jerk for not even calling me.
>
> SUSAN: I'm so *mad* at you for ruining our wonderful evening.
>
> *(Bob continues to repeat each line as Susan expresses all of her angry feelings. Then she begins to feel and express her* hurt *feelings.)*
>
> SUSAN: *It really hurt me* when you didn't seem to care about our romantic date! It makes me so sad when we argue like this.
>
> *(Bob repeats and Susan continues to express all of her hurt feelings and then goes on to the next level,* fear.*)*
>
> SUSAN: *I'm afraid* that you are getting tired of me.
>
> *I'm afraid* I'll always be the one who tries to keep our relationship working.
>
> *I'm afraid* we will both always be so busy that we won't have time for each other. *(Susan has just*

realized why she blew up tonight—what her real upset was about.) (*Bob continues to repeat as Susan gets in touch with her* remorse.)

SUSAN: *I'm sorry* I jumped on you the minute you came home without waiting for an explanation.

I'm sorry I get so jealous sometimes. (*Now Susan can feel the love that was covered up by all those other feelings.*)

SUSAN: I really *love you*, Bob, and I love spending time with you. *I need you* so much. I just miss you when we are both working so hard. (*Bob repeats until Susan is finished.*)

Let's look at what just happened . . .

TO SUSAN: 1. Susan allowed herself to express the Complete Truth by following her Emotional Map down through all the levels *until she got in touch with what she was really upset about:* that she missed Bob, because they were both working so hard, and she needed more time with him.

2. As Bob duplicated Susan's emotions, Susan not only got a chance to *hear what she was feeling* but also *felt truly listened to and understood by Bob*.

3. Now Susan can work on clearing up the *real issue:* She was wrestling with her wish to spend more time with Bob and her fear of losing him.

TO BOB: 1. When Susan expressed the Complete Truth about her feelings, Bob, too, perceived what the real issue was.

2. As Bob duplicated Susan's feelings aloud, *he could really see her point of view and even get in touch with some of his feelings of anger at himself.*

Step Four: Bob's turn.

Even though both Susan and Bob are feeling better, Bob should also take a turn expressing the Complete Truth about his feelings, with Susan duplicating his lines:

BOB: Susan, I *hate it when* you attack me the minute I get home.

SUSAN: Susan, I hate it when you attack me the minute I get home.

BOB: *It makes me so angry* when you criticize me no matter what I do. I *hate when* you act like you don't trust me.

(Susan continues to repeat Bob's lines until he gets in touch with his hurt feelings.)

BOB: *It hurts me* so much when you call me irresponsible, because I work so hard for us. It makes me *feel terrible* when you yell at me like I'm your enemy.

(Susan repeats each of Bob's "hurt" lines until he expresses his fear.)

BOB: *I'm afraid* I'll never be able to make you happy.

I'm afraid I can't make up for all the ways you've been hurt before.

I'm afraid you'll never trust me and think I'm good enough. *(Bob has just realized that this is what he was feeling underneath all his anger. Susan repeats as Bob continues with his remorse.)*

BOB: *I'm sorry* I was late tonight. This client just wouldn't stop talking. *I'm sorry* you feel neglected. I never want you to feel that way. *(Susan repeats as Bob completes his duplication with the love.)*

BOB: *I love you* so much, Susan, and nothing is more important to me than our time together. I just *need you to* trust me and to believe I can make you happy. *(Susan repeats until Bob is finished.)*

Let's look at what happened here:

TO BOB: 1. Bob expressed the Complete Truth by following his Emotional Map through all the levels until he got in touch with what he was really upset about: that *he is afraid he can't make Susan happy, and he needs Susan to trust in his love*.

2. *As Susan duplicated Bob's emotions, Bob felt listened to and understood by Susan*.

3. Now Bob can work on clearing up the real issue—his fear that his wife won't trust him and be happy with him.

TO SUSAN: 1. When Bob expressed the Complete Truth about his feelings, Susan could see what his real issue was.

2. As Susan duplicated Bob's feelings, *she could really see his point of view, and even get in touch with some of her angry feelings at herself.*

Step Five: Susan and Bob discuss what they learned.

Now that Susan and Bob have uncovered the real issues—that they are missing each other and need to plan more time together, and that Bob needs to know that Susan trusts him and his love—they can sit down and figure out ways to accomplish these two goals. But the real accomplishment is that they avoided a huge fight and ended up even closer than when they started. And the whole process took ten or fifteen minutes, instead of the hours they would spend fighting and then not speaking to each other.

Note: When you and your partner are practicing duplication, notice which lines your partner gives you that you *hate saying the most*. These are almost always your own negative thoughts about yourself, such as "I hate when you are so insecure," or "I hate the part of you that's irresponsible."

Don't get angry at your partner for mirroring your own thoughts back to you. Work on those parts of yourself you know need refining.

▶ How to Use the Duplication Technique with Family, Friends, and in Business

You can also use the Duplication Technique to resolve the Emotional Tension you feel between yourself and someone other than an intimate partner: a family member, a friend, a business associate. In this case, you would *not* practice the technique *with* the person you are upset with, but with a friend or your partner. You talk to your friend or partner *as if he or she were the person with whom you are upset*.

▶ How to Practice the Duplication Technique with Your Children

The Duplication Technique works like a charm with children. I've heard countless stories from grateful parents about how much better their family is getting along using the Duplication Technique.

Children love playing the Duplication Game, as I usually call it with them, because it gives them an opportunity to say the things parents often get angry at them for saying, and gives them a sense that their feelings are important, too. It's wonderful to teach your children at an early age about the Complete Truth and all the different levels of feelings in their Emotional Map. They grow up to be wonderful communicators and compassionate human beings.

You can use the Duplication Game with children in three ways:

Method A: The Child Duplicates the Parent

When you are upset with your child, ask him to play the Duplication Game with you, with your child duplicating your feelings.

Example: Francine was angry with her nine-year-old daughter, Ginger. Ginger had been annoying her little brother and his friends until the boys finally got angry and began to hit her. When she hit back, Francine interceded and took Ginger into the other room.

> THE OLD WAY: Francine reprimands Ginger for misbehaving by yelling at her, punishing her, or explaining what she did wrong. *But the Emotional Tension will still be there.*

> THE NEW WAY: Francine practices the Duplication Technique with Ginger so that she can express the Complete Truth, and so that Ginger gets a chance to vent some of her own anger *at herself* when she repeats what her mom says.

FRANCINE: Ginger, I am *so angry* at you for bothering those boys.

GINGER: Ginger, I am so angry at you for bothering those boys.

FRANCINE: *I hate when* you misbehave and make me yell at you.

GINGER: I hate when you misbehave and make me yell at you.

FRANCINE: It makes me *really angry* when you hit, because everyone gets unhappy and upset.

Ginger continues to repeat her mother's lines as Francine expresses all the levels from the Emotional Map. Examples:

> *It hurts me* to have to reprimand you.
> *I'm afraid* I will always have to yell at you to get you to listen.
> *I'm sorry* that I was too busy to pay attention to you today.
> *I love you,* and want you to learn to ask me for what you need.
> *I'm really happy* you played this game with me.

The Result of the Duplication Game

Francine and Ginger both realized why Ginger was acting so badly: *She needed attention.* Now that they have released Emotional Tension, they can discuss how to handle similar situations in the future. *Instead of just reprimanding her daughter, Francine used the problem as a learning opportunity for both of them.*

Method B: The Parent Duplicates the Child

When your child is upset, ask him to play the Duplication Game and you will duplicate your child's feelings.

Example: Paul's seven-year-old son, Jason, comes home from school in a terrible mood. When Paul asks him what's wrong, Jason mumbles, "Nothing." For the next hour, Jason is rebellious and cranky.

> THE OLD WAY: Jason acts more and more upset until Paul sends him to his room.

> THE NEW WAY: Paul asks Jason if he wants to play the Duplication Game so that he and Jason can figure out what is wrong and heal it.

When your child expresses his feelings during the Duplication Game, help him talk about feelings at each emotional level by asking:

"What do you feel angry about?"
"What makes you so sad about that?"
"Does that make you afraid of anything?"
"Do you feel sorry about anything?"
"How would you like things to be?"
"Underneath, how do you really feel about [person or situation]?

You can adapt the Duplication Game so that it can be used even with children who are quite young and may not be able to articulate how they feel. Sally, a single mother whose ex-husband had called at the last minute to cancel his weekend with their five-year-old son, Brian, was able to send Brian a message of support and love in this way: "Brian, if I were you right now, here's what I'd be feeling . . ." and then she went through all the levels of the Emotional Map with her little boy.

Method C: Children Duplicate One Another

If you have more than one child in the family, there are bound to be fights and bickering. The Duplication Game is an ideal way to help your children learn to express themselves completely and, at the same time, release the built-up tension between them.

Example: Pat's two sons, Jimmy and Johnny, were fighting over who got to sit up front in the car with Pat.

THE OLD WAY: Pat yells at both boys to be quiet.

THE NEW WAY: Pat lets both boys take turns expressing their feelings to each other. The result? Both boys realize they want the same thing: not the front seat, but to feel close with Mom. Pat can now plan some special time or activity with each boy. Now they all know what the *real problem* was.

Taking the time to duplicate your child's feelings makes your child feel loved, important, and understood

▶ How to Use the Duplication Technique to Be a Good Communicator

Whenever you are dealing with people, you are dealing with their emotional levels. Understanding the Emotional Map can help you become an effective communicator with others.

> *People want to know that you understand how they feel. This will help them trust you.*

When you are dealing with another person, ask yourself: "How is this person really feeling? How can I show him that I know what he is feeling?"

Example: Cynthia was a well-known television reporter who attended one of my Making Love Work seminars and learned the techniques I'm sharing with you in this book. She decided to put them to work right away in a situation with one of her writers. The week before, Cynthia had snapped at her writer in a nasty way, and since then, the writer had been ignoring her. Cynthia felt terrible about what she'd done, but didn't really know how to heal the situation.

The day after the seminar, Cynthia called the writer into her office, determined to use the Duplication Technique to heal the rift between them.

"You know," Cynthia began, "you must have been pretty angry at me the other day when I snapped at you. If I were you, I'd probably feel: 'Cynthia thinks she's hot stuff. How dare she treat me like dirt, when I have written her material for four years.'" The writer looked shocked that Cynthia was expressing all of his anger and resentment toward her.

Cynthia continued: "And if I were you, I'd also feel really hurt: 'I thought Cynthia respected me. *I'm hurt* that she is so brusque and cold to me. *I'm afraid* our relationship will never be friendly again. *I'm afraid* I've been kidding myself all this time that we ever had a good rapport.'"

The writer nodded. "That is exactly how I felt."

"I know," Cynthia replied, reaching out her hand. "And I want you to know *I am really sorry* for snapping at you. It had nothing to do with you, and we've been so close over the years, it must have felt awful. I love working with you, and don't want anything to come between us."

The writer reached out to hug Cynthia. "Thank you," he said. "I really feel as though you understand me, and I feel even closer to you now than before."

Cynthia could have said a simple "I'm sorry." But it wouldn't have been nearly as effective as duplicating all of the emotions the writer had about the incident. This dissolved the tension between them and created an even deeper connection.

I hope you practice the Duplication Technique in all the forms I've suggested here. It will help you to get to know your own feelings, and to have compassion for the feelings of others. And we can all use more of that!

9

The Love Letter Technique

The Love Letter Technique is the best method I know for resolving deep emotional conflict, both within yourself and in your relationships. It is a powerful tool for healing Emotional Tension that has become too strong to be dissolved through the Duplication Technique.

I have used the Love Letter Technique in my own relationships for many years, and have seen thousands of people who have attended my seminars and used it to resolve emotional conflicts that it would have taken them days, months, even years to unravel.

The Purpose of the Love Letter

The purpose of the love letter is to express and resolve all the negative feelings that prevent you from experiencing and sharing the love you feel deep inside.

The Love Letter is similar to the Duplication Technique: You express all five levels of the Emotional Map, starting with anger, then progressing through hurt, fear, remorse, and finally love.

▶ Why Write a Love Letter Instead of Using the Duplication Technique?

1. When you write a Love Letter, you can express your feelings without interruption. If you are using the Duplication Technique, your partner's facial expression, the tone of his voice or his attitude, may interfere with your getting fully in touch with your own emotions, especially if there is a lot of Emotional Tension between you. When you write a Love Letter, you are alone, and can feel safe to explore your own feelings without fear of how they will be received.

2. When you write a Love Letter, you can experience deeper levels of emotion and thus experience deeper levels of release and healing. When you sit down to write a Love Letter, you don't have another person standing there waiting for you to express how you feel. You have time to delve as deeply as necessary into your feelings to achieve the emotional healing you seek. It may also be easier for you to be honest with yourself when you are writing, as opposed to talking.

3. Part of the Love Letter Technique, as I'll explain, is to have someone read your Love Letter back to you. This serves several purposes:

- You hear your own emotions expressed and externalized, and this makes it easier for you to let go of them.
- The person reading your Love Letter, especially if it is an intimate partner, will feel his own emotions as he reads yours. When you move from anger to love in your letter, your partner will feel himself moving through to love as well.

• If the reader was feeling distant or emotionally shut down before reading your love letter, he will certainly start to feel once he reads all of your feelings out loud.

4. Although having your partner read your Love Letter aloud has great benefits, it isn't necessary for him to participate with you or even to know about the letter—you can write it by yourself. If you and your partner are having a disagreement and you want to practice the Duplication Technique but he doesn't, you can write a Love Letter and release your own tensions even if your partner doesn't want to work together with you.

▶ Step-by-Step Description of How to Write a Love Letter

First decide that you want to write a Love Letter and *begin right away:* Whenever you are feeling Emotional Tension between yourself and your partner, and the Duplication Technique isn't enough to resolve that tension, then it's time to write a Love Letter.

Sometimes the hardest part of writing a Love Letter to your partner is deciding to sit down and do it. The last thing in the world you may want to do is spend time thinking about your feelings. Remember: *What you feel, you can heal. Your relationship is worth the time it takes to write the Love Letter and get back to the love again.*

Caution: Don't wait to write the Love Letter until you feel loving! That's the whole purpose of the Love Letter—to resolve the emotions like anger, resentment, and hurt that are preventing you from experiencing love. Just start expressing the anger and you will see how naturally your emotions will progress through your Emotional Map back to feelings of love and understanding.

Allow yourself to move through all the emotional levels as you write the letter.

Each Love Letter has six parts:

1. Anger and blame
2. Hurt and sadness
3. Fear and insecurity
4. Remorse and responsibility
5. Intention and wishes
6. Love, forgiveness, understanding, and appreciation

You'll notice that part 5, "Intention and Wishes," is an addition to the Emotional Map levels I introduced earlier. Normally, these feelings ("I want . . ," "I wish . . .") are included in the love section of the Duplication Technique. But in the Love Letter it works better to express these emotions in a separate section.

Section One: Anger and Blame

Whenever you feel upset, you are experiencing some anger. You may not be aware of the anger; you may be suppressing it. You may even feel emotionally numb. It is absolutely essential to begin each Love Letter by expressing that anger and blame. Without expressing and *releasing* the anger, you can never get to the deeper levels of love inside you.

When you begin the letter with anger and blame, don't be nice! This is the time to indulge in that part of you that feels you are right and the other person is wrong. Have a tantrum on paper. Let the wounded, angry child inside you come out.

Don't Try to Be Rational

Even if only one percent of you feels angry, in this first section express it as if *all* of you feels that way so you can get rid of it. It is perfectly all right to use all sorts of "no-nos" you were told by other relationship experts never to say, like: "*You always* do that," "*You are never* on time," "*You should* grow up."

Be Specific

Even though it is important to allow yourself to generalize and indulge in blaming, make sure to be specific, too. For example, instead of just saying: "I hate when you are mean to me," write, "I hate when you are mean to me. How could you leave me standing there for two hours waiting for you!"

The more specific you are, the bigger your release will be.

Don't Explain or Organize Your Feelings—Express Them

An explanation: "When you came home and told me what your boss said, I thought you meant you would have to work late, so naturally I got upset. But I thought if I told you I was upset, you would get angry. So I decided to wait until after dinner."

This person is "explaining" to her husband how she felt. She is "in her head," not "in her heart." Here's how she would *express her feelings* in a Love Letter: "I hate when you don't come home on time. I'm furious at you for breaking our date. It hurts me to see you work so hard. I felt awful tonight when you didn't show up for dinner. I'm afraid we'll never spend enough time together. I'm afraid you will get tired of me . . ."

See the difference?

Don't Edit Your Feelings

One part of your mind might disagree with your emotions, and some statements you write might not even make any sense, but *don't edit what you write*.

You'll never be able to see your feelings clearly until you sort out all the incoherent, negative emotions cluttering up your heart.

Remember: It may be a new and scary experience for you to express *consciously* your feelings of anger and blame, but by doing so, you are preventing yourself from *unconsciously* expressing them by *acting them out.*

So write it out, don't act it out:

"I hate when you treat me like you don't even care."

"You are such a jerk for forgetting our date tonight."

"I am furious at you for criticizing me in front of my boss."

"How can you be such an insensitive dope?"

"I am so angry at you for throwing a temper tantrum at the party."

"I hate you when you get so needy and clingy."

What to Do When You Feel Stuck or Numb

If you feel "stuck," having a hard time expressing your anger spontaneously, you may want to use any of these "lead-in phrases" to help you express and release your anger. (This is not a formula to follow, but simply a guide if you need some help.)

"I hate it when . . ."
"I get so angry when . . ."
"I'm fed up with . . ."
"How could you . . ."
"I'm so tired of . . ."
"I resent . . ."

Just repeat one of these phrases in your mind and complete the sentence with whatever comes up. Here is an example using the lead-in phrase "I hate it when . . .":

"I hate it when *you don't compliment me and then notice other women.*"

"I hate it when *you don't do anything to show me
how you feel.*"

"I hate it when *you expect me to take care of the
kids and do all the housework.*"

While writing the angry feelings, you will eventually start to notice some feelings of hurt and sadness
surfacing. You may even start to cry. Congratulations!
You have released enough of the anger in the first part
of your love letter to begin feeling the deeper feeling of
hurt.

When you notice this transition, go on to Section
Two: Write out your feelings of hurt and sadness.

Section Two: Hurt and Sadness

In this section let the vulnerable part of you write
your feelings. Allow that little girl or little boy inside
you to express herself or himself. Some phrases to help
you are:

"I feel sad when . . ."

"It hurts me when . . ."

"I felt awful because . . ."

"I feel disappointed that . . ."

"It makes me sad to think . . ."

"It makes me sad to see you . . ."

For instance:

"It hurts me when *you act like you don't care
anymore.*"

"It hurts me when *you tell me I'm not as smart as
your ex-wife.*"

"It hurts me when *you pull away when I try to kiss
you.*"

"I felt so sad when *you didn't want to make love.*"

After some time of writing out the hurt and sad
feelings, you will begin to notice yourself feeling vul-

nerable. This is the time to go on to Section Three of the Love Letter.

Section Three: Fear and Insecurity

Allow yourself now to express the fears and insecurities you normally bury under a confident and strong front. *The more you let them out, the stronger you will feel afterward!* Some helpful phrases are:

"I'm afraid that . . ."
"It scares me that . . ."
"I'm worried that . . ."

For instance:

"I'm afraid that *you don't love me as much as you used to.*"
"I'm afraid that *when we go away on vacation, we will fight a lot.*"
"I'm afraid that *you won't want to work on the relationship as much as I do.*"
"I'm afraid that *we'll never work out our problems.*"

Note: These may be feelings you never talk about. Don't edit them: They are vital to the healing power of the Love Letter.

When you feel a release on this level, go on to the next level: remorse and responsibility.

Section Four: Remorse and Responsibility

Now that the emotional turbulence is being smoothed out, you should have a clearer perspective on the *real problem* and your part in it. This is the time to take responsibility for your contribution to the conflict or situation, and to say "I'm sorry" for whatever you feel remorse about. Put your pride aside.

Many people believe that to feel remorseful, or "guilty," they must be "wrong" or solely responsible. "I'm not sorry; *you* started it," they'll insist. They are afraid that if they say "I'm sorry," they are admitting they're wrong. This is not the case.

"I'm sorry" simply means, "I'm sorry I hurt you. I don't want you to suffer." Saying you are sorry gives your partner an opportunity to love and forgive you.

You don't have to be wrong to feel guilty or sorry.

I feel sorry if my mother is ill, even if I'm not responsible. I feel sorry if something I said hurt my partner, even if I didn't mean to hurt him. *Let go of your pride in this section and forget about who is right or wrong.*

> "I'm sorry *I don't always comfort you when you need me to.*"
> "*I didn't mean to hurt you.*"
> "I'm sorry *we are fighting.*"
> "Please forgive *me for saying . . .*"
> "I'm sorry *I lost my temper.*"
> "I'm sorry *I waited so long before writing a Love Letter.*"
> "I'm sorry *I push you away and make it difficult for you to want to make love.*"

When you feel you have completed this section, it will be very easy and natural for you to get back in touch with your wishes and desires in Section Five, and with your love in Section Six.

Section Five: Intentions and Wishes

Now it's time to focus on "changing the situation." What do you *want* to have happen? What do you *wish* will happen?

This is the time to let your dreams and hopes out:

"I want *us to be loving again*."

"I want *to learn to control my temper*."

"I wish *we could spend more time talking about feelings*."

"I want *to find a way to prove how much I do love you*."

"I hope *we can break down our walls and fall in love again*."

And now you are ready for the love.

Section Six: Love, Forgiveness, Understanding, and Appreciation

If you have written the other five parts of the Love Letter, you will definitely begin to feel your heart open. You will experience a renewed connection to your love, forgiveness, and appreciation of the person and will have a better understanding of the situation. *You won't have to fake it or force it—the ice will have melted, and the connection to love will be back.* You may not agree with what the other person did, *but you are ready to love him/her again.*

Forgiveness doesn't mean, "I agree with what you did to me." Taking a little liberty with language, I like to think that it simply means to "give as before," to forgive. *Allow yourself to really let go in the love section.* Don't be too intellectual . . . write from your heart. Let the poet in you come out. Let your partner know why you love him or her and what you appreciate. No one ever gets tired of hearing that they are loved, so don't worry about being redundant!

"I love *the way you want to work on our relationship*."

"Being married to you *means everything to me, and I promise to work harder at it*."

"I love you because *you are so sensitive*."

"Thank you for *always being there to listen to me.*"

"I love *making love with you and being close.*"

"Thank you for *putting up with my cranky moods.*"

Writing a Love Letter to Someone You Aren't in Love With

If you are writing a Love Letter to someone you aren't in love with, your love section will obviously be a little different.

Here are some lead-in phrases for this kind of Love Letter:

"*I really appreciate you for* being such a good friend."

"*I like it when you* are honest with me."

"*I'm grateful that* we work together."

"*I love your* sense of humor."

"*You really are* a wonderful boss."

Don't try to force or fake your appreciation. There are some people whom you will never like because you don't have much in common with them. But you can almost always feel at least some goodwill or good wishes toward a person, and try to understand why he acts the way he does.

▶ Hints and Procedures for Writing a Love Letter

1. *Balance the six parts of the letter in length.* You may find the anger and blame section longer, since that is where you express much of your tension, so make sure you express a lot of love at the end.

2. *Never stop writing your love letter until you have gotten to the love.* If you stop writing before you get to the love, you are cheating yourself and your

partner out of the true value of the letter—*the renewed connection to love at the end*. Not finishing your letter or giving up on writing it is giving up on making love work. Remember: *You wouldn't be so angry or hurt if there weren't a lot of love underneath*. Be patient, keep writing, and you'll get to the love.

3. *It's okay to repeat levels*. You may find that you have written out your anger, hurt, and fear, and then all of a sudden you feel angry again. Just go back to expressing your anger and write a few more sentences for each level until you get back to where you left off.

4. *Don't reread your Love Letter as you write it*. The best way to write a Love Letter is just to let it pour out. If you stop and reread what you wrote and think about it, you will be back in your head and out of your feelings.

5. *Make sure to write your letter clearly; you can even type it*.

How to Make Writing Your First Few Love Letters Easier

1. *Don't write your first Love Letter to your partner. Write it to someone else, and ask your partner to read it back to you*. Couples are often nervous about beginning to write Love Letters and really letting out the anger and hurt they've held inside for so long. If you want to feel more confident about using the Love Letter Technique, I suggest that each of you write your first Love Letter to someone other than your partner (e.g., your mother, your boss, your ex-husband). Then exchange Love Letters and read each other's aloud.

When you see how good you feel reading and writing Love Letters, and how much more loving you feel toward the person you wrote the Love Letter to, even though that person isn't present, you will begin to trust the Love Letter Technique as a tool you can use to improve your intimate relationship.

2. *In your first Love Letter, don't try to include every emotion you ever felt toward the person*. Sally learned the Love Letter Technique at my seminar and could hardly wait to write her husband her first Love Letter. Three weeks later, she called my office and said she was having problems finishing the letter. "It's taking me too long," Sally complained. "I've already written thirty pages of the anger and blame part, and I still have more things I'm angry about."

I explained to Sally that the purpose of a Love Letter was *not* to write every emotion of anger you have ever felt at your partner, but to deal with the *present* conflict or *one particular* issue.

You may have to go through the same cycle on that same issue ten or twenty times before you have fully resolved the conflict once and for all. That means you may have to write ten or twenty Love Letters—but do not try to jam it all in one Monster Love Letter!

How Long Should a Love Letter Be?

The length of a Love Letter will depend on the intensity of your feelings about a particular issue. For instance, you may write your partner a Love Letter about how neglected you are feeling, a big issue for you, and your Love Letter could be ten pages long. On the other hand, you may write your partner a Love Letter about his making fun of you at last night's party, a small issue for you, and your Love Letter might be only two pages long.

(You may notice that the *first* Love Letter you write is on the long side, especially if you have been carrying around a lot of stored-up anger, or if you were in the four R's.)

You know your Love Letters are *too short* when:

1. You don't feel in love again when you are done.

2. You have to force yourself to write the "I'm sorry" and love section.
3. You have written only a few paragraphs about some major issues in your life.

"But I Don't Have Time to Write a Love Letter . . ."

Do you have any idea of how much time we waste arguing, giving our partner the cold shoulder, and not being in love? Too much time! Taking the time to sit down and write your partner a Love Letter is an investment in the future of your relationship.

You can't afford *not* to take that time. What's half an hour when it will produce a week of happiness, closeness, and love?

▶ Reading the Love Letter

What to Do After You Have Written a Love Letter to Your Partner

1. *Give your partner your letter and ask him to read it to you aloud, as if he/she were the author of the letter.* This step is just as important as writing the letter so that you will hear all your feelings expressed aloud as a way to understand them fully. It is important for your partner to read your emotions so he can fully understand you and, most of all, so he can feel your movement from anger to love.

2. *If your partner also wrote you a Love Letter, read it aloud to him after he has taken a turn reading yours.* You may want to take turns reading the letters aloud a few times, in case you don't feel completely better after the first reading. You may also try reading your own letter out loud to your partner the second time.

3. *When you have both finished reading each other's letter, you should:*

- Feel much more emotionally connected
- Feel much less anger and tension
- Understand the Complete Truth about what was really upsetting you
- Understand the Complete Truth about what was really upsetting your partner

4. *Now it's time to discuss what you learned from writing Love Letters with each other and to make any new agreements in your relationship that will help you be happier.* And don't forget to kiss and make up.

What to Do If You and Your Partner Exchange Love Letters, and You Still Don't Feel Better

Sometimes there may be so much Emotional Tension between you and your partner that you won't feel better right away. If this happens to you, don't panic—try the following:

- Write another Love Letter—you may not have gotten out the deeper feelings that are blocking the love.
- Read your own Love Letter out loud to your partner. This may help you get more in touch with your feelings.
- Take turns rereading your Love Letters until you feel the ice start to melt and the love warming up again.
- Put the Love Letters aside for an hour and plan to meet again to read them. *Do not communicate with your partner at all until then.* Give each other some time to think and recover.

What to Do If Your Partner Won't Practice the Love Letter Technique With You

Suppose you and your partner are experiencing some tension, and you suggest writing Love Letters, but your partner refuses to participate.

1. *Don't use your partner's refusal as an excuse to hang on to your own negativity. Write your Love Letter, anyway.* Your real intent in writing a Love Letter should not be to change your partner or to prove a point:

You are writing a Love Letter to resolve *your own* Emotional Tension, tell yourself the Complete Truth, and get back to feeling love again.

So even if your partner refuses to write you a Love Letter, you can still begin to heal the conflict from *your* side by writing a letter.

2. *When you are finished with your Love Letter, present it to your partner and ask him to read it back to you.* If your partner reads your Love Letter, he is sure to feel better because:

* Your emotions will duplicate many of his own emotions and release some of his tension.
* Your taking responsibility for your part in the conflict will help him do the same.
* Your expression of love and appreciation at the end of the Love Letter will help him get back in touch with his own feelings of love for you.

3. *Your partner may be ready to write his own Love Letter to you, now that he is "warmed up" by having read yours,* or you may both feel so complete from your Love Letter and discussion afterward that there is no need for him to write a letter.

Rules for Reading Love Letters

1. *Never stop reading your partner's Love Letter until you have gotten to the love at the end.* Let's face it: You aren't going to like a lot of what you read in the first few parts of the Love Letter. Who wants to have to say out loud, "You insensitive jerk! I hate you for being

so damned cold," when the "jerk" being referred to is
you? In taking the time to write you a Love Letter,
your partner is performing an *act of love*—it demonstrates his willingness to work through all the negative
emotions that were in the way of his loving you.

So keep reading . . . no matter what you read or
how you feel. The good part is coming at the end!

2. *Do not make any comments while reading your
partner's Love Letter.* The whole purpose of Love Letters is to *avoid the back-and-forth verbal attacks that
take place in most arguments.* So don't comment on
what you read in your partner's Love Letter, even if
you strongly disagree with what he has written. Your
chance to express yourself comes when he reads *your*
letter.

3. *Notice which lines in your partner's letter upset
you the most.* I have found that the things you read that
"push your buttons" the most are usually your own
negative thoughts about yourself. For instance, when
Carla is reading her husband's Love Letter to her and
gets to the line: "I hate when you boss me around just
like your mother bosses your father around," Carla
notices her body tightening up and anger burning inside her. Why? Because Carla hates that part of herself
that is like her mother, and her husband has reminded
her of it.

**Remember, your partner is a mirror, reflecting all
the parts of yourself you may not want to see.**

Use the Love Letter as an opportunity to determine
which parts of your personality you still need to polish.

What to Do If Your Partner Refuses to Read Your Love Letter

If your partner refuses to read your Love Letter,
do not, under any circumstances, continue to commu-

*nicate with him until he has read it. If you do, you are
sure to get into an argument, because all those feelings
are still unresolved.*

Simply tell your partner: "I feel much better since
I wrote this letter. I'd like you to read it so we can make
up. If you are too angry to read it, I wish you'd write
me a Love Letter so you can feel better, too.

"Until you are willing to read my letter or write
your own, I don't want to communicate with you, because I know we will start fighting. So I'll check back
with you in a while."

Take the letter back and go about your business.
Come back in an hour, or whatever amount of time you
feel your partner may need. If he still refuses to read
the letter, leave and try again later. By this time, your
partner will either get tired of resisting or become
curious enough about what your Love Letter says that
he will agree to read it.

If your partner continually refuses to practice the
Love Letter Technique with you, you may need to
reevaluate your relationship and decide whether it is
viable for you to live with someone who repeatedly
will not participate with you in trying to heal conflicts.

▶ What to Do When You Have Read Your Love Letters

Never throw those Love Letters away! I suggest you
keep them all in one place, in a special drawer or
notebook. You'll be surprised to find that the majority
of your Love Letters are about the same issues. Each
couple has its own repertoire:

TOPIC ONE: We don't make love enough.

TOPIC TWO: You are too critical of me.

TOPIC THREE: You don't spend enough time helping me around the house.

TOPIC FOUR: You spend too much time at work and
not enough with me.

In a pinch, you can pull out an old Love Letter on the same topic you are fighting about and read it out loud to your partner and then have your partner read it back to you. Don't rely solely on this method, however, since it is always better to write a "fresh" Love Letter that shows your most recently evolved feelings on the subject.

My partner and I often reread our old Love Letters when we *aren't* upset, to get a perspective on how much we have grown. It's wonderful to see how conflicts disappear from our relationship once we have worked on healing them through the Emotional First-Aid Techniques.

The other benefit of rereading old Love Letters is that the next time the same conflict arises, remembering the Love Letter you previously wrote may help you not to overreact to the present situation.

▶ What to Do in an Emotional Emergency

Have you ever started fighting with your partner just as you were about to enter a restaurant? Did you ever plan a party or family gathering, and just before the guests arrived, you had a blowup with your husband or wife?

What can you do when you need to write a Love Letter, but only have five minutes in which to do so? Write a mini-Love Letter! Here's how:

1. Take out a piece of paper, a napkin, an envelope; anything will do.
2. Write one or two sentences on each of the six levels.
3. Exchange letters with your partner.

If you still feel a residue of tension after the mini-Love Letter, you can sit down and write a longer version later on.

▶ The Five Different Kinds of Love Letters

You can use the Love Letter Technique not only with an intimate partner but with family, friends, and even yourself. Here are the five different kinds of Love Letters you can write:

1. Love Letter to your intimate partner
2. Love Letter to someone other than your intimate partner (friend, relative, boss, etc.)
3. Love Letter to yourself
4. Love Letter in which you pretend to be someone *else* writing a Love Letter to *you*
5. Love Letter in which you pretend to be someone close to you writing a Love Letter to someone that person *needs* to write to but hasn't been able to

You have just learned how to write type 1: Love Letter to an intimate partner. Let's look at type 2: Love Letter to someone other than your intimate partner.

Writing a Love Letter to Someone Other Than Your Intimate Partner

Writing a love letter to people other than your intimate partner (a parent, a friend, your ex-wife, your boss, etc.) is a wonderful way to keep your relationships as loving and harmonious as you'd like them to be. Here are some rules to follow in writing this type of Love Letter:

Do not, under any circumstances, give your Love Letter to the person you wrote to unless:

1. You have explained the Love Letter Technique to him, and *he is willing to read your Love Letter*.
2. You give him an opportunity to write a Love Letter back to you.

For example, don't write a Love Letter to your ex-husband and send it to him in the mail. Don't show up for Thanksgiving dinner at your mother's house with a ten-page Love Letter to read to her. Don't dump all your resentment toward your unsuspecting best friend into a Love Letter and hand it to her after you finish playing tennis one day. If you wish to heal your relationships with these people, you have two options:

OPTION A: Ask for permission to exchange Love Letters with your friend, parent, etc.

1. Write a Love Letter following the format described earlier.
2. Explain the Love Letter Technique to the other person, and, if he agrees to read yours or to write one of his own, go ahead and exchange Love Letters.

OPTION B: Write a Love Letter to your friend, parent, etc. and ask someone else to read it back to you.

1. Write a Love Letter following the format described earlier.
2. If the person is unable or unwilling to exchange Love Letters with you, ask someone who is close to you to read your Love Letter back to you out loud.
3. After you have written your Love Letter you should feel a renewed loving connection with the other person. Now you can communicate the Complete Truth to that person either verbally or in an *informative* type of letter. For instance:

You know, Dad, last week I was so *angry* at you for a while for calling me up and sounding so tired and complaining about your health. I realized that it really *hurts* me to think of you in pain and getting older. I never admitted how *afraid* I am that you will die and how helpless I feel because I can't make you better. So I want to tell you I'm *sorry* I get so impatient on the phone sometimes. *I love you,* Dad, and want you to get better.

Notice how this communication contained all the levels of emotions. This person was able to express his feelings to his father effortlessly because:

1. He had written a Love Letter and was in touch with his *real feelings*.
2. He had released a lot of the emotional charge these feelings originally had, thus making it easier for him to express himself to his father from a loving place, not an angry one.

You may want to write Love Letters to the following people in order to heal your relationships with them:

- Ex-spouses or partners
- Parents, brothers and sisters, other family members
- In-laws
- Bosses and authority figures
- Your children
- Friends
- Business associates or co-workers

Writing Love Letters to Yourself

Writing Love Letters to yourself is one of the most powerful ways to heal your relationship with the most important person in your life—you. Suppressing your negative feelings about yourself prevents you from connecting with your natural self-love and self-esteem.

Writing a Love Letter to yourself will help you to forgive yourself for your imperfections, motivate yourself out of self-recrimination and into action, and move you from depression and despair to hope and clarity.

To write a Love Letter, simply *imagine that you are standing outside of yourself, looking at the person called "you."* What are you angry at that person about? What hurts you when you look at him? Be sure to include all six levels of feeling.

Example: Mary is angry at herself for giving up her power to her boyfriend, and not speaking up when he criticized her during a date. She comes home from the date and writes herself a Love Letter:

Dear Mary:

I am furious with you! I hate when you act so pathetic around Jim. I hate when you feel like you don't deserve to be treated wonderfully by a man, and let Jim treat you like dirt. You make me sick. It makes me so angry to see you doing this to yourself, and then feeling, "Poor me; Jim is so mean." Well, it's your own damned fault for being such a victim.

It hurts me to see you hurting yourself. It makes me so sad that you don't think you deserve any better. It hurts me when you let Jim say mean things and don't defend yourself.

I'm afraid you will never be strong. I'm afraid you will never stand up for what you believe in. I'm afraid you'll end up alone without a man. I'm afraid that you will get hurt in this relationship.

I'm sorry you are so hard on yourself. I'm sorry I pick on you and make you feel nothing you do is perfect. I'm sorry you don't have someone in your life who treats you really well.

I want you to know you deserve all the love in the world from a man. I want you to tell Jim how you feel. I want you to go after your dreams.

Mary, I love you. I am proud of you for all your accomplishments, and for working so hard on yourself. You have really been growing and I admire you for your courage. You are beautiful and powerful and deserve a man who will adore you.

Love, Mary

When to Write a Love Letter to Yourself

- When you feel *depressed*
- When you feel *angry* at yourself for something
- When you feel you *aren't asking for what you deserve*
- When you feel *guilty* about how you've treated someone, including yourself
- When you feel *confused* and *stuck*
- When your *self-esteem is low*

What to Do With Your Love Letter to Yourself

1. Have a friend or your partner read your Love Letter back to you. It is powerful to hear your own feelings about yourself read back to you, all the way down to the love. This helps you release the Emotional Tension inside.

2. If you can't find anyone to read you the Love Letter, read it out loud in front of a mirror, or into a tape recorder, and play it back. This will help you "own" all your feelings about yourself and experience an emotional release.

Writing Love Letters From Someone Else to You

Have you ever wanted to show someone that you understood how he felt, but you weren't sure how to convince him? *Love Letter Technique 4* is a powerful way to heal your relationships with people close to you by looking at *yourself* from *their* point of view.

THE TECHNIQUE: Write a Love Letter to yourself, pretending you are someone else (your husband, daughter, father, etc.).

EXAMPLE: Felicia and her husband, Tom, attended one of my Making Love Work seminars. During the weekend, Felicia confessed to Tom that she had been unfaithful to him several years earlier. Naturally, Tom was very upset, and felt betrayed.

Felicia and Tom decided to write Love Letters to each other to heal their marriage. One week later, Felicia called me for help: "Tom and I do feel closer," she began, "but I still can't seem to get him to forgive me. I've tried to show him that I know how he feels, but I can't find the right words."

I suggested that Felicia imagine she was Tom, whose wife had just told him she'd been unfaithful, and write a letter starting out with anger, and moving through all the emotional levels until she arrived at love and forgiveness. Then I asked her *to give the letter to Tom and ask him to read it back to her.* Here are some excerpts from that letter:

Felicia, how could you do this to me? I hate you for ruining our marriage and breaking my trust in you. I hate you for not coming to me for love, but letting some other jerk touch you. It makes me sick to think of what you did, and I feel like never touching you again.

I feel so devastated, Felicia, by what you have done. My heart is crushed. I feel as though all our dreams are gone. I feel so sad thinking about how much I believed in you. It hurts me to think I wasn't making you happy.

I'm afraid everything is over now. I'm afraid I'll never trust you again. I'm afraid you don't love me. I'm afraid I'm not what you want.

I'm sorry I didn't give you what you needed and you had to get it elsewhere. I'm sorry I didn't see the signs and do something. I'm sorry I worked so hard and was away so often. I'm sorry all of this happened.

I want to be together again as we once were. I want to forgive you. I am really trying. I want to heal this and rededicate ourselves to each other. I want to be happy with you.

I love you, Felicia. You mean everything to me.
I know we can make our marriage work. You are the
most wonderful woman I know, and I know you feel
as terrible as I do about this. Thank you for being so
honest with me and being willing to work on this
together.

What Happened After Felicia Wrote Her Love Letter

- Felicia felt a big emotional release because she
  had a chance to write out all her angry feelings
  toward *herself.*
- When Tom read Felicia's letter, he felt a tremendous sense of release in reading his own feelings,
  and he felt more able to forgive Felicia.
- Most important, *Tom felt that Felicia really understood him.*

When to Use Love Letter Technique 4

1. When you feel *guilty* about hurting someone
   and need to *forgive* yourself
2. When you want to *heal past guilt* (from a
   divorce, argument, homelife)
3. When someone you care for is *angry* with you
4. When someone you care for is having trouble
   forgiving you
5. When you and your partner want to *really
   understand each other's point of view*

Writing a Love Letter to Someone From Someone Else

Love Letter Technique 5 is great *for helping someone you love to heal his/her relationships with others.*

THE TECHNIQUE: Pretending to be someone close to you, you write a Love Letter to someone with whom that person needs to heal.

Examples of How to Use Love Letter Technique 5

Your daughter is angry and cold toward her father, who happens to be your ex-husband. She refuses to acknowledge her feelings, let alone write a Love Letter. You write a Love Letter from your daughter to her father and ask her to read it back to you.

Your mother is angry at your father, but can't express herself. You write a Love Letter from your mother to your father and ask her to read it back to you.

Your husband is angry and hurt because his best friend has been talking behind his back, but your husband refuses to confront the situation. You write a Love Letter from your husband to his friend, and ask him to read it back to you.

THE LOVE LETTER FORMAT

Here is a summary of each section of the Love Letter:

Begin by expressing your anger, resentment, and blame, and allow yourself to move through the other emotional levels until you get down to the love.

The following lead-in phrases may help you if you get stuck at one level and can't move on to the next.

1. ANGER AND BLAME
I hate it when . . .
It makes me furious when . . .
I'm fed up with . . .
I'm tired of . . .
I resent . . .

2. HURT AND SADNESS
It hurts me when . . .

I feel sad when . . .
I feel awful because . . .
I feel hurt because . . .
I'm disappointed that . . .

3. FEAR AND INSECURITY

I'm afraid that . . .
I feel scared that . . .
I am worried that . . .

4. REMORSE AND RESPONSIBILITY

I'm sorry that . . .
I'm sorry for . . .
Please forgive me for . . .
I didn't mean to . . .

5. INTENTION AND WISHES

I want . . .
I wish . . .
I hope . . .

6. LOVE, FORGIVENESS, UNDERSTANDING, GRATITUDE

I love you because . . .
Thank you for . . .
I'm proud of you for . . .
I understand that . . .
I forgive you for . . .
I love it when . . .

▶ Sample Love Letters

Here are two samples of Love Letters from a husband and wife who attended my Making Love Work seminar. (These are fairly short Love Letters.)

Robert and Ellen have been married for seven years. Robert sells corporate real estate, and Ellen takes care of their young son. They are having an argument about spending more time together.

Ellen's Letter to Robert

Dear Robert,

You are so self-centered. I hate you for acting like you don't want to spend time with me. I'm furious at your burying yourself in your work and ignoring our relationship and our family. If I were a client, you would love to talk to me now, but I'm just your wife, so you act like you couldn't care less. I hate when you come home and act so cold. I hate when you are too tired to make love night after night. I hate it when you make me seem neurotic for wanting to spend time with you. Grow up and stop being so damned numb.

It hurts me when we fight like this. It hurts when I am so excited to see you, and you walk in the door and talk down to me. It makes me so sad to lie in bed with you and not have you reach out to me. I miss you, Robert, and I miss making love with you as much as we used to. I feel sad to see you working so hard and not letting yourself play. It really hurt me tonight when you called me "a demanding bitch," because I wanted to spend time with you after dinner. It hurts when you push my love away. It hurts when you close your heart down to me.

I'm afraid you will always work hard and we will never be together. I'm afraid it will destroy our marriage. I'm afraid our little boy will grow up feeling unloved. I'm afraid you are getting tired of me and hiding behind your job. I'm afraid I will never feel loved enough by you. I'm afraid you won't open up enough for me, and I will feel so alone. I'm afraid I want to be closer than you do.

I'm sorry I don't always tell you how much I appreciate how hard you work. I'm sorry you had a hard day today. I'm sorry I jumped on you tonight with my own problems as soon as you came home. I'm sorry we are fighting. I'm sorry I make you feel you can't trust me with your worries. I want you to trust me.

I want us to be close again. I want us to be a team. I want to spend special time together like we used to. I want to help you so you don't feel so alone in supporting us. I want to know you love me, and never feel insecure about us. I want to make it safe for you to open to me and let your feelings out. I want us to be so happy together.

I really love you, honey. I miss you so much when you work at night. You mean everything to me. I feel so lucky to be sharing my life with you. And I am really proud of you for working so hard and doing so well. You are a wonderful man, and I love how clear your mind is and how much other people admire you. I know you want to be with me, too, and just not feel so pressured. Let's work together to make our marriage wonderful, because it really is wonderful. I've loved you since the day we met, and I just love the times when we play and are close. Let's make up and be close again.
Ellen

Robert's Letter to Ellen

Dear Miss Insecure,

I hate you for being such a big baby. I can't even work hard one night without you going into total panic. It makes me so mad when I come home from working hard and have you nagging me. Why don't you lay off for once, and let me be? All you think about is yourself and what *you* need. Well, what about me, Ellen? I hate you when you get so needy. I hate when you get so critical of what I do, and tell me I'm not doing things right. Look who's talking. Well, if you think I'm so bad, go back with your old boyfriend from college. I hate when you expect me to be energetic at the end of the day. I hate when you act like our relationship is over just because we aren't lovey-dovey. Grow up, Ellen.

It really hurts me when I feel you don't appreciate how hard I am working for you. It hurts me to think you feel like I don't love you when I do, and I feel frustrated and sad that you feel so unloved. I feel awful when you walk around looking so mopey-eyed, like I have just committed a crime or something. It hurts when you don't seem to believe in me. It feels awful to fight and not to feel close like I know we can.

I'm afraid you will never be happy or satisfied with me, that I will never be enough for you. I'm afraid I will always have to work harder than anyone else to get ahead. I'm afraid I won't have the time in my life to do all the things I want to do. I'm afraid if I give to you and my job, there will never be anything left for me. I'm afraid to show you how much I need support sometimes.

I'm sorry I work so hard. I'm sorry I don't put aside special time for us. I really want to. I'm sorry I called you names tonight. I didn't mean it, I just get scared when I feel I can't make you happy. I'm sorry you feel so abandoned sometimes. I'm sorry I get cranky and lose my temper with you. I feel terrible when I yell at you like that. Please forgive me.

I want us to be close just like you do. I want to spend more quiet time. together. I want to become really successful so I can be with my family more. I want to know what you need and find ways to give it to you. I only want to make you happy, honey.

I love you, Ellen. I am doing all this hard work for you. You make it all worthwhile. Please feel how much I mean that. I love coming home to you and sleeping next to you at night. I love how much you need me, because I need you just as much. Thank you for being such a good mother and wife and for always being willing to write Love Letters and make up quickly. I promise to try harder to take more time to be with you. I love how much you want us to

be close, and think you are adorable, even when you are angry. Sorry, baby . . .
Robert

The more you work with the Love Letter Technique, the more confidence and certainty you will feel that *underneath all negative emotions, love is always waiting to be expressed and enjoyed!*

CONGRATULATIONS! YOU HAVE JUST CHOSEN LOVE OVER SEPARATION AND ACCOMPLISHED THE GREATEST FEAT OF ALL—LEARNING TO MAKE LOVE WORK!

10

The Power Process

Do you ever procrastinate about doing important tasks?

Do you ever get nervous before you have to give a presentation, make a sale, present your ideas, or ask for what you want?

Do you ever feel so lethargic that you can't find the energy to get going?

Do you ever make a mistake and feel so bad about it that you become more and more depressed?

Do you ever feel frustrated and angry with yourself and can't snap out of it?

If you answered yes to even one of these questions, you are going to really enjoy practicing the third Emotional First-Aid Technique: the Power Process.

The Power Process is the easiest of the three techniques I've taught you, and it takes the least amount of time—only about three to five minutes! It is a powerful way to *turn your anger and criticism of yourself into motivation and personal power.*

▶ Why the Power Process Works

Your angry feelings toward yourself can be a tremendous source of inspiration and power if you know how to use them properly. *Most people think that their anger at themselves is the result of low self-esteem, but that couldn't be further from the truth.* The real source of your anger at yourself is revealed in what I call the Anger-to-Power Chain.

THE ANGER-TO-POWER CHAIN

ANGER
↓
I DIDN'T GET
↓
I WANT
↓
I DESERVE
↓
SELF-LOVE
↓
PERSONAL POWER

When you get angry about something, it is because you *didn't get something.* You wanted a raise; you didn't get it; you got angry . . . You want your husband to make love to you; you don't get it; you get angry, and so on.

Obviously, you wouldn't be angry if you hadn't wanted the thing you were denied. So underneath your frustration about not getting what you want is the feeling "I want." This is the level of your dreams and desires.

When you want something, you have to feel you *deserve* it. So underneath all the dreams you have is a feeling that you deserve to have them come true, or you wouldn't dream them in the first place.

And why do you feel you deserve all you dream of? Because you love yourself . . . because you have a strong sense of self-worth. This is your source of personal power. Underneath the feeling that you deserve to have your dreams come true is your love for yourself and your sense of personal power. If you didn't love yourself so much, you wouldn't care when you didn't get what you wanted, and you wouldn't ever feel angry.

So when you deny your feelings of anger, you are also denying your true source of power, a source that says, "I deserve to be happy, successful, and loved!"

▶ How the Power Process Works

The Power Process has three sections, each one repesenting a step back toward your own natural state of power:

Step One: Expressing anger at yourself
Step Two: Expressing what you want
Step Three: Expressing positive, loving support of
    yourself

When to Practice the Power Process
Whenever you:

- make a mistake
- miss an opportunity
- disappoint yourself
- don't keep commitments
- do something foolish
- feel frightened or nervous
- have an important appointment
- want to make a good impression
- want to boost your energy

Where to Practice the Power Process

- In the shower, in the morning, before you start
  your day

- In your car on the way to or from work
- Looking into a mirror
- Talking into a tape recorder
- Anywhere you like

How Long Does the Whole Process Take?
Three to five minutes.

How Will You Feel When You Are Finished?
Fantastic!
Example: Dennis is in computer sales, and he isn't doing very well. He freezes up during sales presentations; he doesn't make the calls he should; he isn't aggressive enough.

Dennis is fed up with being such an unaggressive, unsuccessful salesman. He finds he is putting himself down all the time, anticipating failure, and thus making matters worse. So Dennis decides to do a Power Process before he goes to work. Let's follow him through it, step by step.

Step One: Get angry at yourself.

Verbalize *out loud* your anger and blame at yourself for the situation you are angry about. Use phrases like:

"I hate it when you . . ."
"You are such a . . ."
"I'm tired of you . . ."

You may find yourself yelling, or you may just use a very angry, firm, deliberate tone. *Note:* Don't scream at the top of your lungs—this is actually a way we *avoid* our feelings and just blow off steam. On the other hand, don't do the Power Process in a quiet, gentle voice. Unless you are firm and forceful in what you say, you will not feel a full release from your anger.

Be sure to use "you" statements, and not "I"

statements. *This allows you to direct the anger out and not in.*

Don't say:
"I hate myself for being a wimp."

"I am such a lazy jerk."

"I am so fed up with failing."

Do say:
"I hate *you* for being a wimp."

"*You* are such a lazy jerk."

"I'm fed up with *you* being a failure."

Spend two to three minutes of unedited, unadulterated anger at yourself. Dennis's anger:

"Dennis, you are such a wimp. I hate getting up every morning and watching you screw up your day. I despise that part of you that is so damned weak and scared. I hate when you give a presentation in a little mousy voice and act afraid of your customers! Act like a man! Quit being such a nobody!"

Step Two: Become the motivator by expressing what you want.

Maintaining the same tone of voice, *begin motivating yourself by saying what you want yourself to do.* Dennis's motivation:

"I want you to grow up! I want you to take charge at work! I want you to go in there today and really shine! I want you to project your voice in meetings! I want you to convince those customers how lucky they are to know you! I want you to be on time for your appointments! I want you to believe in yourself! I want you to have the greatest day you have ever had!"

Step Three: Become your own cheerleader by expressing love and support for yourself.

Now it's time to cheer yourself on. Using that same positive, firm tone of voice, *express your love and support for yourself.*

"*I love you* when you shine."
"*I know you* can be successful."
"*You deserve* to have everything you want."

Dennis's love and support:

"Dennis, you have so much potential! I know you can be a powerhouse! I love you when you show everyone how smart you are! You deserve to make tons of money! You deserve to be the best salesman in the company! I know you can do it because you are a natural! People love being around you! I believe in you! I love you!"

You have to try this technique to experience what an empowering and energizing effect it has on you for hours afterward! I do at least one Power Process every day, usually in the morning, in the shower, and another if I have an important situation to face. Instead of letting my negative thoughts and fears build up, I can walk into the TV show, interview, or meeting charged-up, confident, and clear!

▶ Some Variations on the Power Process

1. Take turns doing a Power Process with your partner or a friend. Instead of talking straight through, stop every few sentences and have your partner duplicate what you said. Having your words yelled back will feel great to you, and to your partner, too.

2. Tape the Power Process on a cassette, leaving blank space after each sentence. Play the tape in your car or at home, and after you hear yourself say each

sentence, duplicate it and fill in the blanks. This is a great way to do an instant Power Process.

3. If your partner or friend is angry at you, do a Power Process at yourself, and have her duplicate what you say to yourself. Any anger she has toward you will be released as *you* express it for her!

The Power Process in a Nutshell

STEP ONE— **Express anger and blame at yourself**
"I hate it when . . ."
Etc.

STEP TWO— **Express what you want for yourself**
"I want you to . . ."
Etc.

STEP THREE— **Express positive, loving support of yourself**
"You are . . ."
Etc.

So the next time . . .

You're out on a date, and you are angry at yourself for acting so unexpressive and feeling so nervous, excuse yourself, go to the rest room, do a Power Process, and come back looking and feeling magnificent!

You are nervous about a job interview, do a Power Process on the way there and walk into the office shining!

You are moping and uninspired to get anything done, go over to the mirror, do a Power Process, and find that source of energy and power that's the real you!

▶ Now It's Up to You

It may take you a little while to become familiar with the techniques I have outlined in this section, but after a while they will become second nature. When you and your partner have an argument, you will sit down and write a Love Letter as naturally as you used to walk out and slam the door; when you are feeling angry and disappointed with yourself, you will do a Power Process as easily as you used to eat three cartons of ice cream and watch five straight hours of TV to suppress your sorrows. When your children are misbehaving, you will sit down and play the Duplication Game with them as effortlessly as you used to send them to their rooms to control them.

I know that as these techniques become a part of your life, you will begin to have the same experience that thousands of other people have. *It feels wonderful to know how to make love work!*

11

Keeping the Magic of Love Alive

Kathy unloaded her packages from the car. She wondered if her husband was home from work yet. "I guess he isn't," she thought, heading toward the kitchen. And then she saw the balloons: a dozen colored, helium-filled balloons floating in the kitchen. Hanging from one were two envelopes. One said, "Open me first." It read: "Go to the living room and push the 'play' button on the cassette player, then sit down and read card two."

Laughing, Kathy went into the living room and pressed "play" on the recorder. She was greeted with "Only You" by the Platters.

This was great! The song brought back many happy memories of when she and Louis had just started dating. Then she opened the other envelope:

Congratulations! You have just won a Dream Date down Memory Lane with a really swinging guy who loves you to pieces. Follow these instructions carefully:

1. Take a nice, long bath. Close your eyes and remember how exciting it used to be to get ready for your dates in high school.

2. Get dressed for a casual night out. You *must* wear shoes or sneakers with socks, and a skirt. While you dress, play the rest of the tape to put you in the proper mood.

3. Leave the house by 6:30. Go to Main Street and Pier Avenue. Proceed to the drugstore on the corner and wait. Look for a cool-looking guy with love in his eyes.

Now, get going and don't be late! You're in store for a wonderful evening.

Your lover, Louis

Kathy could hardly wait to find out what was in store! She ran a hot bubble bath and soaked in it until she felt completely relaxed and pampered. She found an old plaid wool skirt in the closet and added a pullover sweater, white socks, and sneakers. "I look just like I did in high school," she thought.

Later, standing outside the drugstore, she felt butterflies in her stomach—she was excited and even a little nervous. Then she saw Louis, smiling as he walked toward her. He was wearing his high school jacket. He had even slicked back his hair!

"Hi, baby," Louis said. "Want to do the town tonight with me?"

"Sure," giggled Kathy.

"You look great," Louis added.

Kathy blushed. "Why am I blushing?" she thought to herself. "This is my own husband!" But she was having so much fun! "Where are we going?" she asked.

"You'll see," Louis answered.

First, Louis took Kathy to a little malt shop, where they ate at the counter, just as they used to when they were dating. Then they got in his car, and he put a cassette of their favorite fifties songs on the tape machine. It was just getting dark when Louis pulled up to a drive-in movie! "We haven't been to a drive-in for years!" Kathy exclaimed. Louis bought some popcorn, and he and Kathy snuggled in the back seat to watch the film.

"Do you still have some energy?" Louis asked at the end of the movie.

"Definitely!" said Kathy.

So Louis drove to a little nightclub where it was Fifties Night. Louis and Kathy laughed and danced together.

Later, instead of driving home, Louis turned off the freeway into a rural area.

"Where are we going?" Kathy asked.

"You'll see," said Louis with a sly smile.

Then Kathy realized Louis was taking her to go parking! He stopped the car on a ridge overlooking the city, turned on the tape deck playing the Platters, and turned to Kathy with a twinkle in his eye. "Want to go steady?" he asked.

"Forever," she answered as she fell into his waiting arms.

This is a true story. And what is most wonderful about it is that Louis and Kathy have been married for twenty-five years! They are more in love today than they were when they got married twenty-five years ago, because they know the secret of making love all the time.

Having a magical relationship won't happen just because you are in love. You have to work to make the magic keep happening.

▶ How to Celebrate Your Relationship

Think back to when you did something you enjoyed that you hadn't done in a long time. Remember thinking to yourself, "I forgot how much I enjoy doing this!" The human mind is very fickle: *We tend to forget how much we enjoy something when we stop focusing our attention on it.*

This same principle applies to your intimate relationship:

▼

SECRET:
> *When you stop focusing your attention on your relationship, you forget how much you enjoy the magic of love.*

▲

Isn't it strange that *the longer you and your partner are together, the less effort you put into enjoying the magic of your love?* Yet this is one reason why the divorce rate is so high, and why couples get tired of one another after a few years: They don't know how to celebrate their relationship.

Okay, so you've decided you *do* need to focus on enjoying your relationship with your partner more— you are ready for the magic! What do you do now?

You apply what I call the *Team Principle*.

▶ How the Team Principle Works

The Team Principle defines the four ingredients that will help you celebrate your relationship and turn you and your partner into a real *team,* with both of you committed to making love all the time. Make sure to include all four of the ingredients, and watch the magic happen!

Recipe for Making Magic
1. Time
2. Environment
3. Attitude
4. Materials and props

1. Time: *"When can I set aside some special time for my partner and me?"*

Your intimate relationship is the most precious gift in your life. It deserves some time every day to be celebrated. Naturally, you can't give your relationship large quantities of time *each* day. Using the team approach, however, you can give love to your partner *in some small way each day*.

Small Doses of Magic

Spend five minutes giving your partner a foot rub first thing in the morning, after work, or before bed.

Spend five minutes combing your wife's hair.

Help your partner get dressed (or undressed) for fun! (Watch out—this can go on longer than five minutes!)

Ask your partner to unload his cares of the day while you give him a shoulder rub.

Write a special love note and place it where your lover can't miss it—in his wallet, in her makeup case, on the steering wheel of her car, in his briefcase, in the refrigerator.

Keep a stack of humorous or amorous greeting cards at home. When you want to express your love, but don't have a lot of time, leave a special card for your partner. (My partner and I buy cards by the dozen, and each of us has our "secret" card drawer. Sometimes I save a card for months until the perfect occasion—there are cards to say, "I'm sorry," "Last night was fabulous," "I love waking up with you.")

Don't throw those cards and notes away—keep them in an album and read them occasionally to remind yourself how loved you are!

Call your partner from work with an erotic phone call. Tell him what you'd rather be doing than working—even if it's not so erotic—like lying on the beach together or watching old movies on a rainy day. *It's fun to dream together.*

Make your partner a "Love Coupon Book" with slips of paper redeemable for loving moments: massages, hugs and kisses, five minutes of compliments.

Larger Doses of Magic

For larger doses of magic, you need to put aside special time for your partner. I suggest that you and your partner take turns planning these events, but make sure to schedule the time together so both of you know about it. It's fun to keep your plans a secret, and drop hints for days or weeks beforehand.

Minimum dose for keeping the magic alive: one surprise each month.

That means you plan something special once a month—a weekend or an evening—and once a month your partner plans something special.

It is such a wonderful feeling to know that every month your partner is planning something special for you. You feel loved and appreciated, and, in turn, you feel more loving and more appreciative. So *even before the event happens, the magic starts happening!*

2. Environment and Theme: *"How can I create a wonderful environment in which to celebrate our love?"*

For his surprise date with Kathy, Louis selected a fifties theme, which he knew would remind Kathy of their early days together. He didn't just write her a note about going out; he instructed her to listen to a special tape, take a bath, and meet him on the corner. All of this helped to get her in the mood for having fun and was part of the mystique of the evening. He also planned the whole surprise from the beginning (the balloons) to the end (necking in the car). It was *an event,* not just a date. That's what made it so romantic, and helped Kathy appreciate Louis's efforts so much.

You don't need a theme for a small surprise, just a nice environment. One night I arrived home quite late from a seminar I was giving. I walked in the front door and found the living room glowing in candlelight. A fire was roaring in the fireplace; there was a comfortable pile of pillows on the floor and a special snack prepared on a tray. Soft music played in the background. Next to the tray I saw a note that read: "I'm so proud of you for working so hard—but I really missed you." My partner popped out from behind the couch and gave me a hug. What a treat to come home to!

It would have been considerate for him just to ask me if I wanted a snack when I got home. But with five extra minutes of preparation, he created a special and memorable experience. And even though I had come home exhausted and not in the mood for romance, you can be sure that my mood changed quickly once I was given the *time,* put in the right *environment,* felt my lover's *attitude,* and was helped along with the *materials,* such as candles and fire.

I'll give you some more ideas for creating a theme and environment at the end of this chapter.

3. Attitude: *"How can I remind myself of how much I love my partner?"*

If you have the attitude that you are having a lifelong love affair with your partner, you will be well on your way to keeping the magic of love alive. Remember how excited you were to meet your lover for a date? You spent time getting ready, making sure you looked all right, fantasizing about how much fun you were going to have. When you meet your "wife" or "husband" for dinner, do you turn it into a special occasion, or is your attitude one of: "Oh, I'm not doing anything special tonight, just having dinner with my husband"? How much magic do you think you will experience with that attitude? Not much!

---------------------------▼---------------------------

SECRET:

> *If you treat your partner as a lover, you will experience him/her as a lover. If you treat your partner as a spouse you take for granted, you will experience him/her as uninspiring and boring.*

---------------------------▲---------------------------

You may be thinking, "Oh, that's easy to do in the beginning, but you get so comfortable with each other that it's difficult to keep that excitement." My answer to that is: *Continually making an effort to rediscover the magic in your partner is the true creative challenge of a monogamous relationship.* It's nice sometimes to feel "comfortable"—to be able to walk around in an old flannel nightgown or to be grumpy and not have to perform to be loved—but not all the time!

---------------------------▼---------------------------

SECRET:

> *Keeping the magic alive and becoming a true team means always remembering that you would like this person to fall in love with you over and over again.*

---------------------------▲---------------------------

Be a continual surprise to your partner—don't always get dressed in front of him. Ask him to wait in the other room while you get dressed and *then* come out and show him how lovely you look. Don't always take your wife to the same restaurant—do a little research and find a romantic restaurant that *you* chose especially for that evening.

For big surprises, having the right attitude means knowing that *you are planning this event as a gift to the person you love*. Allow yourself to get excited about it, too! Let yourself surrender to giving to your partner without any expectations of receiving in return.

4. Materials: *"What materials or props do I need to help create this event?"*

Use materials or props to build suspense and curiosity about the surprise you have planned. Once, when it was my turn to plan a special surprise for my partner, I bought two tickets to the musical *Cats*. For one week before the event, I left little cat stickers and cut-out magazine pictures of cats all over the house. My partner had no idea what was going on, since he didn't know we were going to a show and therefore couldn't make the connection. Finally, on the evening of the show, I cut the ad out of the newspaper and also cut out different phrases, including the title, and pasted them on a card inviting my partner to the theater. He loved it, and finally understood why our house was covered with cat stickers!

Sometimes, your materials or props will constitute a whole environment. One of my favorite places in the world to visit is the Hawaiian Islands. Last year, I was working very hard on my book, and my partner was working hard on his book. We daydreamed about going to Hawaii, but knew it was impossible. That Saturday night, when my partner arrived home, he found himself on Maui instead of in Los Angeles. I greeted him at the door with a lei of flowers and led him into the dining room. The table was decorated with coconuts and Hawaiian flowers; Hawaiian music played on the stereo. I had made a Hawaiian meal for dinner. And guess what I was wearing? A hula outfit! *"Aloha,"* I said with a smile. "We couldn't go to Hawaii, so I brought Hawaii here." My partner loved it! And more important, he loved me for caring enough to go to all the trouble of creating such a wonderful surprise.

▶ Ideas for Celebrating Your Relationship

You may be thinking that you aren't the kind of person who can be this creative. Well, forget about who you have been in the past. The question is, Do you want to learn to be creative in love *now*?

Here are some ideas for themes or environments you can create for your partner:

- *Outings or visits to places* your partner always wanted to see. (If you don't know, find out!)
- *Fun activities* you can do together to allow your inner child to come out and play (miniature golf, amusement parks, renting Three Stooges movies for your VCR).
- *Romantic activities* such as dinner in a special spot, a picnic in a park, a moonlit walk, your partner taking you to a lingerie specialty shop and picking out items for you to model for him (you don't have to buy—just looking is fun).
- *New and different activities*—things you normally would never do. Take your partner to a square dance; stay in a hotel in your hometown and do things tourists do; go to a store and try on clothes you would never buy because they are too "far out" for your daily life.
- *Surprise vacations*—my personal favorite. Plan a vacation (from one night to several weeks) from start to finish without your partner knowing it. Tell him what to pack and how long you will be away. He won't know where he is going until you get to the airport or off the train or arrive in the car. This kind of surprise is extremely exciting and makes the other person feel very taken care of.

When my partner and I started out creating magic time, we weren't nearly as creative as we are now. The more we practiced, the better we got. Now when I go into a store or leaf through a magazine, I am always on the lookout for props or ideas to help keep the magic of our love alive.

It Doesn't Cost Anything to Be Romantic

It doesn't have to cost anything to be romantic. All you need is your imagination.

One of the most exciting surprises my partner ever planned for me cost him very little money. He told me to keep one Saturday morning free and that I would receive my "instructions" then. That Saturday I woke up as he was leaving the house. Next to the bed was an envelope. The note inside instructed me to go to a certain street and look for an envelope taped under a newspaper box on the corner. I felt so excited; it was like a treasure hunt. I went to the appointed spot and checked every newspaper box until I found the envelope. (I must have looked pretty strange groping under the boxes.)

This note told me to proceed to a phone booth five blocks away and wait for a call at exactly 9:34. That phone rang, and a voice (my partner) said, "You are being followed. Can't talk now. Go to the coffee shop at the corner of Fifth and Wilshire and ask for Jan." I drove to the coffee shop, asked if I could see Jan, and a waitress came out and handed me another envelope.

This went on for an hour, and I became more and more excited until finally I was told to wait on a corner, and my partner drove up in his car and greeted me with a big hug and "Congratulations!" Then he took me out for breakfast. I still laugh thinking about each leg of my adventure.

▶ The Seven Levels of Love

When you are planning activities to share with your partner, be aware that there are seven major spheres in your life that need nurturing.

1. *Physical:* sports, walks, dancing, massage
2. *Recreational:* things done just for fun—films, games, sight-seeing, music, social activities
3. *Sexual:* talking about sex, being affectionate, and creating intimate time
4. *Educational:* learning new things together; seminars, lectures; sharing a book, creating new recipes
5. *Intellectual:* sharing your mind with your partner; discussion of politics, religion, other important issues
6. *Emotional:* time just to nurture each other and to support the other in the changes he/she is going through
7. *Spiritual:* sharing your experience of spirit together; attending religious service, practicing meditation, going for a silent walk together

The more of these areas your relationship includes, the more fulfilled you will feel.

▼

SECRET:
You and your partner will be affected by the level of Emotional Tension in the couples you spend time with.

▲

It will be difficult for you to enjoy being in love when you are with a couple who is not enjoying each other. You may feel strange and almost guilty about being happy when they are not happy, and you will *duplicate some of their tension in order to make them "feel better."* You may identify with the partner of your own sex, so when you hear that person criticize his partner, you may feel you are "betraying" him if you are nice to your own partner in that moment. You may start to feel insecure seeing another couple fighting, and become hypersensitive to your partner's reactions to you.

The more time you spend with couples who aren't loving and respecting one another, the more difficult it will be for you to keep the magic of love alive. This same principle applies to your single friends as well. If your girlfriend is always complaining about men, it will be difficult for you to enjoy loving your husband in her presence without "betraying" her. You'll either have to disagree with her strongly, or go along with what she says and shut down your own feelings.

▶ Your Relationship Deserves All the Support It Can Get!

Treat your relationship as you would your own newborn baby. You wouldn't let just anyone hold your baby—you want only those people near your baby who will be a loving, supportive influence. The same goes for your relationship. *Surround youself with other couples who are willing to work on making love all the time and who support you in making love work.*

As for the couples and friends who are *not* supportive, tell them the Complete Truth about how you feel when you are with them, and offer your support to help them heal their relationship and make love work. They deserve it, too!

Your relationship won't transform overnight. Sit down with your partner and create a plan for rejuvenating your relationship. Your plan might include:

1. One Love Letter each week (Chapter 9)
2. One surprise each month
3. Three sessions of Planned Intimacy a week (Chapter 16)
4. Two twenty-second kisses a day (Chapter 16)
5. Reviewing this book together and discussing important points

6. Taking the Making Love Work seminar if it is being offered in your area

Start today! And be patient . . . the results will come. And they will definitely be worth waiting for.

PART THREE

▼▼▼▼▼▼▼▼▼▼▼▼▼▼▼▼▼▼▼▼▼▼▼▼▼▼

Secrets About Sex

▲▲▲▲▲▲▲▲▲▲▲▲▲▲▲▲▲▲▲▲▲▲▲▲▲▲▲▲▲

12

Your Secret Sexual Classroom

When I was in college, I wanted to have every sexual experience imaginable. Eventually, I realized I did want a committed relationship with a woman. That's when I met my wife. We were really into having the ultimate sexual experience. We had all the books on how to do it, and we used to make love for hours. Yet, for the past few years, sex just isn't as important anymore. If it's there, fine. If not, no big deal . . . I have a good job and a solid family. Do I miss the old days? Well, sometimes I think it would be great to feel that much passion again. But I can't stay young forever.

—Thirty-seven-year-old attorney

As a culture, we are preoccupied with sex. We use it to sell perfume and pantyhose, to boost TV ratings and our egos. Books about sex sell. Why? Because the public is hungry to unravel the puzzling mystery of sex and its significance in our lives.

And so we buy books about having phenomenal sex. And the books sit on the shelves by the bed, and the couples lie in bed wondering why they still aren't satisfied with their sex lives.

Like the man in the opening quote, we may tell ourselves that sex is just not important anymore. But recent statistics show that as many as 80 percent of married men and 50 percent of married women have extramarital affairs, or something close to it. That means there are a lot of people telling themselves it doesn't matter whether or not they have a fulfilling sex life with their partners who are going to a lot of trouble and risk in order to have wild sex with someone else.

▶ Why Sex Is So Important to Us

Why are we willing to get married and divorced over sex; pay for it; sacrifice our own values and even our better judgment for one night of it? Here are the key reasons:

- *Sex is physically satisfying.* We all have the need to be touched, held, and to release the sexual tensions that build up inside of us.
- *Having sex with someone we love creates more intimacy and closeness between us.* Having sex with a partner, especially when we are *making love* and not just having sex, makes us feel special, valued, and cared for.
- *A healthy sex life builds our self-esteem.* When we feel we are good lovers and are desired by another, our sense of self-worth increases.

The *real power* of the sexual experience, however, has a much more profound effect on our entire lives.

The Secret Power of Sex in Your Life

Whether you know it or not, the way you make love may be affecting how you talk to your boss at work, how you get a point across to your husband or wife in an argument, what action you take when others confront you, and how well you pursue success in life.

▼

SECRET:
The way we make love inside the bedroom directly affects how we feel about ourselves and others, and how we behave outside the bedroom.

▲

▶ Your Secret Sexual Classroom

Imagine that you are lying curled up in a very dark, warm place. Your eyes are closed, and you are naked. You do not speak, but make sounds that express your joy and contentment. You are being gently touched, stroked, and told that you are loved, and it feels wonderful.

Many people would say, "It sounds like I am being made love to." You're right, but it also describes a scene that you experienced over and over again in your childhood.

As an infant, you were constantly held naked, hugged against your mother's body, and nursed or cuddled in the darkness of the nursery or in your parents' bed. In fact . . .

The experience of making love is the closest experience to the circumstances of our infancy that we have in our adult life.

The first few years of your life virtually were your classroom. As an infant, you learned your major lessons about how loved and accepted you were, how to get approval from others, and how much to trust or fear other people. The whole field of psychology is centered around unraveling many of those childhood messages we received, and reprogramming ourselves to feel lovable and deserving.

The Power of Touch

One of the reasons you were so vulnerable to being "programmed" as an infant was the power of touch. If you want to make an impression on someone, just touch his arm below the elbow while making your point. Studies show your listener will be more apt to remember you and what you said than if you hadn't touched him. *We are more susceptible to being conditioned, either positively or negatively, when we are touched by another person.*

Research has indicated that early touch deprivation can cause irreversible personality disorders, as well as serious physical problems. One study compared a group of premature babies, given routine care, with another group who were stroked for five minutes an hour, ten days in a row. The babies who were touched gained weight faster, cried less, and, even eight months later, were healthier than the untouched group.

From birth, we all need touching to feel good about ourselves. Sex is one way we bring touching into our lives as adults.

Re-creating Your Childhood Classroom

When you make love with someone, you are re-creating the same conditions you experienced in infancy:

Warmth	Darkness	Nakedness
Physical touching	Vulnerability	Non-verbal communication

In this way, *sex creates the perfect atmosphere for being emotionally reprogrammed or reconditioned.*

Each time you have sex, you are opening yourself up to a whole new set of associations or "lessons" about yourself and love. You have entered the Sexual Classroom.

What You Learn in Your Sexual Classroom

We learn two kinds of lessons in the Sexual Classroom:

1. We draw conclusions about our relationships with others.
2. We draw conclusions about our relationships with ourselves.

Conclusions About Your Relationships With Others

I like to call sex a training camp for how to behave with people. Just making love with someone is, in itself, an act of trust: I offer you my naked body; I trust you will not hurt me; that you will be loving to me. When you make love with someone, you make yourself completely vulnerable to them. What happens during the sexual act becomes highly significant when we think of it in this way.

> *The Incident:* You make love with someone, and he or she isn't sensitive to your needs. Instead of asking for what you want, you lie there and feel unloved.
> *You Conclude:* No one ever gives me what I need. No one loves me or really understands me.

> *The Incident:* You make love with someone, giving him or her instructions about what to do and how to touch you, etc. Your partner becomes overwhelmed and doesn't do what you requested.
> *You Conclude:* People always let me down. No one does anything right.

In both of these instances, *you have used the power of the sexual experience to reinforce negative beliefs about your relationships with others.*

Conclusions About Yourself

Sex is one of the most powerful ways in which to establish your self-image.

> *The Incident:* You make love with someone, fearful of doing it wrong or being rejected. To be on the safe side, you end up giving practically no response to his/her lovemaking.
> *You Conclude:* I have to suppress how I feel or what I want in order to be accepted and loved.

> *The Incident:* You make love with someone, and do everything you can to please her, asking her over and over what she wants. She responds by wanting to see you again.
> *You Conclude:* I have to perform in order to get someone to love me.

Each time you have sex with someone, you strengthen the behavior that emerged during your sexual experience. If you were passive, you strengthen your passivity. If you were controlling, you strengthen your tendency to want to be in control. The secret power of the Sexual Classroom puts you into a very vulnerable, infantlike state of receptivity, so that the lessons and behaviors you learn there are played out in your life *outside* the bedroom as well as *in* it.

Don't Get Discouraged

As I was writing this chapter, I presented the information about the Sexual Classroom to some of my staff. I was amazed to see their faces tighten up with embarrassment—even fear—and to hear groans of despair. "What's wrong," I asked, "don't you like my theory?"

"Like it!" one answered, "Of course we like it. It's just that it's so true it's frightening. I am sitting here thinking about all my sexual complaints, and suddenly I realize how I have been using my Sexual Classroom to perpetuate my negative patterns."

If you share my friends' feelings of discouragement, don't despair. Use the next section, on sexual diagnosis, to understand your personal sexual patterns and, through understanding them, take the first step in changing the way you make love and make your life work outside the bedroom.

▶ Making Your Sexual Diagnosis and Cure

The first thing I want to tell you is that *there is no right way or wrong way to make love,* so please don't read this section expecting to make yourself or your partner feel bad. Sex is "right" when it supports you in feeling good about yourself and the relationship and leaves you with a sense of peace and happiness. It is "wrong" when it adds to your negative feelings about yourself or your partner and leaves you feeling unhappy and disturbed.

Here is a six-step program for creating your own sexual diagnosis:

Step One

Let's look at what you have been teaching yourself in your Sexual Classroom. On a sheet of paper, make a list of your general sexual complaints—the ones that seem to resurface over the months and years and pop up again in each new relationship.

Here are two sample lists from a husband and a wife who attended one of my seminars:

Lisa's List

My partner never knows what to do to satisfy me.

I feel as though I am not "doing it" right.

My partner finishes and I'm not satisfied yet.

I don't have as much sexual desire as I would like to.

I have a hard time communicating how I feel in bed.

I don't feel as close to my partner as I would like to feel.

Greg's List

We don't have sex as often as I want to.

My partner takes a long time to get turned on.

I get bored with the same partner after a while.

My partner always does the same thing; there is no variety.

My partner takes things so seriously. We don't have enough fun in bed.

Step Two

Read over your list, and write down any similarities you see between the way you feel and behave while making love and the way you feel and behave in your life outside the bedroom. Make these into a second list.

This is the hard part, because it means you have to be completely honest with yourself. You might want to ask a partner or friend to help you with this step.

Lisa's Second List

I always feel let down by people.

I have a hard time asserting myself at work.

I never feel that people really are pleased with me or my work.

I get angry at others for not being more sensitive to me and my feelings.

I am afraid to complain or give someone feedback because I don't want them to get angry at me or dislike me.

Greg's Second List
I get easily impatient with other people and myself.
I am easily bored with my work, friends, activities.
I have a hard time relating well to others and prefer to do things my way.
I work best on my own.
I have a short attention span.
I tend to use alcohol and drugs to feel high when I'm not having fun.

Step Three

Compare both of your lists and notice the similarities between them. Let's use Lisa's list as an example.

Lisa the Martyr
In comparing Lisa's lists, we can see that both in and out of bed, Lisa doesn't ask for what she wants and then ends up feeling unloved, unappreciated, and eventually resentful. She has a hard time communicating how she feels and then complains that in bed her partner doesn't know what to do to satisfy her. In life she also has a hard time asserting herself and then feels angry that others aren't more sensitive to her needs.

Lisa is using her Sexual Classroom to train herself to be what I call a Sexual Martyr. *She never asks for what she wants; then she resents not getting it*. Each time she has sex, she reinforces this behavior pattern, going back to her everyday world an even stronger martyr.

Is Lisa doomed to be unsatisfied forever? Certainly not! Once she changes her behavior in her Sexual Classroom, that behavior change will begin to affect her behavior outside the bedroom, until she is no longer a martyr in or out of bed.

Greg the Sexual Self-indulgent

Greg has a very different pattern from Lisa. Greg tends to be self-absorbed and not very open to how his partner is feeling in bed. He is looking for pleasure and fun, and he gets impatient and eventually bored, needing to look elsewhere. This behavior pattern carries over into his life outside the bedroom as well. He has a hard time focusing on what he is doing. When he isn't experiencing pleasure or fun, he often uses alcohol or drugs to feel better.

Greg is using his Sexual Classroom to train himself to be what I call a Sexual Self-indulgent. Greg knows only how to take, not how to give. Each time he has sex, he reinforces his tendency to live in his own self-indulgent pleasure world.

Greg needs to use his Sexual Classroom to retrain himself to give as well as receive, and find pleasure in sharing love and intimacy with Lisa.

Step Four

Now that you have compared both your lists, write down the lessons you are presently learning in your Sexual Classroom.

> Lisa's List—Lessons I Am Learning in My Sexual
> Classroom:
> To not ask for what I want
> To feel like a victim
> To feel sorry for myself
> To feel that I can't get what I want from others in
>   life
> To give up and be passive

Greg's List—In My Sexual Classroom I Am Learning:

That no one can satisfy me or keep me happy

That I'll never find anyone as fun-loving as me

That I can't get what I want

To be indulgent and think only of myself

To tune other people out

To take and not give

Once you become fully aware of how your sexual behavior does not support your personal happiness and success, you can use your Sexual Classroom to teach yourself positive lessons rather than unhelpful ones.

Step Five

Make a list of ways you could change your behavior in your Sexual Classroom that would train you to pursue your happiness and personal power.

Lisa's List

1. When I don't like what Greg is doing, I'll let him know, rather than lying there complaining to myself and feeling sorry for myself.
2. When I feel Greg isn't really there for me and is indulging, I will ask him to connect with me or remind him of my love for him. If he refuses to pay attention to me, I will stop making love rather than be a martyr.
3. If I feel Greg is rushing me, I will ask him to slow down so I have time to get fully turned on to him.
4. If after lovemaking, I feel tension or withdrawal, I will talk it over with Greg and see if we can clear up any distance between us.
5. I'll let Greg know all the things I really like about sex.

Greg's List

1. I will be alert to the times when I am overindulgent of my own pleasure and give some attention to Lisa at those times.
2. I will ask Lisa what turns her on and gives her pleasure, with the aim of learning to experience pleasure from giving her love.
3. I'll try expressing my feelings more to Lisa when we make love, and not just keep them inside and be in my own world.
4. When I feel she isn't participating or is being a Sexual Martyr by just lying there, I'll tell her so and ask her how she is feeling.
5. I will tell Lisa what I want and then "let go" and trust that I will get it without having to grab it all at once.

Step Six

When you are in your Sexual Classroom with your partner, begin practicing the goals you set in Step Five. Here are some tips to help you along:

- Share your lists with your partner.
- Agree to work together on practicing the goals on your lists when you are sexual together.
- Set aside time for regular discussions when you may give each other feedback on how you are making progress in your Sexual Classroom. (Be careful *not* to have these discussions right after sex when you're both feeling sensitive.)
- Make sure to express your appreciation and encouragement for your partner when you notice improvements.

How Lisa and Greg Revived Their Sex Life

Lisa and Greg had been married for six years and had been acting out their "parts" in their Sexual Classroom for that entire time. They wanted desperately to revive their sex life, but they were afraid they would fail and their marriage would then come to an end.

After sharing their lists, Lisa and Greg agreed to work together to monitor themselves for any tendency to fall into their "Sexual Characters."

The first major change both Lisa and Greg made was to express much more of how they were feeling *during* lovemaking, using the communication techniques for telling the Complete Truth from the first part of this book. Lisa began asking for what she wanted from Greg instead of hoping he'd figure it out himself. Greg worked on telling Lisa more of what he was feeling inside while they made love, rather than just thinking about how wonderful it was. At first, they were embarrassed to be so open and vulnerable. But they soon noticed that their feelings of intimacy and trust for each other deepened. The more Lisa asked for what she wanted, the more she received it, and the happier she felt. The more Greg expressed his love for Lisa along with feeling his own pleasure, the more turned on Lisa got, and the more pleasure Greg felt.

As Lisa's and Greg's behavior changed in their Sexual Classroom, it naturally began to transform their rapport outside the bedroom. Lisa became accustomed to asking for what she wanted and giving Greg feedback. Much to her surprise, she also found herself speaking out more at work and becoming more assertive. Greg was learning how to listen closely to Lisa and be concerned about her feelings, thus breaking out of his self-indulgent shell. He also noticed that he was feeling much more connected to everyone in his life. His friends at work commented that he seemed to be "warming up."

One month passed, and Lisa and Greg returned to see me. They were beaming. "We deserve straight A's in our Sexual Classroom!" Greg proclaimed proudly.

"Lisa says I'm not so caught up in myself anymore, and I can tell you that she has never been so expressive and passionate!"

You, too, can use your Sexual Classroom to teach you the lessons about loving that you need to learn. The first step is creating your own sexual diagnosis to determine what lessons you have been learning in your Sexual Classroom and what new lessons you need to learn. Then read through the next chapter and learn how you may be playing a Sexual Character that is limiting your chances for the wonderful, fulfilling love life you deserve to have.

13

Your Sexual Cast of Characters

In order to help you understand how you have been operating in your Sexual Classroom, I want to introduce you to ten Sexual Characters I have discovered through working with many different people in my practice. See if you can find a little bit of yourself in some of the characters, or maybe a lot of yourself in one (I know you will recognize former and present lovers!). *Warning: Do not try to typecast yourself.* Most people are a combination of several characters at one time or another. The real solution to having a wonderful sexual relationship is *not* figuring out which type you are, but in using that knowledge to tailor the six-step program I described in the preceding chapter to your unique needs.

SEXUAL CAST OF CHARACTERS

1. The Sexual Traffic Cop
2. The Sexual Martyr
3. The Sexual Self-indulgent
4. The Sexual Performer
5. The Sexual Corpse
6. The Sexual Animal
7. The Sexual Procrastinator
8. The Sexual Pleaser
9. The Sexual Idealist
10. The Sexual Tease

▶ The Sexual Traffic Cop

The Sexual Traffic Cop must be in control of love-making, or he will be angry and/or withdrawn. You may find it difficult to remember what the Sexual Traffic Cop likes and doesn't like—that's how many *instructions* you get!

This character is equally demanding outside the bedroom. He can be critical and controlling of others. *Inside, he secretly doesn't trust others to love him and meet his needs.* So he tells them exactly how to love him without waiting to see if they will give their love freely.

Larry told me a story about his night with Denise, who was a definite example of a Sexual Traffic Cop:

> Denise owned an art gallery near my office. One day, I stopped in and she came on to me very strongly. We went out for dinner and then back to her place. She seemed outspoken and intelligent, and I was excited about the possibility of having a relationship with her.
>
> I should have suspected something when she spent twenty minutes searching for the *perfect piece of music*. Then she spent five minutes adjusting the lights to the right dimness.
>
> I'm embarrassed to tell you that she talked me right through every step of our lovemaking. "Faster," she'd say, and I'd go faster. "No, that's too

fast," she'd insist, "a little slower . . . now draw your nails across my stomach . . . No, not like that . . . like this . . ."

The worst part, though, was when I made a "mistake." I thought maybe she'd like it if I kissed her neck. Boy, was I wrong! She shrieked, "No! No! Don't do that now, you idiot. You are ruining everything." Apparently I had broken her concentration. But I hadn't ruined everything . . . it was already ruined.

Sexual Traffic Cops need to learn to let go, to let their partners choose how they want to make love sometimes, to trust that their partners will care enough to discover what pleases them. *Sexual Traffic Cops need to let themselves be taken care of, which is, after all, what they secretly really want.*

How One Sexual Traffic Cop Turned in Her Badge

Jody and Peter needed help. "I love Jody," Peter began as the couple sat in my office. "But in bed she becomes tremendously bossy and picky. I can't do anything right."

Jody didn't trust men to give her what she needed, in or out of bed. Jody's father had left her and her mother when Jody was very young. Jody's mother taught her to "look out for herself" and not count on men for anything. So Jody became very controlling and authoritative, never waiting to see if her husband would give her what she wanted, and assuming that he, like all men, would let her down.

I helped Jody get in touch with the little girl inside her and asked her what that little girl wanted more than anything else in the world. "I want someone to take care of me," Jody answered, her eyes filled with tears. "I'm so tired of taking care of everything myself." What a relief it was for Jody to admit how much she needed to be nurtured! Suddenly Peter felt needed, instead of used. He embraced Jody, telling her how much he loved taking care of her and how he loved seeing the vulnerable side of her as well as the strong, self-sufficient side.

I suggested that Peter and Jody follow the six-step plan for sexual diagnosis described in the preceding chapter, and that Jody practice lying still and allowing Peter to seduce her. This was difficult for Jody, but almost immediately she began to notice that Peter was doing things she liked—some of which she never thought of asking him to do—and she was becoming very aroused. Even more important, Peter was loving her without being told to. This made Jody feel safe and loved as she never could when she demanded Peter's love.

Jody was learning to trust in bed *and* out of bed, thanks to the power of the Sexual Classroom.

PROFILE: THE SEXUAL TRAFFIC COP

Characteristics in bed

Tells her partner step by step what to do in bed
Is very critical
Doesn't pay much attention to pleasing her partner
If something goes wrong, she may just stop and
   refuse to continue

Characteristics in life

Very picky and impatient
Constantly gives advice or "mothers" people
Corrects others if they don't do things right
Not very good at taking orders or advice
Hard on herself

What she is really feeling during sex

Fears not getting what she wants
Mistrusts her partner's ability to satisfy her
Wants to be taken care of, even babied

How her partner feels

Controlled
Pressured to perform
Inadequate

Lessons she can learn in her Sexual Classroom

Trust that others will care for her and please her
Patience with herself and others
Acceptance of her own and others' imperfections
Flexibility when things aren't under control
Surrender to the other person and his way of loving

▶ The Sexual Martyr

The poor Sexual Martyr always seems to meet the wrong men and is always being taken advantage of. *She tends to meet the same kinds of partners over and over again, none of whom ever satisfies or loves her enough.* She dreams that one day, she'll meet a man who will know just what she wants and will be the perfect lover.

In her life outside the bedroom, the Sexual Martyr frequently plays the victim. She feels used and taken advantage of, never quite finding the courage to speak up for what she wants.

When you make love with a Sexual Martyr, you may sense that something is wrong, but don't count on your partner to fill you in. She'll never tell.

Here's how one Sexual Martyr described her sex life to me:

> I went out with a very attractive man from my sports club last night. We went back to his apartment and started making out on the couch. I thought that maybe this time a man would turn out to be great. In the bedroom, however, he became very insistent, unbuttoning my blouse and rubbing himself against me. *Ugh!* I hate it when men do that. I hoped he would slow down.

Then he started sucking on my breasts so hard that it was painful. I tried to let him know I didn't like it by moving away a little, but I guess he didn't get the message. He entered me, and I knew I wouldn't have an orgasm. I just wanted him to finish.

Finally it was over. We just lay there, and I felt so far away. I know he won't call me again. It doesn't matter anyway . . . he just wasn't very *sensitive*, you know?

When I asked this woman to tell me about a great sexual experience she had in her life, she couldn't think of any. Not one! Sexual Martyrs rarely have wonderful sexual experiences, because they do nothing to make sure they turn out to be wonderful. They go from partner to partner, feeling increasingly helpless and hopeless.

In her Sexual Classroom *the Sexual Martyr must practice owning her power and asking for what she wants.* She'll find that she usually can get it and that people really do care for her.

How Linda Stopped Playing the "Victim"

If you listened to Linda's list of sob stories about how terribly she'd been treated in and out of bed by all the men in her life, you would feel sorry for her until you realized that she chose these men in the first place. No one forced her to go to bed with them.

Linda's first step was to make a list of what she wanted in a man and what she liked and disliked sexually. This was very difficult for her, because she had been brought up to be "seen and not heard" and was taught that girls who like sex were "bad." Asking for what she wanted in bed would mean that she *did* like sex, and Linda had to accept that this was okay.

Linda's list was one and a half pages long! Once she got free of her Sexual Martyr role, she knew exactly what she wanted—she had just been afraid to ask for it. I told Linda that this list was her new rule book—that she should not go out with a man who didn't closely fit most of the qualities on her list, and that she should tell her partner at least three things she liked if they made love. I also reminded Linda to make sure to say no to the things she didn't like and not lie there like a victim.

Two months later, Linda called me. "I'm so proud of myself," she bubbled. "After we talked, I met two different men whom I liked. I went out with each one once, but they weren't even close to what I had on my list. I actually said no when they each asked me out the second time. Then three weeks ago, I met a wonderful man. I've told him what I need in a relationship, and he said he wanted the same things. Last night, we made love, and for the first time in my life, I asked him for what I wanted, and even asked him a few times to slow down when he was going too fast for me. It was wonderful."

Linda had used her Sexual Classroom to learn to own her power around others. She was transformed from a victim into a winner!

PROFILE: THE SEXUAL MARTYR

Characteristics in bed

Often doesn't enjoy what happens during sex, but just grins and bears it

Wants to get sex over with

Feels that nothing she can do could change what is happening

Complains that she rarely has good sexual experiences

Feels that her partner doesn't know how to satisfy her

Often has trouble having an orgasm

Characteristics in life

Doesn't ask for what she wants from others
Feels unappreciated
Blames others for her lack of success, happiness, etc.
Tells a lot of "poor me" stories
Acts meek and timid around the opposite sex
Is always asking advice from others and not taking it

What she is really feeling during sex

Angry at not getting what she wants
Afraid to express herself
Afraid of abandonment
Has low self-esteem: "I don't deserve it, anyway"

How her partner feels

Afraid he cannot satisfy her
Pressured to figure out what she is feeling ("psychic sex")
Resentful because he can't read her mind and because she somehow makes him feel guilty for not being able to do so

Lessons she can learn in her Sexual Classroom

To own her power and ask for what she wants
To say no to what she doesn't want
To trust herself and her feelings
To take responsibility for creating her own reality by communicating

▶ The Sexual Self-indulgent

Unlike the Sexual Traffic Cop, who often doesn't enjoy sex because he's too picky, the Sexual Self-indulgent is a professional at enjoying himself—once he gets you to do what gives him the most pleasure, he becomes self-absorbed, lost in sensation. The Sexual

Self-indulgent usually masturbates frequently when there is no one to have sex with. He may even do it when you are there to make sure he gets maximum pleasure.

In his life outside the bedroom, the Sexual Self-indulgent is equally oblivious of others. He may over-indulge in food, alcohol, or drugs because they feed his need always to feel good.

Here is how Ted, the lover of a Sexual Self-indulgent, describes his experience:

> Karen is like a machine in bed. She sets things up so they work to make her feel good, and then she just goes into herself and I can't feel her with me at all. If I start to change what I am doing, she will gesture for me to keep going. Sometimes I will do the same thing for fifteen, twenty minutes, and the whole time she'll be in her own pleasure world, biting her lip and moaning to herself. It's as though I'm not even there.
>
> If I climax and she hasn't, she even will take her vibrator out of her drawer and masturbate herself to orgasm.

The Sexual Self-indulgent is so afraid to need anyone else that he has learned to depend on himself for love and pleasure. Sexual Self-indulgents also usually have a low tolerance for pain, using pleasure to numb themselves to feelings of vulnerability and fear.

In his Sexual Classroom *the Sexual Self-Indulgent can learn to open up and feel his need for others, thus making others feel needed by him*. He needs to get turned on from his heart, not just from his genitals, and must learn to find joy in giving pleasure as well as in receiving it.

How Karen Learned to Be Less Self-centered

When Karen and Ted came to me for counseling, Karen was very defensive. "I think Ted is just hung up about sex," she snapped. "What's wrong with my enjoying myself?" When I asked Karen if she had always made love in this way, she became very quiet. "No," she answered, "with my first husband, I didn't really like sex. It was an unhappy marriage. He hurt me a lot, and it took me a while to recover from the divorce."

Karen's sexual-indulgent character grew out of that painful relationship. Lost in her own world of pleasure, she didn't have to face her need for Ted or her fear of being hurt by him. She carried this behavior outside the bedroom by drinking too much, using too many drugs, and overeating—she indulged in everything in order not to feel.

The first step in Karen's healing was for her to share her sadness and hurt from her first marriage with Ted. Karen talked and cried, and Ted held her, amazed and moved to see a whole new side of the woman he loved.

I then told Karen and Ted to practice lying in bed for twenty minutes without having sex, just talking about feelings, dreams, and their past. Karen also agreed not to make love when she had been drinking or using drugs. She also planned to set aside times when Ted wasn't allowed to touch her at all, but when *she* could make love to *him*.

Karen and Ted had wonderful results in their Sexual Classroom. By talking more, being sober when they made love, and being aware of Karen's tendency to become self-indulgent, they created a new level of intimacy which tremendously enhanced their lovemaking. Karen found that she could get turned on by turning Ted on—something she had never taken time to do. She also noticed that she was more sensitive to other people and their feelings at work, and that she no longer felt alone and cut off from the world.

PROFILE: THE SEXUAL SELF-INDULGENT

Characteristics in bed

Absorbed in her own pleasure

Pays little or no attention to her partner's feelings

Uses fantasy if necessary to sustain her own pleasure

Very goal-oriented about what she wants

Doesn't get turned on by her partner's excitement

Doesn't talk much in bed, but if she does, it is to turn herself on

May need stimulants (drugs, alcohol) to make love

Characteristics in life

Self-centered

Not a good listener; may interrupt a lot

Can be pushy

Uses other people to get ahead

Appears cold or insensitive

May have addictive habits (food, drugs, alcohol)

Lacks self-discipline

What she is really feeling during sex

Fear of intimacy

Fear of being alone and unloved

Fear of not getting enough; was deprived in past

Afraid to need another person

How her partner feels

Unimportant

Unloved

Left out

Angry at being used

Lessons she can learn in her Sexual Classroom

To give to others

To find joy in other people's joy

To increase her sensitivity to her own and to
    others' feelings and not just pleasure her body
To let love in again

▶ The Sexual Performer

The Sexual Performer makes sure you know that
she is the most passionate person you have ever met.
This person is hot, you tell yourself. Yet there is something not quite right about her passion, and often you
are left with a strange feeling that you have just been
taken for a ride. You are probably right.

*The Sexual Performer feels the need to appear
passionate and sexy to cover up her feelings of inadequacy as a lover and her fear of abandonment*. She is
paying you what she believes is the ultimate compliment: "See what you do to me?," hoping you will stick
around to keep satisfying your ego.

Out of bed the Sexual Performer needs constant
attention and approval, is wildly enthusiastic about
whatever she does, and does not enjoy being upstaged.

Harriet described her boyfriend Fred—a classic
Sexual Performer—to me:

> Fred is a warm and loving man whom I've been
> seeing for four months. The first time we went away
> for a weekend, it was very romantic. Fred made a
> big production of slowly undressing me, kissing me
> all over. "Wow," I thought to myself, "this is the
> kind of man I've always wanted." As we got closer
> to having intercourse, Fred began groaning and
> chanting, "Baby, I want you," over and over again. I
> thought he was overdoing it a little, but tried to
> overlook it. Then he entered me, and the sound that
> came out of his mouth was like that of someone
> who was on a huge roller coaster on its way down a
> steep drop. What we were doing was nice, but it
> didn't feel *that* good . . . I thought maybe I was
> missing out; maybe I was undersexed. I became

very depressed. Fred just kept going. When he finally came, it sounded like World War III had broken out. I began to hear pounding. "Oh, no," I thought, "he's ruptured my eardrums." Then I realized that the pounding came from the guests in the hotel rooms on either side of us, who could hear every ecstatic scream Fred made. Of course, Fred didn't hear a thing.

Each time it's the same. I really love him, but I feel so confused about our sex life. Part of me isn't sure if he is faking it or not. Part of me thinks there is something wrong with me for not being like him.

As long as Fred kept putting on a show, he would never be sure if his partner loved *him*, or only his performance.

Bringing Fred Down to Earth

When I met Fred, I could see why Harriet felt so torn—he was very charming and warm. As we talked, I noticed how hard he tried to get me to like him.

Fred was a performer, both in and out of bed. He came from a family of six, and had learned that in order to get attention he had to stand out. His lovemaking style evolved from a combination of his need for love and a fear of being sexually inadequate. Harriet and Fred's first "lesson" was to lie in bed together while Harriet told Fred all the reasons she liked him that had nothing to do with his charm or sexual passion. Next, the couple decided that for a while, Fred would be as quiet as possible during sex, in an attempt to feel Harriet's love rather than block it with his own sensations.

One week later, Harriet telephoned me to thank me. "Fred is doing wonderfully, and so am I," she reported. "Just telling him what I love about him seems to relax him enough during sex so that he is really there *with* me. And I find that as he becomes a little quieter, I am becoming more expressive! It's as though we are balancing out. Outside the bedroom I notice he is telling fewer jokes and turning on the charm less often, but expressing real warmth from the heart. I like him so much more this way!"

Fred used his Sexual Classroom to learn that he could trust Harriet to love him even when he wasn't "on," and that in the quiet moments of lovemaking, the greatest love can be felt.

PROFILE: THE SEXUAL PERFORMER

Characteristics in bed

Very dramatic in his expression of passion
May make a lot of noise and movement
Will tell you over and over how fabulous it is
May fake or exaggerate his pleasure

Characteristics in life

Is easily excited and talks a lot
Has a hard time sharing the stage with others or
    learning from others
Needs a lot of approval

What he is really feeling during sex

Fear of being sexually inadequate
Insecure
Fear of abandonment
Desperate need for love and attention

How his partner feels

Left out
Used
Confused and mistrustful
Eventually resentful

Lessons he can learn in his Sexual Classroom

Doesn't have to perform to be loved
Trust that others can see his inner self

Relax and be himself

Give love and approval to others

▶ The Sexual Corpse

The Sexual Corpse's favorite game is "psychic sex": "See if you can guess how I am feeling, or if I like this. See if you can figure out what I want—or if I even like you." They lie there and do nothing and you are the aggressor.

Some Sexual Corpses are unresponsive during sex because they are frozen with fear of displeasing their partners or of being abandoned. Other Sexual Corpses are so angry at males or females in general for hurting them, letting them down, and not loving them enough from childhood on that they play dead as a way to get even and to humiliate.

Sexual Corpses may use food, alcohol, or drugs to further numb themselves. They are experts at repressing their emotions; they appear "cool," and they don't forgive or forget easily.

Harold and Maureen were on the verge of ending their relationship when they came to me. Here is Harold's description of Maureen:

> Maureen seemed so sweet when I met her. I knew she was very quiet and deep, but I had no idea how serious it was.
>
> From the beginning, I always had to initiate sex. At first I thought that was kind of nice and old-fashioned. But I was wrong to think it was just her shyness. She isn't shy—she is *dead*. I approach her and say, "Do you want to make love?" "I don't care," she'll answer. I keep thinking I will break through to her, to get her to feel again. So we start making love, and I'll be stimulating her. "Do you like this?" I'll ask. "It's fine," she says, lying there completely limp. If I move her, she will stay in that position. She never makes a sound. It makes me feel

like some sort of sex maniac. I hear the sounds of
my own moans and Maureen's silence, and I feel
embarrassed. Not once in four years has she initi-
ated sex.

After making love, we often fight. I am angry at
her for being so dead, and I think she is pretty angry
at men, and so we pick a fight about something, and
end up not speaking. I can't go on like this anymore.

Maureen's passivity left Harold feeling frustrated,
inadequate, and angry at her for not being as fully
involved in the relationship as he was. The Sexual
Corpse is a more extreme version of the Sexual Martyr—the former has given up completely and is usually
a very angry person.

Bringing Maureen Back From the Dead

I began working with Maureen to discover what
she was angry about, and why she was so frightened of
living. Within a few weeks, Maureen confessed that as
a young girl she had been sexually abused by a relative.
Unable to express her anger at the time, she had shut
down sexually and emotionally. She appeared very
gentle and loving, but she was full of rage and mistrust
for men. Her deadness in bed was a "safe" way for her
to get even with men.

Maureen's first step was to transform her relationship with Harold from one of enemy to that of
friend. She had to share all her feelings, memories, and
fears with him, and feel his warmth and empathy. This
was an act of trust for Maureen and an important part
in reviving her Sexual Corpse.

Maureen took the risk and told Harold why she
had become so numb and how angry she was. Harold
was relieved—now he understood the cause of
Maureen's deadness and didn't have to worry that it
was his fault. Harold gave Maureen permission to get
as angry as she wanted at men, and even at him for
little things he did that bothered her. The angier

Maureen allowed herself to get, the more alive she became. Slowly, her heart began to wake up, and she found herself wanting to be held, then touched, and even wanting to make love for the first time in her life.

In her life outside the bedroom Maureen's personality underwent a wonderful change: She became warmer, less guarded and nervous, and more enthusiastic about living.

PROFILE: THE SEXUAL CORPSE

Characteristics in bed

Gives little or no physical or verbal response to her partner
Usually experiences no orgasm
When asked what she wants, answers "I don't know" or "I don't care"
Almost never initiates sex

Characteristics in life

Nervous
Afraid of others
Represses her emotions
Appears cold and may be cynical
May use drugs or alcohol to escape
Holds bitter and longtime grievances

What she is really feeling during sex

Afraid of making a mistake or displeasing partner
Angry at not getting the love she needs
Hopeless
Self-protective

What her partner feels

Inadequate for not satisfying her
Frustrated
Selfish
Angry

What she can learn in her Sexual Classroom
To take a risk and communicate what's inside
Build confidence that she can get what she wants
Forgive others and give them a chance again

▶ The Sexual Animal

When you make love with the Sexual Animal, you
aren't sure whether you are being loved or devoured.
More aggressive and sometimes more violent than the
Sexual Performer, *the Sexual Animal is not performing
to get attention, but is using sex to express his aggression and his need to dominate*. His panting, grabbing,
pushing, pulling, and primal verbal references (known
as "dirty talk") reduce the sex act to its most basic
level.

Inside the Sexual Animal is actually a very frightened person who perhaps was abused physically as a
child. His anger at not being loved and his fear of being
controlled take the form of intense and very physical
sex play. In his life outside the bedroom the Sexual
Animal is very aggressive and often has an explosive
temper. On the other hand, some types can be quiet
and brooding, using sex as an outlet for their pent-up
hostility. The Sexual Animal isn't necessarily hurtful to
his partner. It's just that his is an angry passion, not a
loving passion.

When you make love with a Sexual Animal, you
may feel a combination of fear, awe, excitement, and
anger. Sometimes it's hard to believe that what is going
on is real. But don't ever make fun of a Sexual Animal.
They don't think their act is funny at all.

Sheela confided her story of being with a Sexual
Animal to me:

> Alan was very seductive when I first met him at
> the party. We ended up at his penthouse suite—I
> knew he was a successful attorney—all set for a

fabulous night. I walked into his living room and was admiring a painting when I felt something literally pounce on me from behind with a growl. I screamed, thinking it must be Alan's dog or cat. It was Alan. He was making very strange noises and grunts as he told me what he was going to do to me in bed.

Alan stalked me into the bedroom and started ripping off my clothes, playfully but roughly. I couldn't tell if he was serious or not. Then he started to talk dirty to me—I mean really dirty—insisting that I talk dirty back. When he kissed me I felt as if he were gobbling me up. He would make wet sounds with his mouth as if he hadn't eaten for weeks.

Finally, he entered me, and started to move and pant so heavily that the sweat poured off his body. I almost felt like laughing. If he could have seen himself, he would have been embarrassed—this straight attorney acting like Attila the Hun. I left as soon as it was over, and that was it. The next time someone tells me his lawyer is a real tiger in the courtroom, I'll believe it.

This character can use the Sexual Classroom to allow himself to feel his vulnerability again and his need to be loved. He needs to learn to trust others not to hurt him.

Taming the Sexual Animal in Scott

Scott was a handsome, athletic young man who came to me for counseling because, as he put it, "The ladies just can't handle my intense energy." After talking with Scott for a while, it was clear that he was a classic case of the Sexual Animal: In bed he was rough, loud and liked to talk dirty; out of bed he was aggressive, domineering, and cynical.

The painful truth was that Scott "leaked" a lot of anger and resentment toward women during sex. Although he wasn't violent, women just didn't feel ·safe with him. They sensed his anger and contempt.

As we explored Scott's past, we found that he had good reason to feel so much anger toward women: His mother had been widowed at a young age, and in order to control her three sons, she had resorted to verbal abuse, physical force, and constant criticism. Scott desperately needed a woman's love, which was why he dated one woman after another. Once in a woman's presence, however, all that old anger at his mother emerged, and he transformed his anger into angry passion.

Using the techniques in this book, Scott discovered the hurt and sadness he had buried beneath his resentment. For the first time since he was a child, Scott cried, finally feeling the loss he had experienced growing up without much love or affection.

At about this time, Scott met a woman through a mutual friend and began dating her. "I feel very attracted to her," he admitted, "but I'm afraid that once I get in bed, Mr. Sexual Animal will come out again, and that will be it." I suggested that *before* they had sex, Scott share some of his recent realizations with his new friend, showing her the more vulnerable part of him.

Scott did share his feelings with his new girlfriend and found, to his surprise, that when they got into bed, he felt passionate, but less forceful than ever before. The more he showed his vulnerability to his girlfriend and received love in return, the less his Sexual Animal needed to come out. He was successfully using his Sexual Classroom to trust women with his heart again.

PROFILE: THE SEXUAL ANIMAL

Characteristics in bed

May talk dirty and very loudly
Is animalistic and likes rough play
The sex act is very intensely performed
Transforms anger into passion
Needs to dominate partner

Characteristics in life

Is very aggressive or very brooding
May be vindictive and unforgiving
Has to be in charge of things
Is explosive and cynical in temperament
May appear to be very controlled

What he is really feeling during sex

Anger or hatred toward the other sex
Fear of not being loved
Pain of deep childhood scars
Resentful for not being loved
Afraid of being controlled or made to feel vulnerable

How his partner feels

Frightened
Unsatisfied
Mistrustful of what is going on
Angry, but not sure why

Lessons he can learn in his Sexual Classroom

To learn to be vulnerable again
To experience the sadness underneath his anger
To trust others not to hurt him

▶ The Sexual Procrastinator

If you love sex, don't get into a relationship with a Sexual Procrastinator—he will avoid sex and sexual contact, and always give you logical reasons why he just isn't in the mood or doesn't have the time. The Sexual Procrastinator makes so much sense in his excuses that you don't really notice he is procrastinating until you look at a calendar and realize it's been weeks since you made love. Sexual Procrastinators hate to be told they don't like sex, or that there is something wrong with them, because that is just the revelation they are avoiding by avoiding sex itself. *They avoid dealing with reality, both in and out of bed.*

Inside, the Sexual Procrastinator is usually a very sensitive, warm person with a great fear of intimacy because of the hurt he is sure it will bring him.

Beth describes her husband, who is a Sexual Procrastinator:

> Albert was the sexiest man I had ever met. The first time he kissed me, I felt I'd never been so turned on. As the months passed, however, I found myself hanging on to Albert and even propositioning him sexually. This was new to me: I had always had men wanting more sex than I did. I'd see Albert at the end of the day and tell him that I couldn't wait to get into bed. He would tell me he felt the same way. Yet after dinner Albert would tell me he was still a little full and would come to bed soon. Sometimes so much time would pass that I would fall asleep. The next morning, I would ask Albert what happened. He would say, "I did some paperwork, prepared my appointments for tomorrow and I guess the time just flew." What could I say?
>
> On other days when I suggested we go upstairs and make love, he'd reply, "I'd love to, but I'm going running in a few hours and I don't want to strain myself beforehand." That made sense to me somehow, until I realized that Albert runs every day, that he can't make love too much before his run, and that he has no energy afterward.
>
> He has dozens of excuses: "I don't like getting turned on before a big business meeting. . . . I don't

like to rush it, when we only have a half hour . . . I have a lot on my mind today; maybe later . . ." I feel like I'm going crazy. All I think about is having sex with Albert.

When I confront Albert with the sorry state of our sex life, he calls me demanding and claims that if I just stopped pressuring him, he would be more aggressive. So I try that, but nothing changes. He insists that our not having sex has nothing to do with sex or with me, but with our schedule.

How Albert Learned to Trust Love Again

Like most Sexual Procrastinators, Albert wasn't conscious of how hard he worked to avoid having sex. When we first met and talked, he insisted that he liked sex, that he loved Beth, and that he really had no intention of procrastinating about making love.

Albert's first sexual experience had been with an older woman who knew his family. Albert was very young and impressionable, and he was devastated when the woman suddenly ended their meetings, frightened that his parents would find out. In this first Sexual Classroom Albert learned to love sex but to fear the pain and rejection it would eventually bring.

Albert lived out this "lesson" when he grew up: The closer he got to a woman, the less interested he became in sex. Frightened by the growing intimacy between himself and Beth, Albert avoided sex, hoping to avoid the pain his unconscious was sure it would bring him.

Making love is a perfect way for a Sexual Procrastinator to learn to trust love again. The first step was for Albert to tell Beth about his childhood experience and his fear of being embarrassed or rejected. Next, Albert agreed to schedule sex into his calendar just as he did other activities. I explained that although this sounded cold and clinical, he was going to have to force himself past his fear and plan time to be close with his wife physically, whether they ended up having sex or not.

Albert and Beth began to practice being intimate—talking, cuddling, and caressing. Each time they did this, Beth reassured Albert about how much she loved and needed him. As Albert took small risks opening up to Beth and received love and approval in return, his wounds slowly healed. He became more seductive, more aggressive, and more relaxed. In his life outside the bedroom Albert noticed he was also procrastinating less about facing business problems and challenges and was taking more risks. His Sexual Classroom was teaching him to live in the present, not be paralyzed by his past. He felt happier than he had in years (and so did Beth!).

PROFILE: THE SEXUAL PROCRASTINATOR

Characteristics in bed

Makes excuses for not having sex
Even during sex, lets little problems or interruptions turn him off and force him to stop
Claims partner is too pushy and demanding for sex
Withholds truth about how he is feeling
Doesn't show a lot of outward passion for partner

Characteristics in life

Avoids feelings and issues he needs to deal with
Procrastinates on doing things he needs to do
Hates being told what to do
Is very rational and reasonable
Talks a lot
Has a hard time facing himself
Takes himself very seriously

What he is really feeling during sex

Fear of intimacy
Feelings of inadequacy and imperfection
Fear of being judged and punished
Unloved and alone

How his partner feels

Neglected
Insecure
Controlled
Desperate
Angry

Lessons he can learn in his Sexual Classroom

To live in the present, not the painful past or the
    feared future
That he docsn't have to be perfect to be loved
To trust love again
To be more flexible
To let joy and fun into his life

▶ The Sexual Pleaser

The Sexual Pleaser is like a sexual Sherlock
Holmes—she will investigate to find out exactly what
pleases you and will check with you every minute or so
to make sure you still like what she is doing, asking,
"Do you like this? Am I going too fast? Is there something else you would like me to do?" *The Sexual
Pleaser doesn't really care about her own pleasure,* just
yours.

The Sexual Pleaser is usually a very insecure person who needs a tremendous amount of love and is
afraid she is inadequate as a lover and a mate. She
compensates for it by becoming Superlover. She will
have a hard time saying no to any request in or out of
bed. In her life outside the bedroom the Sexual Pleaser
is cheerful and nice to everyone; enthusiastic, but

without any real personality of her own. *She is desperate to please, because she feels she must earn people's love.*

Making love to a Sexual Pleaser can feel wonderful—at first. Often feelings of obligation, guilt, and performance pressure set in as you feel the desperation and loneliness underneath her apparent love, and cannot return her feelings in the same intense way.

Robert told me about Linda, a Sexual Pleaser whom he dated:

> Linda was like a dream girl. She adored me and never questioned anything I said. She just loved giving me pleasure, and at first I didn't mind taking it. Then I noticed that she didn't seem to respond when I gave pleasure to her, although she acted as though she did, to please me. She preferred giving me pleasure, which made me feel selfish and guilty. She'd ask me over and over again, "Do you like this, Robert? Tell me what to do. Should I stop or continue?" Sometimes I just wanted to lie there and not say anything, but Linda would panic if I was quiet and start to apologize for turning me off.
>
> The truth is, she never really showed me who she was, just who I wanted to see. I felt pretty bad when I realized how much I had been using her. Breaking up with her was hard—she still calls me and tries to lure me into bed with her. I don't think she likes herself very much.

Sexual Pleasers need to learn they can make mistakes and their partner will still love them—and that they don't have to wait on people to keep them in their lives.

How Linda Learned to Say No

Linda tried pitifully hard to get me to like her during our first appointment by agreeing enthusiastically with everything I said. I knew she hadn't really heard a word—she was too busy making sure I approved of her.

Like most Sexual Pleasers, Linda had grown up in a family where nothing was good enough. She was loved, but not approved of. So she grew up with one purpose—to be liked. She worked hard to be popular, uncontroversial, and nice to everyone. With men, she worked even harder, especially in bed.

Eventually, Linda confessed to me that she felt emotionally drained from trying so hard all the time. She agreed to use her Sexual Classroom to learn that she didn't have to cater to a man in bed in order for him to like her.

Linda's first assignment was to make a list of what she liked and didn't like when she made love. She agreed to say no when a man was doing something she didn't feel comfortable with, and to ask for what she wanted as well.

Linda used her Sexual Classroom to practice being herself. The more she relaxed and responded from her heart and not her head, the easier it was for Robert to like her and not just her lovemaking skills. For the first time in her life, she began to feel that she deserved to be loved just the way she was.

Outside the bedroom, too, Linda was behaving in a more genuine way with everyone. With the help of her Sexual Classroom, she was transformed from a two-dimensional girl into a real woman.

PROFILE: THE SEXUAL PLEASER

Characteristics in bed

Asks over and over, "Do you like this; am I pleasing you?"

Is very hurt if her partner doesn't love what is happening

Will go to any lengths to please

May have difficulty feeling own pleasure
Needs tremendous reassurance

Characteristics in life

A people pleaser
Popular with others
Can't say no to people
Doesn't assert herself
Fears being alone

What she is really feeling during sex

Fear of being sexually inadequate
Desperate to be loved
Fearful of disapproval and abandonment

How her partner feels

Pressured to perform
Obligated to her
Controlled
Guilty

Lessons she can learn in her Sexual Classroom

She doesn't have to please in order to be loved
She can say no when something isn't what she
    wants
She can relax and trust that love will be there
She deserves to be loved just the way she is

▶ The Sexual Idealist

When you make love with a Sexual Idealist, be
prepared to enjoy your lovemaking not once, but twice:
first during lovemaking when you will hear how fantastic it is, and again after your lovemaking, when you
will hear a recounting of your sexual union for days
after it is over. She will tell you you were spellbinding
and that she has never experienced anything like it,

and she believes it. To a Sexual Idealist, each experience must be better than the last one.

The Sexual Idealist *wants desperately to believe in life's goodness and fairness,* only because she probably has experienced so much of the opposite. She may delude herself that her work and relationships are perfect, fearing that to be unsure of this is to fail and that if she looks at her life honestly, her positive outlook might collapse. Deep inside, the Sexual Idealist is frightened that she will end up unloved, alone, and bitter.

Eric told me about his lover, Jeannie, who was a Sexual Idealist.

> Jeannie is one of the most powerful women I have ever met: sensitive, intelligent, and loving. When we make love, Jeannie seems to bask in the feeling of closeness between us.
>
> Often, she weeps after she climaxes. When I ask her why, she explains that she is having a spiritual experience. I feel a little left out at these times. Jeannie says that she wishes I would allow myself to have the same significant experiences she does. That makes me feel put down, as if she were the teacher and I her student.
>
> Somehow my lovemaking just doesn't seem enough for Jeannie. The more inadequate I feel, the less open I become. That just doesn't fit into Jeannie's perfect picture at all. I just want her to accept me for what I am, and accept us for what we are—not try to make us fit her ideal.

The Sexual Idealist needs to accept imperfection in herself and others and to trust more in love and stop trying so hard to make things perfect by force of will. (She can also try writing books about love and sex, teaching others, as well as herself, that they don't have to be perfect . . . !)

How a Sexual Idealist Became a Sexual Realist

When Jeannie came to me for counseling, she quickly admitted that she knew she was a Sexual Idealist. "It is so hard for me to accept things when they don't turn out the way I want them to," she confessed. "I always have an ideal of how I think things should be, even in bed, and when things are less than perfect, I feel like I've failed."

Jeannie was a very creative and sensitive person whose parents were divorced when she was young. Suddenly Jeannie's picture-perfect life turned into one of her parents battling, her father dating other women, and a stepfather moving in. Jeannie seemed to adapt to the new situation, and went on to become very successful. Deep inside, however, a part of her felt cheated. To compensate, she made an unconscious decision that she wouldn't make the "mistakes" her parents had made: *Her* life would be *perfect*. Jeannie put tremendous pressure on herself and her partner to live up to her "perfect" image of how a relationship should be.

I worked with Jeannie on forgiving her parents for not being perfect and on realizing she could love herself even with her own imperfections. I encouraged her to share the imperfect parts of herself with Eric and to give him a chance to love her just for being herself.

Jeannie began to use her Sexual Classroom to make love without the pressure to perform perfectly. The more she allowed herself to be human, the more loved she felt by her partner. And the real love she began to experience for Eric was much more powerful than the idealized love she had always tried to feel.

PROFILE: THE SEXUAL IDEALIST

Characteristics in bed

Sees every sexual experience as being fantastic
Is very complimentary to her partner
Talks a lot about it afterward
Narrates to her partner what she is feeling
Compares her partner with past lovers

Characteristics in life

Sees the world through rose-colored glasses
Denies her negative feelings
Is thought of as being inspiring to others
May delude herself for fear of her life collapsing if
  she admits imperfection
Fears failing and ending up alone

What she is really feeling during sex

Afraid to make a mistake or be rejected
Afraid of being inadequate
Afraid of admitting she is with the wrong person

How her partner feels

Pressured to perform and have similar high experi-
  ence
Inadequate
Not loved for himself
Mistrustful of her emotional claims

Lessons she can learn in her Sexual Classroom

To accept things as they are and let them be
  enough
To trust herself and her destiny in life
To learn to be flexible
She doesn't have to be perfect to be loved

▶ The Sexual Tease

The Sexual Tease is the kind of woman who glances at your husband in a restaurant and makes him wish for a minute that he were single . . . he is the kind of man who gives your girlfriend a look that makes her want to be wild and untamed for a night—with him. The Sexual Tease loves to advertise how sexy she is.

The surprise comes when you actually get into bed, or just before. Either the Sexual Tease will find an excuse not to make love, or she will make love perfunctorily, just to get it over with. Gone is the sexy temptress or powerful stud image. As one of my clients put it, "The Sexual Tease is like a company that hasn't found its product yet, but is doing its marketing anyway!"

The Sexual Tease is turned on by the idea of being wild and sexy, but not by the actual act. She may pride herself on sleeping with powerful, wealthy, or famous people, dropping their names to friends. In her life outside the bedroom she places emphasis on the same kind of material superficiality—clothes, status, and appearance—never really developing herself on the inside. She appears to be very competitive and to have a mysterious side to her, which is part of her intrigue.

The Sexual Tease doesn't really like sex, and that is part of her secret. She was probably very controlled by others when she was young, and fears being hurt again, so she stays in charge. She likes to get people turned on, not as a way to give them pleasure, like the Sexual Pleaser, but as a way to humiliate or control them. Getting involved with the Sexual Tease leaves a person feeling manipulated, embarrassed, used, angry, and often sexually frustrated.

Timothy told me about his encounter with a real Sexual Tease:

I met Allison at a disco. She came on like a bulldozer. Her eyes roved all over my body. As we talked, she controlled the pace of the conversation. Every move I made, she would double. For instance, I'd say, "I have an apartment in the Marina." She would respond, "Is it comfortable?" I'd say, "Yes, I love it; it's right on the water." She'd answer, "Sounds great for nude sunbathing." Wow! My temperature was rising quickly.

We drove back to my place, and she was driving me crazy in the car, crossing her legs so I could see up her dress, stroking her arms—the whole bit. We got to my apartment and began undressing, when all of a sudden she cried, "Wait, wait! I didn't realize you were so close to the ocean. Let's go for a swim." "Now?" I asked. We were practically in bed. "Oh, yes, come on, let's be impulsive!"

I didn't catch on to what was happening until after the swim, when she was suddenly seized with the desire for a pizza. "Won't it be fun," she said, "to eat pizza and watch TV?" After two or three such diversions, I finally fell asleep. We had several dates like this, where on the phone and before we got home she would be this incredibly sexy tease, and then would suddenly freeze up and avoid sex.

Finally, one night, I got her into bed. What a disappointment! As hot as she seemed to be, that's how cold and boring she was to make love to. Gone was the love goddess. I was really depressed, and a little angry, too. I really wanted to believe she was for real.

How Maria Transformed From a Tease Into an Intelligent Woman

I've counseled many women like Allison, who have made a habit of coming on to men very strongly, yet secretly dread sex. Maria was an up-and-coming model who had been living her life as a classic Sexual Tease. At twenty-eight she was tired of playing the same sexual game but didn't know how to stop.

I asked Maria if she had always been a "flirt." "No," she replied. "When I was younger, I was chubby with frizzy red hair and braces. The boys never paid attention to me. I was pretty lonely," she told me with tears in her eyes.

"What happened?" I asked.

"Puberty," she answered with a wistful smile. "I lost the baby fat, developed large breasts, got my braces off, and had my hair styled."

Maria went on to explain that from the day she was thirteen, boys, and even men, began to pay constant attention to her, vying for her favors. On the inside, Maria was still the shy, insecure little girl she'd always been. But she craved the attention she was receiving. She used her looks to get that attention, which she so desperately needed to make her feel good about herself. Even Maria's father, who had always been quite distant, became more affectionate and complimentary when Maria "blossomed," telling her his little girl had grown into a "real beauty." The message was clear: "Men will love me if I'm sexy."

Maria never trusted the approval she got—she knew the men only liked her for her looks, and not for who she was on the inside. She was using her Sexual Classroom to reinforce her negative feelings about herself as well as her anger at men for not loving the "real" Maria.

I helped Maria to see that she needed to let go of her need to control the other sex, and to become vulnerable again. She needed to realize that she deserved to be loved for the sensitive woman she was on the inside, and not just what was on the outside. The first step was to drop the Sexual Tease act and begin to share the real Maria with the men she met.

I gave Maria the homework assignment of wearing very little makeup and more conservative clothes for a month, especially on dates, and encouraged her to talk about her real feelings with the people she met. Within just a few weeks, Maria felt like a different person. "It's amazing," she told me. "I am attracting totally different men. Last week I met a man who is a high school principal, of all things! We've gone out twice already, and all we have done is talk—not even a good-night kiss! He actually told me he thought I was intelligent and articulate!" Maria was on her way to healing the wounded, mistrustful child inside her and becoming a real woman, not just a caricature of one.

PROFILE: THE SEXUAL TEASE

Characteristics in bed

Comes on very aggressively
Tries to act or look like her partner's dream image
May go after conquests who are powerful, rich, or famous
Once sex begins, may get numb and want to get it over with

Characteristics in life

Emphasizes superficiality—clothes, status, etc.
Feels very competitive with members of her same sex
Gets jealous easily
Doesn't accept compliments well
Has a rather mysterious persona and cultivates this aura

What she is feeling during sex

Dislike of sex
Resentful of being controlled by others when young
Insecure
Fearful of getting hurt

How her partner feels

Used
Manipulated
Insignificant
Disappointed and angry

What she can learn in her Sexual Classroom

To let go of control
To trust again
To connect with the deeper meanings of life
To heal the wounded, mistrustful child inside her

▶ Becoming an "A" Student in Your Sexual Classroom

Now that you have an understanding of what kinds of Sexual Characters you may be acting out and what kinds of behavior and feelings you are reinforcing in your Sexual Classroom, you are ready to begin using the power of the sexual experience to become the person you would like to be. This is the exciting part— to put into action the lessons you learned from reading this book. And you can do it!

I have worked with thousands of clients and people attending my seminars who have successfully used their Sexual Classroom to retrain themselves in how to feel and behave in powerful and fulfilling ways. Use the six-step plan I described in the previous chapter, and you will be well on your way to becoming an "A" student in your Sexual Classroom.

14

The Hidden Power of Your Sexual Energy

▶ The Life Force Within You

You have your own magic energy. It is invisible, yet it is as powerful as all the other invisible energies that govern our planet. This energy lies dormant in your body, holding all the power, vitality, and joy you dream of experiencing. This chapter will introduce you to your hidden energy, explain why sex is one of the most effective ways of tapping into that vital energy, or life force, and teach you ways you can use your sexual energy to unlock the potential you have waiting inside you to be discovered and enjoyed.

Sexual activity is one of the times when the life force within us is most apparent. For some people, it is the *only* time they experience the life force inside them. They may actually become addicted to sex; they are so dull and numb most of the time that they rely on the sexual experience to give them some sense of being alive.

Life energy is *not* sexual in nature. It is just energy. But when it moves through our sexual organs, we experience its power in our sexual center and it *feels* like sexual energy. When that same energy is experienced in our emotional center, we experience it as love. When that same energy is experienced in our rational or thinking center, we experience insight or revelation. It is the same life energy being experienced in different ways by different parts of our being.

The Hidden Power of Your Sexual Energy

During sex, another person helps to stimulate and start the flow of life energy inside you. (We even say things like, "You could see sparks fly when their eyes met," or "I could practically feel the electricity between them.") Sexual energy is a special kind of energy: Out of its power, new life can be created.

We can use this powerful life force to create new life in the form of a child, or *we can use this life force to create new life within ourselves. By learning how to use your sexual energy in a conscious way, rather than using it unconsciously, you can turn the sexual experience from one that simply feels good to one that rejuvenates you physically, emotionally, and even spiritually.*

How to Use Your Energy

Each day of your life, you make many choices as to how you want to use the life energies available to you. You can wake up with a certain amount of creative energy and decide to watch TV all day or to clean and organize your closet. One decision would be a waste of your creative energy; the other would be a positive use of that same energy. You may wake up with a certain amount of physical energy and decide to sit around the house and eat, or you can go out for a bicycle ride or to your job and energize yourself even more.

SECRET:
The energy available to you is the same, but what you choose to do with it can either increase your vitality or decrease it.

Similarly, we can have sex in a way that wears our body out or in a way that rejuvenates our body and creates even more energy.

The oldest cultures in the world knew the secret of using sexual energy to promote longevity, higher consciousness, and deep fulfillment. In India this tradition is called *Tantra;* in the Orient, the *Tao.* Both involve using the life force expressed as sexual energy not solely for the purpose of experiencing pleasure, but as a sacred ritual in which both male and female rise to a higher level of awareness, health, and inner peace.

In our Western culture *sex has become synonymous with pleasure and release.* We use sex as a form of ego gratification, as a form of tension release, and as a way to feel good. *We are missing out on the tremendous hidden power sexual energy can offer us if we don't know how to use it.*

▶ **Greedy Sex and Gourmet Sex**

Imagine your body as a big container of energy. When you start to have sex with someone, you feel an increase in the energy inside your body, starting in your genitals. That's called being "turned on," or aroused. As the energy starts to build, you make a choice:

1. To try to focus all of that energy on your genitals for maximum pleasure.
2. To "spread out" the energy all over the body, especially into the area of the emotions.

The human body can handle only a certain amount of energy in one area before it has to release the excess. It's as if the body says, "Hey, there's no more room in here."

For most people, sex consists of making the first choice noted above—trying to stuff as much pleasure and energy into the genitals as quickly as possible, until the body goes into an involuntary explosion or release called orgasm. I call this Greedy Sex.

The alternative is what I call Gourmet Sex.

A real connoisseur of food knows that the wisest way to eat a meal is to eat slowly, allowing time for the food to move down into the digestive organs. A friend of mine who frequents gourmet restaurants can eat about twice as much as anyone I know. "How do you do it?" I asked him once. "Simple," he replied, "I spend four hours eating one meal. The longer I take, the more I can eat."

Learning to have Gourmet Sex means making the second choice of the two I proposed above: *taking the time to integrate the sexual energy throughout the body so you can experience even more energy, resulting in more vitality, more joy—more love.*

▶ Are You Having Sex From the Waist Down?

In my years of research with couples and individuals, I've found that most people recall that their most fulfilling sexual experiences occurred when they experienced intense love energy as well as sexual energy. *Sex wasn't just physically satisfying, but emotionally fulfilling as well.* Yet we continue to have sex from the waist down, focusing on getting as much genital pleasure as possible. Here are the three common ways of having sex from the waist down:

1. Goal-oriented sex
2. Pleasure-oriented sex
3. Release-oriented sex

Goal-Oriented Sex

If you are making love with certain sexual expectations in mind—"I want to have an orgasm with my partner," or "I want to come three times"—you are having sex from the waist down. *You are focusing on genital goals, and not on creating emotional closeness.* There is nothing wrong with having three orgasms or lasting for an hour as long as that doesn't become the goal. *Making love works best when our goal is really to make love.*

Pleasure-Oriented Sex

During pleasure-oriented sex, you may spend the whole time going for an orgasm or trying to give your partner an orgasm or trying to maneuver yourself into the best position for maximum stimulation. *You know you are pleasure-oriented when you feel preoccupied with your pleasure or your partner's pleasure.* Sex often becomes very mechanical when you are pleasure-oriented.

Obviously, experiencing pleasure is a big part of sex. But when pleasure becomes the goal, you are having Greedy Sex from the waist down, and thus you are limiting your true experience of the power of sexual energy.

Release-Oriented Sex

Having release-oriented sex is like carrying a huge bag of groceries from the car to the house—you can't wait to get rid of it! Release-oriented sex has one purpose: *to release pent-up sexual tensions*. It usually has little or nothing to do with love and it is usually fairly brief—just long enough to build up the energy and then release it. The unfortunate person on the receiving end of this kind of sex usually feels like a depository, if she's female, or like a human vibrator, if he's male.

Problems Caused by Sex From the Waist Down

Sex from the waist down contributes to two of the most common sexual problems—premature ejaculation in men, and inability to have orgasm in women. In men all that focus on the genitals builds up the sexual pressure too quickly, producing the need for a quick release. The man needs to learn to let his energy build up slowly, integrating it throughout the body so he can last longer without having to discharge the energy. (Techniques will follow.)

For women sex from the waist down fails to focus the energy and attention on a woman's most powerful erogenous zone: the feelings in her heart. Many studies have shown that women become aroused emotionally first and sexually second. Many women cannot experience orgasm because the emphasis on genital stimulation isn't getting them anywhere—they aren't emotionally receptive and relaxed enough to feel the pleasure. Women need to practice the techniques in this section to make sure they make love from the waist up as well.

▶ Sex From the Waist Up

Earlier I said that your body was like a big container of energy. Imagine now that your body is made of *two* energy tanks, one from the waist down and one from the waist up. The one from the waist down holds sexual energy, and the one above the waist up holds love energy. The two tanks are connected by a channel.

When people have sex from the waist down, they are using only one of their energy tanks. When that tank gets full, they have an orgasm, and the sexual experience is over. Using your full sexual potential means learning to open up your second energy tank, and thus expand your capacity to experience the power, pleasure, and fulfillment that sexual energy will bring you.

SECRET:
> *The longer you allow sexual energy to circulate in your body, the more powerful its effects on your entire being.*

Just think about how you feel after you have a beautiful lovemaking experience with your partner, not one that was rushed or unsatisfying, but one in which you feel totally loved from head to toe. Afterward, you feel refreshed, revitalized, and glowing. You have probably made love from the waist up as well as from the waist down. Unfortunately, this experience of total regeneration and joy is not very frequent for most people.

▶ Why We Have Sex From the Waist Down

You have sex from the waist down for three main reasons:

1. You were taught that sex is for pleasure and you don't know any other way to make love.
2. You have become dependent on sex for release of tension.
3. You are avoiding making love with your partner from the waist up because it involves making yourself emotionally vulnerable.

The emotional walls you build around your heart keep your sexual energy from rising to that second energy tank above the waist. Anger at your partner, fear of being rejected, emotional numbness, and mistrust—all of these can keep the sexual energy from becoming love energy and making room for more sexual energy.

If you want to experience the maximum in sexual energy, you must be willing to become emotionally turned on as well as sexually turned on.

▶ Are You Riding on a Sexual Roller Coaster?

If we drew a diagram depicting the pleasure pattern most people experience during sex, it would look like this:

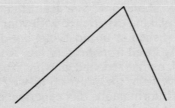

TRADITIONAL PLEASURE PATTERN

Now let's put many such sexual experiences together in a diagram:

THE ROLLER COASTER EFFECT

I call this the *Roller Coaster Effect*. Notice the extreme contrast between the highs and lows. This diagram illustrates one of the problems with trying to experience instant pleasure: It takes our body on a physical roller coaster, and our emotions often follow.

If you own a car that has four gears, you would never start your car in fourth gear, or shift from first to fourth right away—it would be too hard on your engine. Yet many people make love as though they are going from zero to eighty miles an hour in thirty seconds, and then screeching to a smoking halt. This kind of roller coaster sex wears out the body. Usually when you finish, you feel "spent," fatigued, and very attracted to the idea of a nice nap.

In the previous chapter we saw how the way in which you make love in the bedroom reinforces the way you behave outside the bedroom. Taking this one step further, the pattern your sexual energy follows in the bedroom may repeat itself in the pattern your relationship follows outside the bedroom. This means that roller coaster sex may create roller coaster moods and roller coaster arguments in your relationship outside the bedroom.

The solution is to begin to master your sexual energy so that it serves you in every way, contributing to your personal power, not depleting it. And the first step is to understand the habits of your sexual energy.

▶ The Pleasure Wave

Science teaches us that all energy moves in waves. Because it is also energy, sexual pleasure can operate in the same way. Have you ever been making love and felt as if a wave of pleasure had swept over you? That was a Pleasure Wave.

Here is how a Pleasure Wave looks:

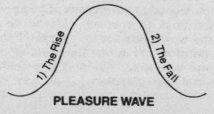

PLEASURE WAVE

The wave has two parts:

1. *The Rise:* The first part of the wave is felt as an increase in pleasure. Pleasure continues to build until it reaches a peak.
2. *The Fall:* The second part of the wave is felt as a decrease in pleasure. Pleasure has momentarily stopped increasing, giving you the sensation that the pleasure is decreasing.

If you don't interfere with the Pleasure Waves, they will continue to flow, each one a little bigger than the last, building in energy and intensity. They will look like this:

CONTINUING PLEASURE WAVE

Why You Interfere With Your Pleasure Waves

If you compare the drawing above with that of the Roller Coaster Effect, the difference is apparent. Why does sex end up looking like a roller coaster rather than an unfolding wave? The answer is: We interfere with the Pleasure Cycle because we are goal-oriented and impatient.

When you are making love and that first wave of pleasure rises, it feels wonderful. "I hope this doesn't go away," you think. And then at some point, maybe only for ten seconds, the intensity of pleasure seems to lessen. You think to yourself, "Maybe he moved his hand to the wrong position . . . maybe I should try a different position . . . maybe I am turning off . . ." In other words, you panic. You think you won't recapture that powerful pleasure! So what do you do? You try harder to create more pleasure. You move faster, touch harder, moan louder, ask for more stimulation, all in hopes of not losing that feeling. But by doing so you have just interfered with the natural Pleasure Cycle. Your body was experiencing the second part of the cycle: the fall. The fall of the Pleasure Wave is not something to avoid—it serves two very important functions in lovemaking. First, the decrease in pleasure gives the body *time to rest,* to integrate all of that powerful sexual energy so the body doesn't get overloaded and have to release the energy prematurely.

Nature works in cycles of rest and activity: The trees bloom with green leaves in spring and then rest themselves in winter; the sun shines during the day while we are active and then disappears at night, so that all can rest. Our bodies also work in these cycles—and sex is no exception.

Second, the decrease in pleasure provides you and your partner with the opportunity to increase your intimacy. When the Pleasure Cycle is in its fall phase, this is the natural time to focus on increasing your love energy. With less distraction from increasing sexual sensation, you can take this time to reconnect with your partner emotionally, to express your love and share your feelings.

This is also the time when you can learn to make use of that second energy tank. *When you share with your partner on an emotional level, you open the channel for the sexual energy to flow up and be transformed into love energy, thus making room for more sexual energy when the next wave rises.*

Making Sure You're Sexually Balanced

Let's look at the diagram of the Pleasure Wave again:

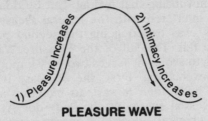

PLEASURE WAVE

Each phase of the wave balances the other: Phase one *takes in* sexual energy. Phase two *integrates* the energy, making room for more. Each part of the Pleasure Cycle is essential to keep the body in balance.

Now imagine that you have a scale. On one side you have *pleasure*. On the other side you have *intimacy*.

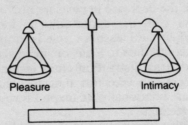

Pleasure   Intimacy

BALANCE BETWEEN PLEASURE & INTIMACY

If you can make love with equal amounts of pleasure and intimacy, your lovemaking will be free of tension, and your body can enjoy greater amounts of energy.

How to Notice If You Are Off Balance

Watch out for the peak of your Pleasure Wave—just when the sensations start to settle down a little bit. That's the time when you usually start trying to increase the pleasure and make it just as intense as it was a few seconds before. Stop! You are creating tension in your body by trying to keep your wave going up like a roller coaster when it naturally wants to settle down and balance itself.

SECRET:

Whenever you are trying to create more pleasure because it feels like what you have is not enough, that is the time to pause and connect emotionally with your partner.

In other words, *learn to ride the waves of love.* Allow yourself to relax and settle down when the pleasure settles down. The next wave will be along soon, and it will be even bigger than the first. And the third will be bigger than the second. You don't have to do anything to create the pleasure—it's all there waiting for you if you just let it flow through you *without trying to control it.*

How It Feels

Sometimes that downward phase of the wave lasts only ten seconds; sometimes a minute or two. It all depends on how aroused you are and how much time your body needs to integrate the energy from your sexual tank into your emotional tank. Here's a description of how the process may feel to you:

> I was making love with my partner. We both were so turned on that I didn't even think about what I wanted or how I felt. Then at some point I noticed that I had stopped just flowing with it and had started *trying* to get turned on—it wasn't coming naturally. I noticed I was thinking too much: wondering if I should turn over or if I should ask my lover to touch me differently.
>
> Then I remembered what you taught me about the two parts of the Pleasure Wave. I realized that our wave must be in a rest cycle and that it was time

to increase the love energy, not the sexual energy. So I said to my lover, "Just hold me for a minute." And we stopped stimulating each other and just lay there breathing together, and I really *felt* him and told him how close it felt. After about a minute, I felt a huge wave of pleasure start to rise again, as if just lying there had made me more turned on. He felt it, too . . . it was amazing. We rode our waves for several hours that night . . . I'll never make love the old way again!

How to Tell When You're Fighting the Waves

If you stay in tune with the natural cycles of increasing sexual energy alternating with increasing love energy, lovemaking will feel effortless and completely satisfying. I have found that there are four warning signs which tell you that you are fighting the waves, and that you need to relax and stop trying to create the pleasure:

1. Thinking About Time

How long has it been since we started?
How much longer do I need to do this before she comes?
How long will it take me to come?

Thinking about time is a sure sign that you are looking outside of the moment for something, that where you are is not enough. The wave is on its way down, and you are up there trying to make something happen. Just ease off a little; let the wave take its own time.

2. Feeling That What Is Happening Is Not Enough

I wish he'd touch me harder.
I wish I were more turned on.
This is okay, but it could be better.
I want *more!*

If your lovemaking has been going well, but suddenly you start to feel that it is not enough, you probably are at the peak of a Pleasure Wave, and the wave is settling down. You may feel cheated, as though you want more. This is not the time to work at creating more pleasure, but to trust that it will be back soon. Hold your partner and let the love be enough.

3. Your Mind Is Wandering

I wonder what I should wear to work tomorrow?
That report is due Tuesday, I'd better get on the ball.
After we finish tonight, I'd like to go out for pasta.

If in the middle of lovemaking, your experience of passion turns into thoughts of pasta, you probably just missed the downward side of a wave. When your mind wanders, it's looking for something, and that something is the intimate connection you have with your partner. Let yourself be absorbed into your heart—get out of your head, and save the pasta for afterward!

4. You Are Making Comparisons

It felt better a few minutes ago.
I liked how he did it last night better.
She seemed more responsive when we started than she does now.

Your mind is comparing what you have now with previous experiences because now doesn't feel like enough. Stop comparing and let go of your search for even more stimulation—it will come back soon. Relax and reach out to your partner and let the love energy reconnect you with what is going on at this moment.

What Happens When You Fight the Waves

As part of their research on the physiology of sex, Masters and Johnson created a model to show the four stages of the sexual experience which most of us have:

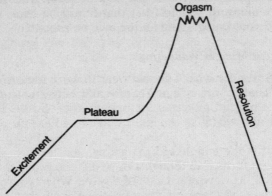

The Four Stages of the Sexual Experience

Excitement Phase: Sexual energy is building
Plateau Phase: Sexual energy has reached a
   plateau: not decreasing, but not increasing,
   either
Orgasm: the release of maximum sexual tension
Resolution: the return to a nonstimulated state

Compare this with how the Pleasure Wave looks in what I call Conscious Lovemaking:

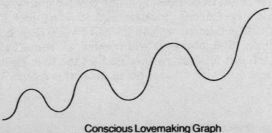

Conscious Lovemaking Graph

In order to understand the difference between Masters and Johnson's model and that of the Pleasure Wave, let's imagine we can visit two couples who are spending the night in two hotel rooms.

Couple number one will be practicing Traditional Lovemaking in room 101. Couple number two, who just finished reading this book, will be practicing Conscious Lovemaking in room 102. We will graph the sexual energy of each couple as we go.

PHASE ONE: Both couples start out in a similar way. Their energy wave begins to rise naturally due to their attraction and affection for one another. So we have half a wave each:

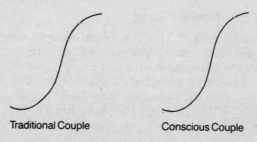

Traditional Couple   Conscious Couple

PHASE TWO: The natural cycles of sexual energy and pleasure have peaked for both couples. The Traditional Couple, noticing a lull in the excitement and stimulation, starts trying harder to turn each other on. They don't get much more aroused, but they attempt to hold on to what they have.

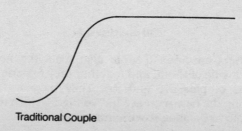

Traditional Couple

In Room 102 the Conscious Couple notices the lull, too, and decides to flow with the natural downswing of the wave. They stop moving for a moment and hold each other, feeling the emotional energy that has been building between them during their sexual excitement. As they lie together, they feel their intimacy deepening.

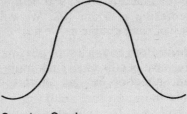

Conscious Couple

PHASE THREE: The Traditional Couple, who didn't stop and take time to integrate all that intense sexual energy by balancing it with love energy, now find themselves hit with a great big Pleasure Wave. This throws their systems off balance—their tanks are already almost full of the pleasure they have been holding on to so tightly, and there is no room for more. So *their energy levels rise drastically, resulting in orgasm and ejaculation.*

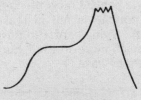

Traditional Couple

The Conscious Couple also feels the new wave rising inside of them, and together they experience new heights of pleasure and joy. They have no problem handling the new increase in "voltage," since they took the time to balance it with intimacy.

Conscious Couple

PHASE FOUR: The Traditional Couple is finished making love. They talk a little and fall asleep.

Meanwhile, the Conscious Couple is continuing to ride the waves of pleasure and intimacy, reaching higher and higher levels each time. Long after their neighbors in the next room are fast asleep, this couple is still making love. They will stop at some point, when they choose to, or when their bodies are so saturated with energy that they experience orgasm and ejaculation.

If we lay these two graphs on top of each other, we get an even clearer understanding of the difference between Traditional Lovemaking and Conscious Lovemaking.

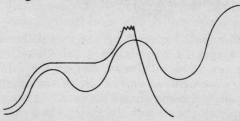

TRADITIONAL LOVEMAKING & CONSCIOUS LOVEMAKING

It's obvious that Traditional Lovemaking is very goal-oriented and does not use the hidden power of sexual energy to create the highest lovemaking experience possible. I like to use a triangle to represent Traditional Sex: Two people start out and go for the goal—orgasm.

Orgasm

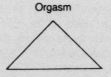

TRADITIONAL SEX

Conscious Lovemaking is like a spiral: a wave spiraling outward, ever-expanding, without a sense of beginning, middle, and end.

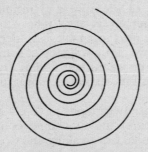

**CONSCIOUS LOVEMAKING
SPIRAL**

I call Traditional Lovemaking sex *for* fulfillment: looking for a specific experience. I call Conscious Lovemaking sex *from* fulfillment: finding the fulfillment in *every* moment, in *each* cycle of the energy, and, most of all, in the love shared between two people, full and complete to begin with, seeking nothing except love's celebration.

▶ How to Create Ecstasy

Ecstasy is more than pleasure—it is the experience you have when you allow yourself to be *full of pleasure and yet also totally relaxed. I define ecstasy as plea-sure without tension.* Most people tense up when they make love—their breathing quickens and their muscles tighten. Learning to relax in the midst of a tremendous power of sexual energy is an art that takes time and practice to learn, but it is worth it. When you make love consciously, staying aware of when sexual tension is building too quickly, you can learn to stay relaxed. And in that relaxed state, while feeling the life force flow through you, you will experience ecstasy.

How to Monitor Your Tension Meter

You have your own built-in tension meter that can help you monitor how much tension you are experiencing when you make love. If you pay attention to your meter, you will be well on your way to creating a whole new kind of joy for yourself and your partner.

Imagine a meter, like a tachometer in your car, with three sections: the green zone, the yellow zone, and the red zone.

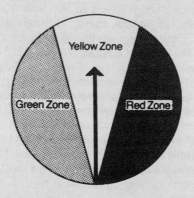

TENSION METER

Each zone represents a different tension level.

The Green Zone indicates "all clear." There is little tension, so you can keep receiving more sexual energy. You know you're in the green zone during lovemaking when you feel as though you could go on forever, and wouldn't be forced to stop.

The Yellow Zone indicates "caution." Some sexual tension is building and you have a limited amount of time before that tension will need to be released. You are in the yellow zone during lovemaking when you have the thought: "If we keep moving like this, I will come in two minutes," or "If she keeps doing that to me, I will ejaculate in thirty seconds." The yellow zone warns you of imminent release of your sexual pleasure and energy unless you do something to minimize the tension.

The Red Zone indicates "release." Your body must unburden itself of all that extra energy. If the yellow zone is the warning, the red zone is the explosion you were warned about. There is no zone after the red zone!

In order to create ecstasy, you need to keep your sexual tension at a minimum when you make love. As soon as you notice yourself in the yellow zone, pause and integrate the sexual energy throughout the rest of your body. That means saying to yourself, "Hmmm, I seem to be feeling some sexual tension. If I continue to do this wonderful thing I am doing now, I certainly will ejaculate or have an orgasm in about two minutes (based on previous experiments!). In order to allow myself to experience even greater ecstasy, I will pause right now, relax, and try to spread the energy throughout my body. When I feel relaxed again, I will resume a more active kind of sexual play."

This pause could last for fifteen seconds or for three minutes: as long as it takes you to decrease the sexual tension.

Warning: Never try to stop and decrease the tension when you are already in the red zone—it's too late, and your body needs the release it is seeking at that point. In other words—in the bedroom at least—don't ever stop at a red light!

Tips to Help You Reduce Sexual Tension

You might try any or all of the following techniques to reduce sexual tension. (You also will come up with your own tricks, which will probably work better.)

1. *Verbally express your love and caring to your partner.* Sharing love dissolves tension and opens up that channel to the second energy storage tank. Open your heart and express love!

2. *Breathe.* We tend to hold our breath or breathe shallowly during intense experiences: when we are angry, afraid, sexually aroused, or frustrated. Breathing moves energy throughout your body. Inhale deeply from your genitals and pull the energy up with your breath all the way to the top of your head. Then exhale and imagine yourself totally relaxed. Do this several times and you will notice the sexual tension diminish. Your partner can do it with you, and that will help relax you even more.

3. *Visualize.* Your mind is your most powerful tool. Visualize all the concentrated energy from your genitals melting and spreading out all over your body. Imagine the channel between your below-the-waist tank and above-the-waist tank opening up, and see all that beautiful sexual energy flowing upward, leaving your lower tank spacious and empty.

4. *Make eye contact with your partner.* Looking into your lover's eyes reminds you that your purpose is to make love. You can exchange a great wave of love energy with your partner when you look into his or her eyes, thus reducing the tension you feel inside you from too much sexual energy.

5. *Stop or minimize all physical movement.* Don't forget this one! The last thing you need is to keep stimulating yourself while you are trying to reduce your sexual tension.

What About Orgasm and Ejaculation?

You may be wondering when you will finally experience a climax if you have been working at staying out of the red zone. There are two possibilities: one, that after experiencing so much ecstasy, you may at times not wish to release all that powerful energy, and choose instead to let it circulate inside of you; and two, on one of your wave cycles, your body may finally decide that it wants to put on a fireworks display for you and you will experience orgasm and ejaculation. But it will probably feel different from what you have been used to feeling. *Your orgasm may be much greater in intensity, since you let all that energy build up over time; and it will be more a celebration than a release.*

Remember: Conscious Lovemaking is *not* designed to give you bigger and better orgasms, or even to prolong the time before ejaculation. Rather, it's a way for you to use the sexual experience to share your most true and tender self with the one you love and to begin tapping into the hidden power of your sexual energy.

▶ Seven Keys to Sexual Happiness

I have developed seven keys to remember that will help you create the sexual fulfillment you desire. I call these the seven C's, because they are all words that begin with the letter *c*.

Conscious: Be conscious of the process of making love: how your partner is feeling, how your body is handling the energy. Sex can be one of the most unconscious things we do—in the dark, with our eyes closed, not talking, numb on alcohol or drugs. Being conscious means being loving.

Choice: When you make love from choice, and not from obligation, you are creating the conditions you need to have a fulfilling experience. Never make love when you don't want to. Sometimes saying no is saying yes to your inner voice. If you are a Sexual Corpse or Sexual Procrastinator, you may never be in touch with your desire to make love. In this case, try saying yes to your partner when you *aren't* totally in the mood, go slowly, and you may find you get in the mood as soon as you are feeling loved.

Commitment: Be committed to a higher purpose when you make love. Be committed to sharing *all* of yourself, committed to healing some old patterns of behavior in your Sexual Classroom, and committed to your relationship, to whatever degree you are. Commitment creates a sense of power and strength in your life.

Connection: This "middle C," placed between the first three and the last three, is the centerpiece for making love. Connection means staying emotionally tuned in to your partner, keeping your heart open, letting the experience be one that is shared, and working toward oneness together.

Communication: Sharing and expressing your feelings allows the connection to become concrete and clear to your partner. Share your inner world with your partner by showing him or her how you are feeling, asking for what you want, and expressing your deepest feelings of love.

Cooperation: Be aligned with your partner in purpose. Lovemaking doesn't work when you are trying to practice Conscious Sex, while your partner just wants to climax and go to sleep. Support your partner in using his or her Sexual Classroom to become the loving person he/she is inside, and share your dreams together.

Come from completion: Lovemaking is not a journey *to* someplace, but an expression of a place you and your partner *already inhabit* together. Coming from completion means making love as a *celebration* of your relationship, and not as a desperate attempt to fill your emptiness. When you come from completion, every moment of making love is complete and perfect just as it is.

▶ A New Adventure Awaits You

You are standing on the threshold of a wonderful journey. The territory waiting to be explored is inside you. The power bestowed on you by conscious use of your sexual energy truly can be called magic—it fills your limbs with aliveness; it teaches you how to feel fully again as you move its force up into your heart, awakening you to the true power of love; it can heal all the old wounds and hurts inside you with the pure stream of joyousness it sends racing up your spine.

A new adventure awaits you. May your travels take you where your heart has always longed to go. And may you journey in peace.

15

Common Sexual Problems and Uncommon Solutions

The sexual problems I will discuss in this chapter are not ones you have never heard of. You may have had to deal with them at one time in your life, whether the problem was yours or your partner's. But the uncommon solutions I offer may be new to you. I hope that by understanding and trying them, you can bring more joy and fulfillment to the sexual part of your loving relationship.

▶ The Secret About Most Sexual Problems

Ninety percent of "sexual" problems aren't sexual at all—they have their roots in the emotional barriers we place between ourselves and our partners. We bring these problems into the bedroom from the dinner table, the office, the den, the kitchen, from our adolescence, from our former husbands and wives, from that awful date we had in college, from what our mothers told us about what kind of a girl to be, from what our fathers told us about how to be real men, from magazine articles on perfecting the three-hour orgasm. Sex also becomes the battleground for expressing the anger, fear, guilt, and hurt we feel between ourselves and our lovers. I see this over and over again in couples who come to me claiming that they have a "great" relationship, but that they just don't have a good sex life. Sex has become a dumping ground for the emotional problems in the relationship.

The secret to solving most of your sexual problems lies in keeping your heart open, honest, and loving toward your partner.

That means understanding and practicing all the techniques you have learned in the previous section of the book: avoiding the Four R's, telling the Complete Truth, watching out for the Seesaw Effect, and dissolving Emotional Tension with the Duplication Technique, Love Letters, the Power Process, and the other exercises in this book.

As for the other 10 percent of sexual problems which we all face now and then, read on.

▶ Making Love for the Wrong Reasons

I'll bet you don't often stop and really think about *why* you want to make love at a particular time. If you did, you may be surprised to find out that the majority of the reasons why you make love have nothing at all to do with making love.

SECRET:
   Some of our biggest sexual problems occur because we are making love for all the wrong reasons!

Here is a list of reasons why we make love that I have heard over and over in my seminars. How many of these apply to you?

Afraid to say no
I felt obligated
To see if it still worked
My parents were away
To get rid of cramps
To get it over with
It was Saturday night
To prove I'm a man (woman)
It was available (didn't know when it would be again)
Lust
Nothing good on TV
To avoid having to talk about us
To rebel against someone
Arrivals and departures (he was leaving for a month or he just returned)
To have an orgasm
To be held
To make a baby
To make up after a fight
To keep warm in a camper
To get a job
To keep a job
As a way of saying good-bye to someone
I was intoxicated or high on drugs
To prove I was as good as his ex-lover
Special occasions (anniversary, birthday)
To get to sleep
The kids were finally asleep
To reward someone
I felt sorry for him (her)
To lose my virginity
He bought me dinner
To get revenge on someone else
For old times' sake with an old lover
To control someone
To prove to myself I still cared
To impress someone
For exercise
So he wouldn't get it somewhere else
To check out someone's reputation for being a good lover
Statistical purposes (how many times we can climax, etc.)
Curiosity (what is it like to make love with a foreigner?)
We were in a strange and unusual place

I'd already put my
   diaphragm in
To try and keep my
   partner

To have fun
To prove to him/her he
   wasn't gay
On a dare
    Why waste a perfectly good erection?

And, of course . . .
Because we were in love
To show him how I felt

If you look at this list, you can begin to see why most sexual experiences leave much to be desired for many people—they are making love for the wrong reasons.

If you go into lovemaking because you don't want to say no, or because you want to control the other person, or because you are afraid he will leave if you don't, you probably won't have a wonderful, emotional, satisfying lovemaking experience. *What you put into lovemaking is what you get out of it . . . if you go into it with anger, fear, or out of guilt or desperation, you probably won't come out of it with love.*

Sex: The Ultimate Cure-all

We expect sex to act as a cure-all for whatever ails us: loneliness, a fight with our partner, low self-esteem, boredom, jealousy, and so on. But that's not what happens. Instead, we confuse and pollute the intimate and healing act that sexual union can and should be with all the emotional garbage we have brought to bed with us. And then we are surprised that it doesn't turn out wonderfully!

Many of the reasons we have sex are actually reasons to sit down and discuss how we are feeling, rather than hoping that sex will wave its magic wand and make all the bad feelings go away. Of course, having sex is easier: You don't have to find the right words to express your feelings, and you don't have to take the *risk* of opening up. Many couples would rather expose their bodies to each other than their emotional vulnerability. You may even find yourself intensifying your sexual activity with your partner when you feel your emotional bond slipping. But this just covers up the real problem.

Stacey's Sexual Garbage Dump

Stacey had just broken up with another boyfriend and was frantic. "I'm thirty-eight, and I've never had a good sexual experience," she moaned. "What is wrong with me?"

If you have read Chapter 13, you may already have guessed that Stacey was a Sexual Martyr. But let's look at her technique. I asked Stacey to describe the last few sexual experiences she had had, and I listened in amazement as she listed the reasons she had made love with each one:

> "Well, Frank was just leaving town, and we hadn't gone to bed yet. I thought if I could leave him with that memory before he went away, he'd miss me and want to have a more committed relationship." (Reason: to keep a partner.)
>
> "Then there was Arnold. Arnold really liked me, but I didn't like him that much. One night we were at his place and he practically begged me to make love with him. I just didn't have the heart to say no. I don't think he'd been with anyone for years." (Reason: I felt sorry for him.)
>
> "A few months later I met Eddie at a friend's wedding. I felt so emotional that day—I guess because I'd like to get married. Eddie and I went back to my place afterward for coffee. I began to feel so lonely and hopeless, and started to cry. Eddie held me, and it felt so good, and then one thing led to another, and he got me into bed." (Reason: wanted to be held.)

Stacey's stories all sounded the same. She kept making love with men for all the wrong reasons. I pointed this out to her and explained that if she waited to make love with someone for the right reasons, her chances of having a nice sexual experience were much greater.

SECRET:
If you make love with someone for the right reasons, the sex will probably turn out right.

▶ The Right Reasons to Make Love

When we make love in order to share our loving feelings with our mate, and not just to have sex, we almost always end up making *more* love. We may also fulfill some of the other things on the list of why people make love: having fun, feeling pleasure, being held, etc. But the main reason for having the sexual experience is solely to make love, because we know from experience that it is really making love that brings the greatest fulfillment, inside and out.

So the next time you are ready to have sex, ask yourself: "Why am I doing this?" If your answer is: "Because if I don't he might call his ex-girlfriend," or "Because we started, so we might as well finish," think again. You deserve to have wonderfully fulfilling love-making, and you are the only one who can make sure it turns out that way!

▶ Don't Fall into the Five Sexual Traps

Most of us make five enormous assumptions about sex. I call them the Sexual Traps because they trap us into behavior patterns that contribute to instant sexual problems.

Sexual Trap One: Making love means having intercourse.

Try this exercise: After you read this sentence, close your eyes and picture a couple making love. When you have the picture in your mind, open your eyes.

If you are like most people, you probably imagined a couple having intercourse. This is the first Sexual Trap: the belief that making love means having intercourse. Anything else isn't "the real thing." That's why foreplay is called foreplay: It is warming you up for the "goal"—having intercourse.

Now, there is nothing wrong with intercourse, but if you think that the *goal* of lovemaking is intercourse, you actually just fell into two traps:

- You deny yourself and your partner innumerable opportunities to make love, thinking, "Why bother if we don't go 'all the way'?" (I call this the All-or-Nothing Pattern.)
- You become very goal-oriented during lovemaking.

So many women complain to me that there is nothing they hate more than a man who falls into Sexual Trap One: They start making love, and you can almost hear the clock ticking in his head: "Okay, we've kissed for four minutes, now I can advance to touching the breasts . . . good, three minutes on the breast, now the other for balance . . . now I can start stroking her thighs, just for a minute or two; now I'll touch her vagina . . . okay, as soon as she is wet, I'll turn her onto her back and then we can get down to business." Sex is not a game of Beat the Clock! *Every moment of lovemaking can be fulfilling if you are sharing and expressing love with your partner. And don't wait until intercourse to share that love deeply. You'll find that with less pressure on intercourse to be the ultimate high,*

*the whole experience of lovemaking becomes more
pleasurable and deeply fulfilling.*

Sexual Trap Two: The purpose of making love is to have orgasm.

John and Susie meet on a Saturday night for a
romantic date. John takes Susie to a quiet restaurant,
complete with candles and a strolling guitarist. At the
table the couple sit hand in hand, stroking each other's
arms, occasionally leaning over and giving each other a
light but promising kiss. Susie feels very much in love
with John, and very much appreciated by him. After
dinner they take a long walk through the park by a lake,
strolling arm in arm, stopping occasionally for a long,
deep kiss and to hold each other tightly. On their way
home they stop at a nightclub to dance for a while.

Their bodies seem to melt together, and waves of
happiness and arousal flow through them.

Finally they return to Susie's house. In the bedroom Susie lights candles and puts on soft music. John
spends a long time seducing Susie: taking off her
clothes one article at a time; kissing her lightly everywhere; slowly building the passion between them.
Naked at last, they move together, full of love, joyous.
As the energy mounts, so does their closeness. Suddenly, John feels his orgasm coming on; Susie seems
just as enraptured as he is. As John comes, he hears
himself call Susie's name and feels as if they are one.

For a while the two lie silently entwined. Then
John turns to his lover and says, "Honey, was it good
for you?"

The Real Meaning of "Was It Good for You?"

What does John mean when he asks Susie if it was
"good" for her? Does he mean, did she enjoy the
romantic dinner? Does he mean, did she feel as turned
on as he did when they were dancing or when they

began to undress? Does he mean, did she enjoy the incredible closeness they experienced during intercourse? Of course not! What John means is: Did you have an orgasm?

I chose to tell you this story because I think it perfectly illustrates the second Sexual Trap: thinking that the purpose of making love is to have an orgasm. You may insist that you are too educated and sensitive to believe that that is what sex is all about. But if you are like most people, you fall under the spell of this Sexual Trap more often than you realize.

Have you ever:

Wished your partner would "hurry up and come" so you could stop?

Felt angry at a partner for taking so long?

Felt like a failure when you didn't come?

Felt like a failure when your partner didn't come?

Felt frustrated at your partner, thinking, "If he keeps this up, I'll never come"?

These are all symptoms of Sexual Trap Two.

There is nothing wrong with orgasm. Orgasm is the natural release of built-up sexual energy in the body. It feels great. But it certainly isn't the whole picture. And it certainly isn't the purpose of making love. The purpose of making love is to share and express love with your partner. This can be accomplished with or without an orgasm.

We have given so much of our power away to that little five-second energy release called orgasm. Let's revisit John and Susie. What if Susie tells John she didn't have an orgasm? He will feel disappointed and wonder what else he could have done. Susie will feel like a failure, embarrassed, and angry at herself for not being orgasmic. They are both caught in Sexual Trap Two. And they are missing the point. They just finished *four hours* of lovemaking, starting from the romantic dinner all the way to the bedroom. Yet, like many couples, they will not remember the evening and the lovemaking as being fabulous, simply because Susie didn't have an orgasm.

Becoming Orgasmic

Breaking this sexual habit means realizing that making love, when approached with complete love and openness, is itself an orgasmic experience. Then the idea of sexual orgasm actually becomes a limitation. If you practice the techniques in the previous chapters and allow yourself to experience sex *from* fulfillment, not sex *for* fulfillment, I know that your *entire* lovemaking experience, from the first glance to the last goodnight kiss, will be the magical experience you dream of.

Sexual Trap Three: If my partner really loves me, he'll know just what to do to make sex wonderful for me.

Did Rhett Butler ever ask Scarlett O'Hara what turned her on? No, he *knew*. Did Dr. Zhivago need his lover, Lara, to tell him what she wanted him to do when they made love? Of course not: He knew too. The problem is that these perfect, all-knowing lovers existed in fiction and not in real life. In real life we don't always know just what our partners like and dislike. We have to ask!

"But," you may protest, "talking about it takes all the romance out of it." I like to look at it differently. First of all, I know for sure that if I don't let my partner know what I like in bed, there won't be any romance to consider! Second, I find it very exciting to know that someone I love wants to please me enough to ask what I like, to remember something I said I liked, or to agree to make love to me in the way that excites me most. To me, that's romantic.

We expect our love partners to be mind readers! This puts a tremendous amount of pressure on your partner, and it's unrealistic. Give up "psychic sex" and tell your loved one gently what you like and dislike. Falling into this Sexual Trap can only lead to resentment and frustration for both you and your partner.

DO YOU RELY ON ESP WHEN YOU MAKE LOVE?

Many people hope their partners will read their minds when they're making love so they don't have to take the risk of asking for what they really want or expressing how they feel. Here is a list of some of the common ways you may be relying on ESP when you make love. Give yourself points for how frequently a statement applies to you:

Often . . . . .3 points

Sometimes. . . . . .2 points

Rarely . . . . 1 point

1. *You* know what really turns you on, but you don't tell your partner.

2. You don't come out and tell your partner you are in the mood to make love, but let him/her know you're interested by how you behave, what you wear to bed, or by "hinting around."

3. When you like something your partner is doing to you sexually, you don't show him how excited you are or let him know what he's doing right.

4. You are on the quiet side when you make love, and don't make much noise.

5. When you don't like something your partner is doing to you sexually, you move your body away or lie there not responding, rather than tell

your partner you'd rather have him/her do
something else.

6. You get impatient because your partner doesn't
   know the "right" thing to do or the "right" way
   to touch you.

7. You don't say "romantic" things during your
   lovemaking.

8. When you feel like stopping your lovemaking,
   you don't tell your partner directly, but respond
   less, hoping he'll get the message.

9. You think talking during sexual play "ruins" the
   mood.

Now add up your score:

9–11 points: You are good at asking for what you
   want in bed. Have fun!

12–21 points: You are relying too much on your
   partner's ESP in bed. Practice talking about
   what you want and how you feel.

22–27 points: Either your partner is psychic or you
   aren't getting what you want in bed. Admit that
   you have a problem communicating and start
   working to change it.

If you answered "often" to even one of the above
statements, you're relying too much on ESP when you
make love. The result will be built-up resentment, frustration, and a decrease of passion in your relationship.

The solution is to communicate with your partner
about what you like and don't like, what you're afraid
of, and what makes lovemaking a "10" for you. At first
you might find this kind of total honesty scary, but the
result will be a more passionate relationship.

Sexual Trap Four: Novelty is the key to an exciting sex life.

Judith cried as she sat in my office, trying to understand what had gone wrong in her marriage to Ted. Ted seemed to feel that he and Judith had to keep a constant sense of novelty going in their sex life. The moment the couple would become comfortable making love in a particular style or setting, Ted would insist that they change. "I've had sex in my kitchen, my den, my basement, even in my laundry room," Judith wept. "Ted insisted I change my perfume, my hairstyle, my clothing. I can't stand it anymore. Why can't he just love me and our sex life for what they are? Rather than bringing us closer, this is driving us apart. Now he's even starting to seem interested in other women."

Poor Ted was a prisoner of Sexual Trap Four, believing that most sex lives between couples fail due to lack of variety and novelty. Ted is partially correct; it's just his *interpretation* that isn't accurate. Ted was afraid that he would get tired of Judith. Unfortunately, this does occur in many couples. Why does it happen?

▼

SECRET:
> *You will tire of a partner when you stop actively loving him or her.*

▲

The reason a man like Ted could be tired of his wife and then go out with someone he hardly knew and be excited by her is that *he is not used to her, so he pays more attention to her.*

When we really pay attention to our partner, we remember why we fell in love with him or her in the first place.

The problem is that most of us stop paying attention to our lover once we've "got" him or her, and soon the magic wears off. The problem is not with the person, but with the way in which we learn to look at that person. How many times have you been in a new relationship and said to your partner, "I can't believe your partner left you. He [she] must have been crazy or blind"? What you are really saying is, "Your ex must have stopped paying attention." You're right!

The Art of Paying Complete Attention

It's not really that difficult to learn to pay complete attention. We all do it with our children, and even with our pets. Have you ever watched a parent play with his or her child? The parent seems fascinated and totally in love with his child; never bored; taking twenty pictures of the same pose, because he is *paying attention to someone he loves,* and that is always exciting. If you can think your dog is cute each time he does the same old trick, you certainly can learn to stay excited with your partner year after year!

> *Learn to look at those you love with new eyes every day.*

Sexual Trap Five: Sex shouldn't be planned—it should just happen.

According to Sexual Trap Five, it is unromantic to *plan* sex; it should just occur. You and your lover should be sitting around after dinner, glance over at each other, and suddenly be seized with passion, retreating posthaste to the bedroom. Well, for one thing, most couples never "sit around" after dinner—one or both of you may be cleaning up, paying bills, entertaining your children, doing extra work you brought home from the office, or going out to a meeting or class.

Second, you may not even eat dinner at the same time. And the only thing that may "seize" you, if you *are* sitting around, is one of your children needing help with homework or a tremendous urge to crawl into bed and sleep.

You get the picture. For most couples, free time just doesn't exist.

What is the solution? To make time. And making time means planning. Yes, *planning*—that boring, predictable task which shuts off many lovers' sexual juices immediately. "You mean, you want to *plan* sex?" your partner may ask you incredulously when you suggest you put aside the time. "How unspontaneous; how uninspiring." "How nice even to do it," you can answer. He'll get the message.

Planning Time for Lovemaking

Why shouldn't you plan intimacy with your partner? It will be boring or predictable only if you fall into the other four Sexual Traps and ignore everything else you've learned in this book. And it is certainly just as important as, if not more important than, many of the other things you make time for each week (like watching a movie, painting your nails, or mowing the lawn). *Planning time for lovemaking means creating the opportunity for it to happen*. It doesn't mean *forcing* it to happen.

When your partner schedules time to be with you intimately, you feel very special and loved. Sometimes it turns out to be a wonderful ritual, simply because you put more effort and care into it than normal. And sometimes you will have high expectations, but may end up falling asleep together. That's lovemaking, too, especially when you share a good laugh about it in the morning! Sometimes, even in the midst of your busy schedules, sex does just "happen." What do you do then? Take the phone off the hook, put a "Do Not Disturb" sign on the bedroom door, and play!

▶ Common Mistakes Men and Women Make Regarding Sex

In our exploration of common sexual problems and uncommon solutions, I want to talk about what I have found to be the most common and damaging mistakes both men and women make when dealing with each other in sex. We continue to make these mistakes because no one ever told us the secrets that help us to understand the other sex. So here are the secrets, and the mistakes we make when we aren't aware of them.

Secrets About Women All Men Should Know

Secret One: Women love to be seduced.
MISTAKE: Men in committed relationships very rarely seduce their own partners.

Women love to be seduced because it makes them feel wanted. *Feeling wanted turns a woman on.* It makes her feel beautiful and desirable sexually, and the more she gets turned on in her head to herself, the more intensely she can get turned on to men.

Seducing a woman doesn't have to be a full-scale effort. It means not taking for granted that she is there. It means starting the lovemaking hours, even a day, before you plan to make love: sending little notes, dropping little hints, making suggestions of intimacy. The longer the soup cooks, the better it will taste!

Seducing a woman means not showing up in the bedroom naked, getting into bed with your partner, and getting speedily down to business kissing and fondling her.

Women often talk about their men among themselves, and believe me, they fondly remember their former lovers who knew how to seduce. It will open a magic door!

Secret Two: Women get turned on in their heads first.

MISTAKE: Men don't talk enough during lovemaking.

Women have been brought up to have higher verbal skills than men. Little girls are encouraged to read and to be social (i.e., talk), while little boys are encouraged to be physical and task-oriented. Women have learned to feel through their minds—to be stimulated by thoughts, images, and allusions. In contrast, men are aroused more through vision and touch.

What this means is that during sex, women generally like to be talked to; to be told how *you* are feeling, men; to be told how they look to you; what you want to do to them; and how you feel about them. This turns women on. It will probably turn you on, too, once you try it. Men tend to be more quiet during sex, more internal. Try expressing your feelings before, during, and after sex, and you will love the results!

Secret Three: Women don't like to be rushed.

MISTAKE: Men "check" a woman to see if she is "ready."

All sexual experts agree that women take longer than men to become fully sexually aroused. But men, you are too impatient! And women know when you are "checking" to see if they are "ready" for entry. How do they know? Because sometimes you take your fingers and explore a woman's vagina just to see how wet she is. When you find conditions less than satisfactory, you remove your fingers and begin intently stimulating the woman with the hope of getting her juices flowing. A few minutes later, there go the fingers checking again. I call this "checking the roast."

Remember what your grandmother used to tell you: A watched pot never boils. When women feel pressured and checked up on in bed, they tend to feel less safe.

▼
_____

SECRET:
When women don't feel safe, they have
a harder time becoming sexually aroused.
_____
▲

Solution: Take your time, enjoy the love in each moment, and please don't check the roast. It will get done in its own time.

Secret Four: Women need to feel emotionally secure in order to become fully aroused.
MISTAKE: Men use other women to make their own partners feel insecure.

Men, if you want to keep your woman sexy and receptive to you, please don't flirt with other women or make your partner jealous. Jealousy may make a woman feel more desperate for you, but it probably will end up shutting her down sexually after a while. Women need to feel emotionally safe and appreciated before they can really open up sexually to a lover. Threatening your partner's sense of emotional security will definitely have a negative effect on your sex life, and you won't feel so good about yourself on the inside either. I have seen women in my counseling practice take months to recover from what I will call their husband's "heavy flirting incident": not an affair, but just an energy leak. (Of course, the same rule applies to you, ladies.)

Secret Five: Having a vagina and a womb makes a woman feel very vulnerable.
MISTAKE: Men don't understand the power of the sexual experience for women.

Men will never know what it is like to have an inside to which other people have access. That's how it feels to be a woman—they are vulnerable, open, and receptive. Taking a part of someone inside our bodies is sometimes very frightening and risky. It is as if women have no defenses; they are in the ultimately vulnerable position. *To respect a woman's body and honor her for her willingness to allow you to enter it is truly to make love to a woman.* This awareness applies to each stage of lovemaking.

- *Before entry:* You wouldn't barge into someone's home without knocking. So please don't do that with a woman's body. Make sure you have been invited in, and even then, enter with respect.

- *During intercourse:* You are in a sacred place where life germinates and becomes a child. No matter how turned on a woman is, she needs time to adjust to your presence inside her, whether she is aware of it or not. Go slowly and allow yourself to feel fully where you are. Think about how amazing it is to be inside the body of the woman you love, to be that close to her essence.

- *After intercourse:* Sometimes after we have had family over and everyone leaves, the house feels empty for a while. When a man withdraws himself from a woman, it is a shock to her system. You were so close, and now you are gone. Please take time to fill in the emptiness with loving words, safe embraces, and assurances that you are 100 percent there for her. (Falling asleep immediately is a definite no-no.)

Secret Six: Women need a lot of verbal appreciation and attention.

MISTAKE: Men take their women for granted and get lazy.

The majority of women do not have affairs. They don't want to have them. Their instinct usually is to preserve the relationship. When I counsel women who are having an affair with someone, and I ask them how it started, it's almost always the same story:

> We were working together on a project at the office, and Frank just seemed to love my ideas. I had tried to talk to my husband about the project, but he just didn't seem interested. One thing led to another and . . ."

> "George and I met at a PTA meeting. We started talking about our kids and ideas for helping them learn better. George seemed interested in my philosophy of child-rearing. Then we started talking about our marriages and how our partners seemed to tune us out. One thing led to another and . . ."

> "Serge was my art instructor at night school. He'd always compliment me on my choice of clothing or on a color I was wearing. I would feel embarrassed, but somehow excited. My gosh, it had been so long since my husband really noticed what I wore, let alone complimented me. One thing led to another and . . ."

These women all had one thing in common: They weren't getting enough attention and appreciation from their partners. Now, men, I know you will insist, "But I was out working to support her—isn't that appreciating her?" Yes, it is. But women need more—they need to *hear* appreciation. I know. I had an affair once; something I'm not proud of. Looking back, I can see how desperate I was to find someone who would pay attention to me and see my magic. Like most affairs, mine started out as a long friendship, and after a while it developed into something more. My husband was traveling most of the time, and I felt he was focusing all his energy on his career and had stopped paying special attention to me. Having an affair was *not* the solution to my marital problems, and I would never do it that way again. But I have used my painful lessons to help thousands of women and men heal their relationships in ways that, sadly, I never healed mine.

Learning to make love all the time means being in a love affair with your partner and making him or her the person you rush to the phone to call or get excited about meeting in a restaurant.

Secrets About Men That Women Need to Know

Secret One: Sex is very important to men to make them feel wanted.

MISTAKE: Women reject men sexually and don't realize what it does to them.

Sex is a primal form of giving for men, a way for them to offer themselves and be received or accepted, physically and emotionally. When a man makes a sexual overture to his partner, he is doing more than asking for sex. Whether he is aware of it or not, he is saying, "Please accept me; please receive me."

I'm not saying you should always say yes, ladies. I am suggesting that as women, you learn to understand the particular vulnerability men have in offering themselves to you, and that you receive them in some way when they offer themselves. Other than having sex, that means holding them, telling them you'd love to make love later, telling them how much you appreciate having them in your life, etc.

Men take sexual rejection very badly. They feel a woman is saying, "I don't want you, I don't love you." Since they don't always know how to express their hurt, they may retaliate by turning off to you, or seeking sex elsewhere.

So if you aren't in the mood for sex with your lover, say no to sex, but yes to loving him. (And men, you should do the same for women.)

Secret Two: Men need to feel they are doing a good job in life.

MISTAKE: Women make men feel like failures.

From the time they are little boys, men are taught to "do well," to get out there and make something of themselves. Thus, when men make mistakes, they feel like failures. And when women take men to task for their mistakes, they are pushing a button in men that may lead to an explosion or a shutdown. When you criticize a man, he hears you saying, "You are bad. You have failed." You may just be suggesting that he stop and ask for directions, since you have been driving for twenty minutes looking for a street. Often he will imagine you are saying much more, and you will end up feeling that you have to "tiptoe" in the relationship because of his temper.

The solution is to express yourself with love and tenderness when you correct or criticize your man, making sure you aren't saying "you're bad," and making sure he knows you still love and admire him. I'm not suggesting treating him like a baby. Just be aware of the lifetime of conditioning he has had to *do things right* and make sure you aren't making *him* wrong just because he may be doing something wrong.

Secret Three: Men like women who like sex.

MISTAKE: Women don't let men know how much they like sex.

As women, we are taught that there are "good girls" and "bad girls." The good girls don't like sex *too much*. Many women I have worked with still have a difficult time asking their partner to make love, showing their partner during sex how much they love it, and/ or talking about it afterwards.

Very often men have affairs with "lusty, earthy women," women who aren't afraid to show the sexual side of themselves.

As a friend of mine put it, "I hate always being the one to suggest sex with my girlfriend. It puts me in a position to be rejected constantly. I want my girlfriend to be the aggressor more of the time."

Don't let the men do all the work, ladies. Show them you want them; tell them how much you love sex. Take a risk, and you will find you are feeling sexier, too!

Secret Four: Men really like a woman with a sense of humor.

MISTAKE: Women act too frightened of men to be able to be fun.

Many men complain that their partners are too "serious." They say they need to go out with the guys to laugh it up. Sometimes going out with the guys includes those certain women who spend time with other people's boyfriends and husbands as "one of the crowd." Often these are strictly legitimate relationships, and when you ask your partner what he sees in that crazy blonde at the bar, he'll answer, "She really knows how to have a good time." I'm *not* suggesting we all become men's drinking partners, ladies. But we do need to lighten up and stop being so afraid of men that we can't be a little more playful.

The Chicken with the Cold Feet

I must admit that I used to have a very bad case of "seriousitis." When faced with a problem in a relationship, I'd either pout or cry. When I started my present relationship many years ago, I vowed to lighten up and overcome my fear of losing the man in my life. Very soon, I had an opportunity to put my newfound humor to the test.

I had just been dating my new friend for a few weeks, although we'd known each other as friends for nine months. I was invited to speak at a meeting for an organization my new love belonged to. Everyone there knew him and knew me, but no one knew yet that we were dating. We talked on the phone and decided that it would be a great way to "come out in public" together as a committed couple.

I dressed up for the big evening, excited to see my partner and even more excited about sharing our new love with friends. I went out to do some errands and then ran back to the house to check my messages. On the machine was a message from him:

"Hi, Barbara. Listen, I have a bad headache, and I really can't handle going tonight. I'm going to try to reach a friend of mine who is an acupuncturist to help me get rid of the pain. Sorry about the meeting. I'll talk to you sometime soon, I guess. Bye."

I was furious! I was sure he didn't have a headache and that he was just chickening out on making a public commitment. I drove to the lecture, cursing all the way, talking to myself in the car: "Barbara, don't let this happen again. Don't be the victim and call him up crying. That's never gotten you anywhere. In this relationship it's going to be different. Don't act desperate!" By the time I arrived at the meeting hall, I had formulated a plan.

After the lecture I drove to the supermarket and bought two items: a whole chicken and a big bag of ice. I went home and prepared my "message." It was a rainy night. I drove through the mist to his house, crept up the walkway to his front door, placed my "gifts" down, knocked loudly, and hid behind a tree. He opened the door and looked up—no one there. Then he looked down. There, on his doorstep, to his amazement, was a chicken and a bucket of ice! Stuck into each one was a little flag. He bent down to read the flag on the chicken: "Someone to keep you company," and on the ice: "Something to put your feet into." He looked puzzled, then he started to laugh. He had received my message: "You are a chicken. I hate you for getting cold feet!"

I sauntered out of the bushes with a big smile on my face. He looked at me sheepishly and said, "Boy, you really busted me," and apologized for being such a chicken that night. He proceeded to tell me how afraid he was of opening up and getting hurt in love again.

I felt great! I had expressed my displeasure and anger and I had showed him—and more important, showed myself—that I had spirit. Now he tells this story proudly all the time to people he meets as a way of bragging about me! So don't be afraid to play a little more, ladies!

Secret Five: Men like to experience the feminine side of women.

MISTAKE: Women cut themselves off from their femininity because it has limited them so much in the past.

This is a very delicate issue. There is a lot about my feminine conditioning that I have found to be useless or even harmful, and have discarded over the years. And there is a lot about my feminine conditioning that I retain because it allows me to express my gender in a way that I enjoy. I enjoy running my own company and being independent, and I also enjoy letting myself fall apart and feel helpless sometimes, allowing my partner to take care of me and give me advice and comfort. I enjoy running around in jeans, sneakers, and a sweatshirt, and I enjoy getting dressed up to go dancing in a sexy silk dress and high heels. I enjoy wearing no makeup and I enjoy wearing makeup. Basically, I want to have it all, and to me, that's the essence of the liberated woman: Without discarding her femininity, she gives herself permission to express "male" qualities of power and aggression.

Men love the contrast and complexity of a woman

who can be powerful, assertive, and independent, and still be "feminine" when she wants to be. Finding a balance is up to you. But if you haven't worn a dress in months, don't pay much attention to your appearance, feel very asexual, and wonder why you and your husband don't have a great sex life, you may want to explore yourself and find the feminine you again, so that all of you can be loved.

Secret Six: Men love competence.

MISTAKE: Women hide their accomplishments from men and from themselves.

As I sit and listen to men tell me what they want in women, what they find in their mistresses and secret flings, and what they don't find in their spouses, I hear one theme over and over:

Men get turned on by competence.

Perhaps this is because men are trained to be competent themselves, and recognizing it in someone else makes them feel attracted to that person. It isn't even a physical attraction. It is an energy attraction. She could be a jogger you pass as you drive, an investment broker you both go to see, or a singer in a band at a nightclub.

The problem is that *so many women are professionals at putting themselves down*. Women have been conditioned to make the man feel like he is smarter, better, and more successful than women, and so they sacrifice their own self-esteem to keep this outdated myth alive.

Start being proud of yourselves, ladies! Bring out that old piece of sculpture and show your man what a terrific artist you are. Sit down at your children's piano and show him what beautiful music you can make. *Find out what you do well, and do it!* He'll appreciate you more, and so will you!

▶ Premature Ejaculation and Impotence in Men

At some time in every man's life, he experiences difficulties with premature or "early" ejaculation (I call it early because it occurs earlier than he would like) or with impotence: having a difficult time getting or staying erect. There are wonderful books that discuss techniques for alleviating these problems, and many sex researchers who specialize in understanding early ejaculation and impotence in men.

In my work with male clients, I've found some causes for these problems not commonly talked about or known, and I would like to offer some new ways of understanding and dealing with these sexual difficulties.

Premature or Early Ejaculation

Early ejaculation occurs because there is a buildup of sexual tension in the body that demands release earlier than the male would like it to be released.

Early ejaculation occurs when a man is too tense physically, mentally, or emotionally.

The solution is to eliminate the source of tension. The popular "squeeze technique" will stop impending ejaculation at times, but this is like putting a bandage on a gash without knowing what caused the bleeding in the first place.

Here is a brief list of what I have found commonly causes tension in men during sex. If you want to avoid early ejaculation, learn to avoid these situations, habits, or ways of behaving:

Trying to Build Up Too Much Pleasure Too Soon in the Body

I call this being *sexually greedy.* Your body will go on overload and release the energy too quickly. Practice the techniques in the previous chapter, and you will last much longer.

Tensing the Body

As most women will tell you, most men tense their bodies, especially their buttocks, during intercourse. This forces more energy into the genitals, causing more pleasure, but also more tension. Relax your rears, guys! You will actually learn to enjoy the pleasure more and there will be more of it.

Withholding Your Emotions From Your Partner

Holding back causes tension. Ever try to hold back a laugh, or hold back tears? *It hurts to hold back.* The same goes for holding back feelings. It creates an Emotional Tension that expresses itself as tension in the body. If you are making love with a woman and holding back feelings of anger, guilt, or disgust, or aren't telling her the truth about something important, you will have more of a tendency to ejaculate more quickly (unless you are so shut down to her that you can't get an erection in the first place).

Practice what you've learned in this book and tell the Complete Truth *before* getting into bed.

Not Wanting to Make Love With a Partner

If you don't really care for someone you are making love with, your body may behave as you would if you walked into a party and didn't want to be there—you'd get out of there in a hurry. Sometimes that's the message your mind gives your penis if you are making love under less than desirable circumstances: "Get out of there in a hurry."

Don't expect to be a great lover with someone you don't really care for. And be careful—making a habit of having sex when you don't care can condition you to being unable to feel caring even when you want to. Your penis may be in such a habit of making quick departures from undesirable partners that it could take awhile to restrain yourself when you are with the woman you really love.

Your Partner Wants to Get It Over and Get You Out

When you are having sex with someone who for one reason or another wants it to be over, you may find it difficult to control your ejaculation. You will feel *her tension*, and your body will get the message. If you are very close to your lover and you want to last longer, talk with her to make sure she doesn't have any buried resentments or fears about intercourse that are making her communicate tension to you.

Dietary Causes

In my work with men I have found that those who eat less animal protein often have more sexual endurance and energy than those who eat large amounts of such protein. This is not a scientific fact, just my observation. Perhaps it's the effect of the hormones injected into most commercial meats. At any rate, you might want to experiment with putting more grains, vegetables, and fish in your diet. It will be better for your heart, too!

Impotence

Impotence is the opposite of premature ejaculation—there is not enough energy in the body to create an erection which sustains itself. Impotence can be brought on by some of the same factors that cause premature ejaculation: withholding your emotions from your partner; not wanting to make love; fear;

anger; resistance to getting close. Practicing all you have learned in this book will help you alleviate the emotional blocks that may cause impotence.

I have found two other common causes for impotence in the men I've worked with:

Alcohol

Alcohol diminishes the mind-body coordination necessary for us to function normally. If you have any difficulty with impotence, don't drink alcohol before you make love, or even that day. It will dull your sensitivity and make it harder for your sexual organs to function.

Diet

I have worked with many men who were impotent and were eating a very high-fat diet: milk, cheese, ice cream, meats, etc. Working with a nutritionist to reduce the fat in their diet, we found that this often restored normal sexual functioning. High-fat diets tend to make our systems sluggish, clogging our blood with fat—and don't forget, an erection is caused by blood flow to the penis. If our blood is full of fat, circulation becomes impaired (this is what eventually can cause heart attack and stroke). Try cutting down on your fat intake to improve the circulation throughout your body. And get some exercise! Exercise will benefit heart and mind, as well as the rest of your body.

▶ Difficulty in Experiencing Orgasm in Women

This is a problem that is becoming less prevalent, thanks to many wonderful books that have educated women about orgasm and given them permission to talk about it and do something about it. I have a few more ideas for you, ladies, that may help if you have this problem.

What Makes It Difficult for a Woman to Have an Orgasm?

Anger

Anger doesn't allow us to feel pleasure, or to feel much at all. And many women are angry at the men they are making love to, or at the men they used to make love to. When you are angry during sex, you may have difficulty having an orgasm. You might not *feel* angry, but believe me, you probably are. I have seen thousands of women locate deep rage against men that has kept them from feeling joy and passion. Use the techniques discussed in Chapters 8, 9, and 10 to express your feelings to your partner, and make sure you aren't holding in any resentment before you get into bed.

Fear of Being Controlled and/or Going Out of Control

Being in control is the opposite of orgasm, which is a total letting go. If you are afraid to open up and be vulnerable because the man might control you or hurt you, you may be controlling yourself so much that your body can't relax enough to have an orgasm. You may also not trust yourself to let go—some women tell me that if they really let go, they are afraid they'd become nymphomaniacs. Learn to trust yourself—give yourself a chance.

The Power Struggle

If you are in a relationship in which you feel you frequently give your power away to your partner, you may withhold orgasm as one of the only ways you can feel "powerful." You are the one who suffers in the end. You are depriving yourself as well as your partner. Think carefully about your feelings of powerlessness, work with the concepts in this book, and give yourself permission to feel powerful *because* you can let go!

Dietary Causes

The same link between a high-fat diet and male impotence applies to nonorgasmic women. Sexual excitement is caused by blood flow. If your diet is too high in fat, you may be creating a sluggish circulatory system, making it difficult for you to experience sexual arousal and, ultimately, orgasm. Consult your doctor about decreasing your fat intake through a program of gradual dietary change combined with exercise.

To complete our look at common sexual problems and uncommon solutions, I want to mention a few final topics and share my thoughts and experiences with you.

▶ Fantasy and Pornography

If you have been reading this book carefully, you probably already know what I am going to say about fantasy and pornography: They work for creating more sexual excitement, but they do not support you and your partner in really making love *to each other.* How connected can you feel to your wife when you are fantasizing about a centerfold? How in tune with your husband can you be when you imagine he is your tennis instructor? *I believe making love works best when there are just two people involved. Three (or more) is definitely a crowd.*

Many people have come to rely on using fantasy or pornography to become sexually stimulated. This is often because they have spent so much energy numbing themselves emotionally that they cannot really feel unless they have a huge amount of stimulation. In my work with couples I have found innumerable sexual problems and resentments stemming from the use of fantasy and pornography: the girlfriend who can't open up to her boyfriend in bed because she knows he has a stack of erotic magazines in his drawer which he looks at frequently—it makes her feel like she isn't enough for him. Or the man who is impotent with his wife because the only way she can get turned on to him is to imagine that he is a lover she had in college. We use fantasy and pornography to escape from the very emotions we need to deal with in order to make love fully with our partner.

Don't make yourself feel bad or wrong if you've had a habit of using these things . . . just resolve to learn to make love fully to the person you love, and work together to create a trust and surrender that will bring you much more joy than any fantasy ever could.

▶ Masturbation

Masturbation is a normal act of self-discovery that most young people go through as they become sexual beings. It teaches us what we need to learn about our bodies so that we can teach our lovers. However, many people have no idea how powerfully continual masturbation may be affecting their sex lives. Let me explain some of the effects of masturbation you might not be aware of.

Addiction to Self-Stimulation

Most people who masturbate frequently know just how to turn themselves on. *The problem comes when they make love with someone else, and their partner doesn't do as good a job as they can do alone!*

Mary came to me for sex counseling. "When I'm alone and I masturbate," she explained, "I have no trouble coming. But when I am with Paul, it takes me forever, and most of the time, it doesn't happen. I feel awful about it. I love Paul, but I just can't seem to respond to him."

Mary was the victim of what I call masturbation numbness. She had desensitized herself to anyone's touch but her own. Mary's body was waiting for her touch, and when it received Paul's, the sensations didn't register as pleasure. Mary would lie there hoping Paul would do just what she did to herself, believing that that was the only way she could reach orgasm. But Paul could never do it as perfectly as Mary, so she was always let down.

I suggested to Mary that she forget all about orgasms for a while and that she stop masturbating entirely in order to give her body a chance to train itself to Paul's touch. I also told her to concentrate carefully on how she felt when Paul touched or kissed her during sex, and to imagine that Paul was the most skilled lover in the world. They agreed to do their homework.

Two weeks later I received a phone call from an elated Mary. "It worked!" she bubbled. "I stopped masturbating, and after a while I forgot what I used to do exactly, and all of a sudden one night Paul seemed to be doing just what I needed to get aroused. It was fantastic, and much better than any orgasm I had alone."

I have had this kind of result with both men and women who were self-stimulators who had a hard time getting turned on by a partner. If you have such a problem, try this technique and see what happens. I think you will be pleasantly surprised.

▶ Afterthought

When I finished writing this section of my book, I showed it to a close friend, who became very excited reading it. "I love this material," he said. "Have you thought about just publishing this as a book about sex?"

"I could never do that," I explained to him. "I truly believe that without the rest of my book, the sex section would have no meaning. In fact, without the rest of the book, I don't even think people would be able to make the sex section work for them."

"Why?" my friend asked. "The techniques seem powerful—what makes you think they wouldn't work?"

"Because the whole point of my book is that making love has to come first from the heart. When you are open to your lover and have torn down your emotional barriers and walls, then you are already making love. The sex section just gives you some more guidelines to play with. If someone is feeling resentment toward his or her partner and is afraid to open up and trust love, what good is the sex section? It becomes a series of instructions, and sex becomes even more mechanical. But really being inspired by the whole book to open up and love, and to keep that magic alive, *that's* the prerequisite for the sex section to have meaning. See what I mean?"

He did. And I hope you do, too. *Making love works best when you are already making love before you get into bed*. The most important sexual technique I can teach you is to be willing to love completely and be loved from the heart. The sex will follow.

16

Becoming the Perfect Lover in and out of Bed

Have you ever had sex with someone who was an expert lover but a failure at making love? He or she did all the right things, was wildly passionate, and everything went well sexually, but you were left feeling empty. That's because the sex was *satisfying*, but not *fulfilling*.

Sex can be truly fulfilling only when it is accompanied by making love—by the sharing of hearts and feelings. Most people are not looking for satisfying sexual experiences—they are looking for sexual fulfillment.

And sexual fulfillment cannot be found by improving sexual performance, but only by improving the emotional connection between two people.

▶ How Do You Rate Yourself As a Lover?

Here's a story about a couple who perfectly illustrates this phenomenon. Jennifer and Howard came to me for sexual counseling. Jennifer seemed to think that she and her fiancé had some serious sexual problems. Howard, on the other hand, thought everything was fine. I asked Jennifer to rate their lovemaking on a scale from 1 to 10, with 10 being the highest score. "Most of the time," she answered, "I'd say it is a two."

"What!" cried Howard, obviously shocked. "A two? I'd say most of the time it is at least an eight!"

Either this couple wasn't making love with each other, I thought, or there was a serious lack of communication.

"All right," I said, "How would you rate the last time you made love?"

"Well, we made love yesterday morning," Jennifer said. "And I'd say it was a three."

"Three!" said Howard. "It was at least a nine!"

"Okay," I said to Jennifer, "tell us why you thought it was a three. Just describe exactly what happened."

"Well," Jennifer began, "I woke up and felt powerful feelings of love for Howard as he lay next to me. I reached out for him and began being affectionate. I felt so happy to be with him. I told him how I felt, but he didn't respond verbally, although he rolled over and started kissing me. As I felt his warm body near mine, I felt lucky to have him in my life. I felt my love for him well up inside me.

"He entered me, and we were moving together, and I realized how much I needed him. I had missed him so much the week before, when he was out of town. I held him tightly, longing to be with him always. Yet, as things got more pleasurable, I felt Howard slipping away from me. It was as though he were going off into his own world. I kept telling him I loved him, but he didn't say anything; he just moaned. After he came, he turned over and lay there for a while. Then he got up and said, 'I guess I'd better go to work now.' That was it. I felt so far away from him, and so alone afterward."

Now it was Howard's turn. He began, "Jennifer woke me up by caressing my back and my thighs. I felt myself getting aroused. I started touching her breasts, and she began stroking my penis and then loving me orally. I felt a strong desire to have intercourse with her. I reached over and noticed she was very wet. I felt really turned on and entered her. I felt engulfed by pleasure. We moved together for a while, and then I climaxed. I rolled over and rested and then, realizing I had to go to work, I got up and took a shower."

As I listened to Jennifer and Howard explain their story, it was obvious to me what the problem was. "Howard, that experience was almost a ten to you, right?"

"Yes," he answered.

"How can you say that!" Jennifer cried. "You weren't even there for me. It was a three!"

"Howard," I said, "when you described what happened during lovemaking, you gave us a strictly sexual description of what happened physically. I want you to describe that lovemaking session again. But this time, express out loud to Jennifer all the *feelings* you were having."

Howard smiled. "That's easy. I woke up and felt Jennifer warm in the bed, curled up next to me. I felt a thrill in my heart, happy to wake up with someone so wonderful. She reached out and started loving me, and I felt grateful to be wanted." (As Jennifer listened to his words, tears started rolling down her face.) Howard continued: "As I started making love with Jennifer, I noticed how beautiful her body was, how soft and tender she was, and I felt lucky to be with her. I felt how turned on she was to me, and that made me feel accepted and safe." (Now Jennifer's eyes were shining with joy.) "As we moved together," Howard went on, "I was feeling closer to her than to anyone ever in my life. I felt a oneness with her."

Jennifer couldn't contain herself any longer. "That's it!" she cried. "That's a ten! That's a ten!" Jennifer and Howard embraced, and we all laughed.

Howard and Jennifer's problem is not uncommon. Howard was feeling all the things that Jennifer was feeling, but he didn't communicate those feelings to her. *Jennifer was left with great sex and no lovemaking.* To her, that was a two or three on a scale. Like many men, Howard was trained to think that if the sexual performance goes well, it is a ten. But Howard felt the experience was a ten because Jennifer was telling him of her love, and he knew he loved her. Jennifer was left out because she had no idea of how Howard was feeling. Once he verbalized what he felt in his heart, Howard and Jennifer felt equally fulfilled.

▶ Are You a Victim of Performance Pressure?

Listen to what these men and women have to say about sexual performance pressure:

> "It all started with my ex-husband. When we were married, he casually mentioned that maybe I wasn't as sexual as I should be. I panicked. I hadn't had much sexual experience before our marriage. So we bought all the sex books, experimenting with everything you can imagine. He seemed happier for a while, but I just felt worse and worse. It was only after our divorce that I realized that our sex life was awful not due to a lack of sexual knowledge, but to the total lack of communication and trust between us. I really resent how sexually inadequate he made me feel because I couldn't respond to his cold, emotionless lovemaking."

"When I was growing up, I thought that the more sex I had, the longer I lasted, and the wilder I made the woman, the more of a man I was. When I met Janet, I acted like Mr. Superstud. I guess I felt I had to give a great sexual performance to make her happy. One day Janet told me she was really tired of our sex life because it felt like work to her. She was right, of course. I was working at being the world's greatest lover. And I had failed miserably."

"Fred's last girlfriend was very sexual and Fred told me how easily she climaxed. Ever since then, I've felt pressured to have multiple orgasms. It turns into the same thing every time: Fred 'working on me' to have an orgasm. The longer it takes, the harder he tries, and the less relaxed I feel. Now he blames my not having orgasms all the time on the fact that we haven't found my G-spot. Sometimes I wish we were back in high school, and could just make out without necessarily having sex."

How can a simple act of physical loving cause so many problems in people's lives?

▶ What Makes Sex Fulfilling for You?

The sexual act is so powerful because it is the closest we ever come to uniting with another being. If that physical union isn't balanced and matched by emotional closeness, the same act that can be so full of joy becomes one that leaves a couple feeling isolated, lonely, and unfulfilled.

So what is it that truly makes sex fulfilling for you? Here is an exercise to help you answer that question. You may want to read through the exercise, and then go through it again with your eyes closed:

Relax, take a few deep breaths, and recall a time in your life when making love gave you a deep sense of fulfillment. Remember whom you were with; what was happening; how you were feeling. Perhaps it was just for a moment, or for one special night, or for a whole relationship. Perhaps you felt as though you were really being loved and as though nothing else in the world mattered except the two of you. Perhaps you felt very safe and protected.

Now complete the following statement and let the answer surface automatically, without thinking much about it: *"The reason I felt so fulfilled was . . ."*

Take a deep breath, and let that memory fade away. Recall another time in your life when making love was completely fulfilling. Re-create that time in your mind, remembering all the details and how you felt, and complete this statement: *The reason I felt so fulfilled was . . ."*

Now take another deep breath, and let those memories fade away. Recall a time in your life when making love was *not* fulfilling. Re-create that time in your mind. Remember whom you were with, what was happening, how you felt. And stay with that feeling of making love and having it feel unfulfilling. Did you feel the other person wasn't really there for you? Did you feel that love was missing? Let these emotions resurface, and complete this sentence: *"The reason I did not feel fulfilled was . . ."*

Doing that exercise may have brought up a lot of feelings, some happy and some not so pleasant. Most of you will notice that when you recalled a time when making love was fulfilling, the cause of it being so fulfilling may have had nothing to do with sex at all, but more with *the feelings you shared with your partner.*

Here is a list I've compiled of responses to this visualization. See if you can relate to what others have experienced.

SEX IS FULFILLING WHEN:

I know I am the only one.

I know I am special to my partner.

It feels like it doesn't even matter what we do sexually, as long as we are together.

We're being honest with each other.

I don't feel pressured to perform.

We're both participating equally and wanting to be there.

I want to be doing it.

I feel safe.

It's spontaneous and unhurried.

I feel completely loved.

I'm not being compared with someone else.

We feel a spiritual oneness.

We can play and not take it so seriously.

My partner is not trying to change me.

We're in love.

We feel safe to say anything to each other.

I trust the other person.

My partner is expressing to me how he feels.

SEX IS NOT FULFILLING WHEN:

I don't want to be doing it.

I know my partner is lying to me.

I know I am lying to my partner.

I'm tired or I'm rushed.

I feel obligated to do it.

I'm afraid of getting pregnant.

I know my partner doesn't love me.

We have to work at it.

I'm angry at my partner about something.

My partner expects me to perform in a certain way.

I'm comparing my partner with another lover.

It's mechanical.

I know my partner just made love to someone else.

I feel my partner is criticizing me.

One of us loves the other more.

I'm just doing it to get it over with.

I get no verbal response from my partner.

I feel my partner is distant or cares only about his own pleasure.

I don't like the other person.

I know I'm not the only one.

We can't talk about it afterward.

I'm afraid that if I don't do it, he/she will get it somewhere else.

If you read over the first list—the fulfilling list—you will notice that most of the answers describe *emotional* realities, not sexual ones. So here is my secret about what makes sex fulfilling:

▼

SECRET:
   Sex is fulfilling when you are not just having sex but also making love.

▲

Chances are, most of the sexual problems you've had in your relationships didn't have much to do with sex at all. No matter how good the sex is, you will be left feeling empty and unfulfilled unless there is also a clear emotional sharing between you and your partner.

▶ Do You Wait Until You Get in Bed to Start Making Love?

You can't expect your lovemaking to be fulfilling when you rush around all week, going to work and coming home, doing house chores, taking care of the kids or the dog, and then get in bed on Saturday night at ten o'clock and decide that now you are going to make love. You will probably end up just having mechanical sex, getting a headache to avoid the unfulfilling experience of having sex without making love, or perhaps having a few drinks first so that you will be too numb to care what happens.

▼

SECRET:
Don't wait until you're having sex to start making love.

▲

Use every moment in your relationship as an opportunity to make love. Then, when it is time to express your love sexually, it won't be such a shift in awareness from walking around caught up in your own world to merging that world in such an intimate way with your partner. I don't mean that you should be sexual every moment of your life. What I'm talking about is keeping a lively emotional connection with your partner, making sure to express your love and attraction all the time, and not waiting until you want to have sex to do it.

Shelley and her husband, Mike, sat in my office

glaring at each other. They came to me to work out what they called their "sexual incompatibility."

"We hardly ever make love anymore," Mike commented. "Shelley complains that she needs more affection from me, but when I am affectionate, she seems to turn off and reject me. I think she just hates sex."

"It's not true," cried Shelley. "But Mike is never affectionate and loving unless he is in the mood for sex. When he starts kissing my neck or telling me I'm beautiful, I always know what's coming next. He will start pushing his crotch against me and saying, 'Baby, I want you.' If I'm not in the mood to go all the way, he just pushes me away and forgets the whole thing. If he gives me even just a kiss, I immediately tense up and think, 'Oh, no, here it comes. How long will it be before he ruins it all by wanting to have intercourse?' "

Shelley and Mike's problem is, sadly, quite common. Women frequently complain that they would actually want to have *more* sex in their relationship if their partner would be more affectionate and loving when they *aren't* having sex. Yet most men are taught that if they start being affectionate with their partner and get turned on, they should go all the way and have intercourse.

I call this dilemma the *All-or-Nothing Pattern:* If you don't intend or have time to go all the way, then don't even start anything.

Be on the lookout for the All-or-Nothing Pattern in your life, because the effect it will have on your sex life will eventually be more in the direction of the nothing than the all! Here are two practical suggestions for combating the All-or-Nothing Pattern:

Planned Intimacy

If you made a list of what you wanted to accomplish on a typical day this week, it might look like this:

Pay last month's bills
Finish project at work
Buy Jill new tennis shoes for gym class
Make dinner for family tonight
Drop clothes at cleaners after work
Schedule baby-sitter for next weekend

If you were in a relationship with a partner, you would have left one of the most important things in your life off the list: putting aside the time for sharing intimacy with the one you love. Think about it: You probably spend time with the person(s) you care about most *after* you have taken care of everything else. Unfortunately for most people, that time doesn't come often enough. *The relationship gets put at the bottom of the priority list, if it makes the list at all!*

There have been times when I was so busy teaching, writing, and taking care of my house, and my partner was so busy with his work, that we often forgot to save time for each other. By the end of the day, we would be so exhausted that we would fall into bed and barely have the energy to kiss each other good night. Finally, I realized that if I waited until I had finished everything else I had to do in my life before I spent time with the people I loved, I would wait forever! There was an endless list of projects to work on and people to help. Once I finished one project, there would always be another project to replace it. It was then that I created Planned Intimacy, or "PI."

What to Do During Planned Intimacy

Planned Intimacy is a time that you and your partner schedule into your lives for sharing intimacy together. You schedule it just as you would a doctor's appointment or a business meeting. In the case of Planned Intimacy, *the time should be at least half an hour together, away from all distractions three times per week. That means no phone calls and no other interruptions.*

Planned Intimacy is *not* planned sex. It is intimacy on the emotional level, and it *may or may not* express itself physically. At times, you may feel so close during PI that you choose to express that closeness through having sex. But it is important *not* to schedule PI with your partner and secretly be thinking that it will guarantee having sex three times a week.

During PI time, you may just lie in bed and cuddle with your partner, give each other a massage, or talk about things you need to share (preferably your feelings, and not which bills you should pay first). You may want to listen to music together (I don't suggest watching TV), or take a walk, or just sit on the couch and do some old-fashioned necking.

If you are thinking that planning to be intimate on a schedule sounds contrived, you probably have been avoiding intimacy with your partner, and the idea of it brings up a lot of resistance and even unconscious fear. Remember when you first met and dated someone you loved? Planning an hour together was something you looked forward to, and it certainly didn't feel contrived just because it was carefully planned. If you feel you are too busy or don't have the time for PI, you may as well forget about your relationship remaining passionate and exciting for any length of time.

The best thing about PI is that it builds a strong flow of intimacy between you and your partner, so that when you do decide to have sex, you are more than ready to enjoy it to the fullest—because you have been making love all week!

SECRET:
The more time you spend making love in your relationship, the better your sex life will be.

Here is another important thing to remember about Planned Intimacy: *If you and your partner aren't feeling especially connected, and have some unexpressed feelings of resentment, anger, or hurt between you, you probably will start fighting when you get together for Planned Intimacy.* If that happens, don't panic! It's wonderful that the tension is now out in the open.

The Twenty-Second Kiss

When is the last time you kissed a partner for at least twenty seconds when you *didn't* plan to have serious sex as a result? I asked this question on a television talk show recently, and received dozens of calls from women complaining that they hadn't been kissed in weeks, months, and even years, except for those times when their husbands wanted to have sex. Most people save those romantic kisses for when they are in the bedroom. If you are in the habit of doing this, you are missing out on many wonderful moments of intimacy and excitement throughout the day.

I suggest that if you are in a relationship, *you and your partner practice giving each other three twenty-second kisses a day.* Why twenty seconds? I've found that if you kiss your partner for twenty seconds, that is long enough to get some feeling of physical attraction and "juice" flowing between you. When you stop at the end of twenty seconds, you will feel very loving toward each other. Go about your day as usual. You will be happy to find that you are thinking more about your partner during the day, feeling more attracted to him/her and looking forward to that next twenty-second kiss!

Most couples don't kiss intensely unless they want to have sex. What they don't realize is that having lots of those twenty-second kisses throughout the week is what will make them want to make love in the first place!

My partner and I have an agreement that either one of us can ask for a twenty-second kiss whenever we want it. If my partner asks me for a twenty-second kiss, and I feel that I don't want to, this is a sign that there is some block in the flow of love between us, and that we need to talk about some unexpressed feelings. So the twenty-second kiss is not only fun; it is also a great barometer for measuring the amount of tension or love present in the relationship. Once you become aware of tension, you can handle it using the techniques in Part Two of this book.

▶ Why the Honeymoon Doesn't Have to End

One of my favorite couples is Jeremy and Karen, who travel all over the United States teaching business seminars together. At least once a week, when they are standing in an elevator or waiting for a table in a restaurant, someone will come up to them and say, "I'll bet you two are on your honeymoon." Their answer is, "You're right—we have been for ten years!"

People assume that this couple is on their honeymoon because Jeremy and Karen look like they are in love.

Jeremy and Karen look like they're so much in love because they use every moment of their relationship to make love, and they treat every day like a honeymoon! A honeymoon is wonderful because the couple focuses on giving and receiving love. Why should that have to end when you return to your "real" life? Of course you can't focus on love all day. *But if you plan moments to share and express love, in those moments you will be falling in love all over again.*

I know many couples who take frequent vacations and need to "get away" in order to enjoy one another. They often don't have much sex when they're at home;

they are waiting until they are on holiday in order to be intimate. The problem is that when they are at home in their ordinary lives, they neglect the relationship. This explains why so many couples fight while on vacation—they don't relate to one another until they go away. Then all the stored-up resentment explodes, ruining their eagerly awaited trip.

▶ Don't Wait Until You're in Love to Start Loving

If you are presently single, everything that applies to being the perfect lover in a couple relationship applies to you as a single person as well, with some minor adjustments. You can be a perfect lover without even being in love with someone . . . just by learning how to make love all the time in your life. In fact, one of the biggest mistakes most people make is waiting to start expressing love until they actually fall in love.

Tina was a classic example of this syndrome. She was a very attractive, outgoing, bright woman who had not been involved in an intimate relationship for several years. Tina couldn't understand what was wrong.

When Tina came to my seminar and listened to me talk about loving, she became increasingly depressed. Finally she stood up to speak. "I haven't had a relationship with a man in two years," she said, "so all this stuff about loving doesn't mean anything to me. I thought I was coming here to create more love in my life."

"Tina," I answered, "your problem is very simple. You decided to drop out of the human race until you fell in love. *You go around looking for love, but you forget about loving.* You are asking others to give you what you are so stingy about giving to them." Everyone in the room looked shocked to hear me saying these tough truths. But the shock soon turned into awe as Tina began to cry and said, "You're right, Dr. De Angelis. I am unloving. I never think of anyone but myself and of who will love me next."

Tina was postponing love until she was being loved by someone else first. She had an image of herself as a loving, sensitive woman, but actually she was "saving herself for the one she loved." Tina had a fantasy that when she found her man, all the love she had saved for so long would come pouring out of her heart. Unfortunately, love doesn't work that way. Suppose you wanted to compete in the Olympics. You would not save your strength for four years, and then, after four years of no practice, show up at the Olympics expecting to win! By not exercising her ability to love, Tina was actually pushing people away from her. The less loving you are, as a person, the less people will be attracted to you. The more loving you are, the more people you will attract.

Of course, Tina wasn't sure that she was being unloving. It manifested itself in very subtle ways. For instance, she would walk into a party all dressed up, hoping to meet Mr. Right. She would take a quick look around the room, perhaps talk to one or two men, and then, when she was certain Mr. Right wasn't there, she would either leave or commiserate with a girlfriend for the rest of the evening. Tina invalidated the party as an opportunity to enjoy herself or to express any love simply because it wasn't the ideal situation.

In another instance, Tina went hiking with several women friends. The other women were feeling very close, very alive, and full of love for nature, for each other, and for themselves. But Tina spent the hike thinking how much better it would be if she were there with Mr. Right. She noticed other couples hiking and felt envious of them, deciding that what she was doing, according to her, was second best.

▶ Are You Postponing a Full Life Because You're Single?

Do you rate your life as second best because you don't have a partner? Do you postpone loving until you fall in love? If so, you are probably pushing the love you so desperately want out of your life. *Using every day of your life as an opportunity to love develops your confidence as a loving person*. When others see you, they will perceive you as being loving, and will feel safe loving you.

Tina took my advice—that very weekend, in fact—and started sharing herself with people again. She made lunch dates with four or five people and phoned several others to give them encouragement and support in their lives. She started making a lot of love in her life. I wasn't surprised when, a few months later, Tina called to tell me the good news: She had met a wonderful man and fallen in love. This man adored Tina and constantly told her that what attracted him to her in the first place was the feeling he got that she was a very loving, giving person! *Being a perfect lover in her life attracted the perfect lover to her.*

Are You Putting Life on Hold Because You're Not in Love?

See if any of these statements apply to you:
You tell yourself that you will lose those extra pounds when you meet your next partner.
You save your most wonderful clothes for those special occasions you look forward to having when you fall in love.
You put off taking vacations to beautiful places until you can go with your ideal mate.

You don't go to the theater or expensive restaurants because it seems stupid to go with "just friends," and not with a lover.

You spend holidays alone, because you don't have a partner, and it seems sad to be with other single friends, rubbing in the fact that you are all uninvolved.

You turn down invitations to social events because you don't have a "special" date to go with.

You sleep in flannel nightgowns and old T-shirts, telling yourself you will buy some pretty nightgowns and underwear when someone is there to appreciate them.

Your house or apartment is a mess, and you figure you won't waste the time to fix it up or clean it until you meet someone special to bring home.

If even one of these statements applied to you, you probably are postponing loving in your life until Prince or Princess Charming comes along. Don't wait! Use every opportunity you can to gain confidence in your ability to give and receive love with others.

If you would like to attract a new mate, here's my tip for you:

▼

SECRET:
Become the person you have always wanted to meet!

▲

Master the qualities you want most in a partner, and you will attract him or her just like a magnet. Remember, like attracts like, and love attracts more love. If you want to attract a giving person, start giving yourself. If you seek a partner who is sensitive and caring, express more of your sensitivity and caring to others.

▶ Being Beautiful From the Inside Out

I'll never forget a seminar I conducted several years ago, because it was there that I learned about what we call "being beautiful from the inside out." Two people stood out in that seminar. One was a woman I'll call Sandra. Sandra was a model. She had a perfect body, an exquisite face, and a sexy, expensive wardrobe. She was the kind of woman at whom you found yourself staring for minutes on end, just because she was so wonderful to look at.

The other very notable person in that seminar was Helen. Helen was about forty-five years old, slightly pudgy, with some gray in her hair. She was plain-looking by anyone's standards.

As the seminar progressed, and more people began to reveal their feelings, something very interesting began to happen. Sandra started to look different—or at least it appeared that way. Her perfect features seemed tight and almost distorted at times. It actually became difficult to look at her without feeling uncomfortable. It turned out that Sandra wasn't very good at loving other people, although she seemed to be well accustomed to having other people love and admire her. Several people who did communication exercises with her said that they felt they couldn't really get through to her. When someone would stand up and express some feelings, most people in the room would be attentive— many crying along with the person—except for Sandra, who looked bored or detached.

Helen, on the other hand, was 200 percent there for those she came into contact with, holding their hands, looking into their eyes, laughing with them and crying with them. If she noticed someone needing attention, she'd go up and give him or her a hug. When she shared her own feelings, she fearlessly let the whole room hear her deepest thoughts and fears. And as time passed, Helen began to look beautiful, even radiant. Her eyes sparkled; her skin glowed. Everyone wanted to sit near her and be near her. Just looking at her was a joy, because when you looked at Helen, you were looking right at her heart. You were looking at love.

Looking at Sandra, on the other hand, was like looking at those walls we put around our hearts. Her beauty on the outside faded as everyone saw that she was unwilling to share her beauty on the inside, whereas Helen's inner beauty started to shine so brightly that it made us see her as beautiful on the outside as well.

By the end of the seminar, Helen had several men interested in her romantically. Sandra had none.

Finally, I had an idea I hoped would help Sandra make the breakthrough I knew she needed. I paired her with Helen in an exercise having to do with expressing our fears of not being lovable. In Helen's safe presence, Sandra finally let down her defenses, and the emotional floodgates burst open. As she sat there sobbing in Helen's arms, Sandra admitted she had always felt unattractive and unlovable as a child. Somewhere along the line she had decided to be beautiful from the outside, but she was afraid to show people the "real" Sandra on the inside, assuming she'd be rejected again.

I was so proud of Sandra when she stood up and, holding Helen's hand, told all of us how tired she was of being liked for how she looked, and how much she wanted to be beautiful from the inside out. Sandra's eyes were swollen from crying, her nose was bright red, her hair was wet with tears, but she never looked more beautiful to us. She had learned how to be beautiful in the truest sense. She had learned how to share her heart.

SECRET:
The way to become the perfect lover is to be beautiful from the inside out.

And the most beautiful thing you have to offer anyone is your love.

Look at every day as an opportunity to share love with yourself and others.

IF YOU ARE SINGLE:

Don't wait until you fall in love to be loving.
   Walk out of the house in love, and others will fall in
      love with you!

IF YOU ARE IN A RELATIONSHIP:

Don't wait until Saturday night or until you and
   your partner go on vacation to be loving.
Make every day count by making love all the time,
   and you can be sure you will stay in love with
   each other.

▼▼▼▼▼▼▼▼▼▼▼▼▼▼▼▼▼▼▼▼▼▼▼▼▼▼▼▼

PART FOUR

What to Do When Love Is in Trouble

▲▲▲▲▲▲▲▲▲▲▲▲▲▲▲▲▲▲▲▲▲▲▲▲▲▲▲▲

17

How to Tell If You Are With the Right Person

Sometimes, no matter how hard you try to make love work, it just doesn't. The walls keep going up, the same arguments erupt over and over again, the silence between you gets emptier, and the feeling of being in love turns into being in pain. Even then, many of us stubbornly cling to our partners, numbing ourselves to the anger, the hurt, and the disappointment, and choosing to ignore the fact that we are in a dead or dying relationship. We are afraid of admitting failure. We are afraid of the confrontation that accompanies breaking up. And most of all, we are afraid of being alone.

The truth is that most of us know as little about what to do when love *isn't* working as we do about how to make it work. Often, we avoid ending a relationship because we aren't sure how to go about it. We let the relationship drag on and on, hoping for a miracle, wishing that one day we would wake up and everything would be wonderful again. Sadly, for most of us, that day never comes.

I believe you should do everything possible to save your relationship or marriage and to keep your family together. *But there are times when staying together is not the right thing to do, because it wouldn't be loving to yourself, your partner, or your children.* In this and the next two chapters I hope to help you gain clarity about the condition of your relationship, and, if you are ending a relationship, support you in making that transition as painlessly as possible.

▶ Are You With the "Right" Person?

Relationships between two people are very complicated. As you have seen in this book, when your relationship is in trouble, you probably are under the influence of the Four R's, the Seesaw Effect, and some troublesome Sexual Characters. It takes time and effort to unravel the emotional messes we get ourselves into. I hope that I have shown you that it is possible. But before you decide to "save" a relationship, one burning question always pops into your head: "How can I tell if my partner is the right person for me?"

I am asked this question more often than any other by people in my seminars and counseling practice. And there is never a time that it creates more concern than during those moments when you are deciding whether or not to end a relationship.

If you have ever ended an intimate relationship, you know that you may have a lot of conflict in one area of the relationship and a lot of happiness in another. For instance, Perry is wondering whether he should stop dating Judy. On the one hand, Perry and Judy have a great sex life and a lot of fun together. On the other hand, Judy is very insecure and dependent on Perry and can't seem to take care of herself. Perry is torn—part of the relationship is wonderful and part of it is terrible. And he keeps asking himself that tor-turous question: "How can I tell if Judy is the right person for me?"

Monica and Phillip are an example of a couple in a different situation but plagued by the same question. They have been married for seven years and have two children. Both Monica and Phillip feel that they are different people from who they were when they met and married. Their relationship isn't bad, but it isn't great either. They are "comfortable" together. They love one another, but they aren't *in love*. And each time they discuss getting a divorce, they both become over-whelmed by the same fear: "How do we know we are doing the right thing?"

▶ Why Your Relationship May Not Be Working

Relationships don't work for two reasons:

1. You are with the *right person*, but you don't know how to make love work.
2. You are with the *wrong person*.

If you fall into category 1, you can use the tools in this book for making love work, and you should be well on your way to creating an exciting and fulfilling rela-tionship. But if you fall into category 2, no amount of work on your relationship will be effective. Problems will always arise because of the inherent incom-patibility between you and your partner.

How to Tell If Someone Is Right for You

There are three elements that form the foundation of a successful relationship:

1. You and your partner give each other the love you both need.

2. You and your partner are compatible.
3. You and your partner are willing to grow together in the same direction at approximately
   the same speed.

If your partner demonstrates all three of these
qualities, he or she is probably the "right" person for
you. You may still have problems in your relationship,
but they come from not knowing how to make love
work rather than from basic incompatibility.

Who is the "wrong" person for you?

1. He won't give you the love you want and need.
2. He won't be compatible with you.
3. He won't be willing to grow with you in the
   same direction at approximately the same
   speed.

▶ To Break Up or Not to Break Up?

Breakup Reason One: You aren't getting the love you need.

Feeling loved is what relationships are all about.
You can live happily by yourself; you can travel by
yourself; you can enjoy the gifts of life by yourself; but
you can't create the same kind of fulfillment you get
when someone other than yourself is loving you.
Knowing you are seen as special and knowing you are
loved and needed validates your purpose in being alive.
It makes you feel that your presence on this earth
makes a big difference in someone's life.

It hurts deeply to be in a relationship with someone who is "supposed" to love and appreciate you, but
who does not feel it or show it as much as you need him
to. Your partner could have the other two qualities
needed for a successful relationship—he could be compatible with your personality and could be growing in

the same direction as you are—but when you aren't getting the love you need, your heart will be left feeling hungry and unsatisfied.

No matter how much you care for your partner or how much you believe in fidelity, you may find it very difficult to turn down the opportunity to be loved by another person if you aren't getting enough love in your relationship.

▶ Why You May Not Be Getting the Love You Need

Let's sum up some of the reasons we've discussed in this book that may be responsible for your not being loved as you want to be.

1. Your partner is emotionally numb or shut down and can't love *anyone* as much as you need to be loved.
2. Your partner is emotionally numb or shut down *to you* due to suppressed feelings, resentment, and emotional wear and tear.
3. You are not what your partner wants in a mate. There is a lack of true compatibility; therefore, he cannot love you enough because he doesn't like you enough.
4. You may be an expert at pushing your partner's love away.
5. Your partner may not know how to show his love.

You can heal a relationship that isn't working when you are affected by *Breakup Reason One: not getting the love you need*. Your chances for success depend on which of the five reasons listed above is responsible for the lack of love in your relationship.

When the lack of love you feel is due to reason 1 (your partner is emotionally numb or shut down and can't love *anyone* as much as you need to be loved) or reason 3 (you are not what your partner wants in a mate; therefore, he cannot love you enough because he doesn't like you enough), then I feel it will be very difficult for you to get the love you need. You are in the wrong relationship—it's time to move on and find someone more suitable for you.

Joanie and Ed: A Relationship That Was Saved

Joanie and Ed were certain that their relationship was over, and they asked me to help them divorce amicably. As I listened to them talk, however, I had the feeling that these two people still loved each other very much.

"Joanie," I asked, "can you sum up in one sentence why you want a divorce from Ed?"

Joanie began to cry. "I just don't feel loved," she said. "He says he cares for me, but I don't feel it."

"What about you?" I asked Ed, who sat there staring at the floor.

"Joanie is right," Ed said softly. "I can't love her the way she wants to be loved."

"Ed, would you *like* to love Joanie the way she asks to be loved?"

"Well, sure," Ed answered, "but I'm just not that kind of guy."

Ed and Joanie were a perfect example of reason 5: Ed didn't know how to show his love. He wanted to, but couldn't.

Joanie and Ed agreed to come to see me for counseling, attend my seminar, and do a lot of talking for one month before making any decisions about divorce.

Joanie and Ed were very fortunate. Their relationship improved tremendously! Ed was learning to show his love, and Joanie felt more loved than she had during their entire seven years of marriage. They still had a long way to go, but their relationship was going to work.

Ed and Joanie salvaged their marriage because they had two out of the three criteria for a successful relationship: They were compatible and they both wanted to move in the same direction at the same speed. Once Ed had learned how to open up emotionally to Joanie, they fulfilled the third criterion: Joanie felt loved as much as she needed to be.

Tracey and Herb: A Relationship That Couldn't Be Saved

Tracey and Herb are an example of a couple in which Breakup Reason One, not getting enough love, was a factor which couldn't be overcome. Herb wanted desperately to save his relationship with Tracey, his girlfriend of three years. Tracey, however, wasn't in love with Herb as deeply as she wanted to be. "I have always cared a lot for Herb," she said, "but I've never been *sure* about him. I hoped that by living together, I would feel closer to him, but in the last six months I've realized that we are different people. I would be happy if I could love him totally, because he is sweet, and he loves me so much, but I can't make myself feel what isn't there."

Tracey and Herb were in the wrong relationship. Herb was settling for less than he deserved, and Tracey hadn't been honest with herself about what kind of man she really wanted. Their relationship served as a learning experience for them both, inspiring them to go on and find a partner who could give them what they needed.

Breakup Reason Two: You and your partner aren't compatible.

Most of us don't fall in love with someone solely because he/she is a good match for our background, life-style, and personality. Yet in my research with couples, *I've found that most partners in successful relationships are enough alike in who they are, what they believe, and how they live to get along with each other harmoniously.*

It took me until I was thirty-two years old and had been in several very serious relationships, including marriage, to know what I really wanted in a man and what would make us compatible. Discovering what kind of man I would be happy with was an outgrowth of discovering who I was. *Who you are and what you want in a partner is always changing as you grow and change.*

▼

SECRET:
> *You will have difficulty knowing what you want and need in a partner if you haven't taken the time to get to know yourself.*

▲

▶ Making Your Compatibility List

Whether you are in a relationship, ending one, or looking for one, you should have a Compatibility List to help you stay focused on creating the partner you want in your life. If you are in a relationship that is working well, your Compatibility List can help you locate problem areas as well as remind you of how much you have to appreciate about your partner. If you are deciding whether or not to end a relationship, your Compatibility List can help you understand what is and isn't working between you and your partner. If you are looking for a new relationship, your Compatibility List can remind you of what you want in a partner, and keep you on track as you seek him.

Find some quiet time by yourself and make a list of

all the qualities you would like in a partner. Make sure to include the following:

> Personal interests (hiking, art, raising animals, music)
> Practical information (age, appearance)
> Health practices (exercise, diet choice, use of cigarettes, drugs, alcohol)
> Philosophical and moral attitudes
> Educational background
> Taste in art, entertainment, clothing, etc.
> Social style (outgoing, introverted, wild, family-oriented)
> Spiritual and religious interests
> Love style (likes affection, pragmatic, romantic, not demonstrative)
> Professional and financial goals

Be as specific as you like while making your list. One way to be thorough is to remember *qualities that were missing from past relationships which caused conflict or problems.*

Here are two sample lists:

JANET'S LIST

Personal Interests
Loves to read, learn
Loves classical music, art, and theater
Loves to travel, especially to beaches, and water
Likes riding horses

Practical Information
Tall, good-looking
30–40 years old
Nice eyes
Has healthy relationship with his family
No dark events in past like ex-wife who hates him

MICHAEL'S LIST

Personal Interests
Likes mountains, hiking
Loves to dance
Likes to take long walks
Likes movies, watching TV
Likes pets in the home
Loves to cook

Practical Information
Petite; good figure
Preferably blonde with blue eyes
Doesn't wear much makeup
Pretty smile

Health Practices
Physically fit and healthy
Not interested in drugs,
    alcohol, junk food

**Philosophical and Moral
    Attitudes**
Interested in world affairs
Old-fashioned values
Positive attitude
Ethical, honest

Educational Background
College education
Well read, sophisticated
Interested in seminars,
    personal growth

**Taste in Art, Entertainment,
    Clothing**
Enjoys everything refined
    and classical
Loves to shop for and wear
    nice clothes
Very selective

Social Style
Warm and friendly to others
Well respected
Loves children, home,
    animals
Feels comfortable with
    people
Has friends Janet likes
Knows how to play and
    have fun

**Spiritual and Religious
    Interests**
Introspective
Preferably Jewish
Wants to help those less
    fortunate

Health Practices
Likes eating in all kinds of
    restaurants
Athletic and healthy

**Philosophical and Moral
    Attitudes**
Not overly analytical
Not too picky

Educational Background
Smart but not an intellectual

**Taste in Art, Entertainment,
    Clothing**
Likes country music, jazz
Down-to-earth taste in
    clothes

Social Style
Easygoing, loves parties
Loves children
Likes Mike's family
Popular with others
Can make Mike laugh, good
    sense of humor
Confident in herself

**Spiritual and Religious
    Interests**
Not important

Believes in God,
  metaphysical teachings

Love Style
Expresses feelings easily
Has a healthy attitude
  toward sex and cherishes
  it
Supports Janet in her goals
  and career
Loves special occasions
Romantic, even "mushy"
Wants a committed
  relationship

Love Style
Makes Mike feel important
Warm, affectionate
Loving, giving
Uninhibited in bed
Believes in Mike and his
  dreams

**Professional and Financial
  Goals**
Financially stable and
  conservative
Successful in his career,
  hard worker
Good at planning for
  achieving his goals
Ideally in a field that helps
  others

**Professional and Financial
  Goals**
Not important as long as
  she is happy at her job

You can see that although there are some similarities in Janet's and Michael's lists, there are too
many differences that would come between them if
they were ever to form a relationship.

Does this mean that Janet shouldn't be with anyone who doesn't have every quality on her list? Of
course not! No one is Mr. or Ms. Perfect. The important thing is to notice the *trend* in your compatibility
list. Janet leans toward a sophisticated, intellectual,
and introspective man, while Michael is looking for a
more down-to-earth, fun-loving woman. So if Janet
meets a man who is loving, warm, interested in growth,
but not very sophisticated, intellectual, or ambitious,
she will probably end up dissatisfied in the rela-

tionship. In the same way, if Michael meets a woman who is fun-loving, athletic, and warm, but highly educated, ambitious for her own career, and interested in philosophy, he will probably end up feeling pressured by her to "change" and be more like her.

We get into trouble when we meet someone and try to fit him into our "picture," rather than accepting him as he is and, if we aren't happy, moving on.

▼

SECRET:
   Don't make the mistake of falling in love with someone's potential.

▲

A relationship is not designed to be a rehabilitation center. If you find yourself falling in love with someone in order to "change" him and turn him into the person *you* think he should be, stop! You aren't being a lover, you are being a repair person. All of us are always changing. The key is: *Your partner should have the desire to become many of the things on your list and should already be moving in that direction.*

Never change in order to please someone else rather than yourself. And never ask a partner to change for you if it is against his nature.

▶ How to Tell If You and Your Partner Are Compatible

Determining whether you and your partner are compatible is essential to the success of your relationship. For this reason, I've written an entire book dealing with the subject in depth, *Are You The One For Me?* It contains all the information you need to really understand compatibility.

The following is a simple compatibility test that will give you a general idea of the degree of compatibility you have with your mate. It won't be as accurate as the Compatibility Formula in *Are You The One For Me?*, so if you really aren't sure whether you and your partner should be together, *read that book before you make any final decisions!*

STEP ONE: Take out your Compatibility List. For each quality your partner expresses *most of the time* give him a yes. As an example, let's look at an abbreviated version of Janet's list as she evaluates her boyfriend, Michael:

Successful in his career	Yes
Warm and friendly to others	Yes
Respected by people	No
Financially stable	No
Loves to read and learn	No
Loves classical music, art	No
Healthy and physically fit	No
Old-fashioned values	Yes
Wants a committed relationship	Yes
Has a healthy relationship with his family	No
Likes horses and camping	Yes
Sophisticated	No
Introspective	No
Romantic and "mushy"	Yes
Tall and good-looking	Yes

STEP TWO: Count the number of *yes*es on your list. Then count the number of qualities on your list. Determine what percentage of *yes*es your partner received. For instance: Your list has 40 qualities, and your partner received 33 *yes*es, or about 80 percent. Janet's list has fourteen qualities. Michael received 7 *yes*es, or 50 percent.

STEP THREE: This is the moment of truth. *I have found that the percentage you come up with is an accurate reflection of the percentage of fulfillment you are experiencing in your relationship.* According to this measurement, Janet is having a 50 percent relationship with Michael. Granted, the 50 percent she has that is working is wonderful. But 50 percent of Janet's interests and qualities aren't being reflected back to her in Michael. This makes it difficult to experience harmony in the relationship.

For example, whenever Janet and Michael go out with friends, Janet notices herself criticizing Michael silently for not being sophisticated enough and for not having much to contribute. Janet and Michael could argue forever about this without making any progress. Michael is just not intellectually inclined, especially compared with Janet. Janet will never be satisfied with Michael's level of sophistication or his background. Their differences lie in an area that is too important to Janet for her to overlook.

Neither Michael nor Janet needs to compromise, and neither is right or wrong. They just aren't compatible enough to spend a lifetime together and fulfill each other's needs.

One way Janet could handle her lack of compatibility with Michael would be to *overlook* it by constantly reminding herself of how much she and Michael have in common in other areas—they have a lot of sexual chemistry; they are both romantic; they love horses and camping (which they spend most of their free time doing). Then she could fall into the "Rehabilitate Your Partner Trap." In this case, Janet would end up going through the Four R's repressing her dissatisfaction with Michael's inability to change. Michael would feel very resentful and not appreciated for who he was, always feeling pressured by Janet to fit into her "picture."

Janet and Michael's relationship could work only under two circumstances:

1. *If Michael truly wanted to grow and develop the same qualities Janet wanted to see in him.* None of us begin a relationship as a finished product. Part of being in love is supporting your partner to grow in the

ways he or she wants to grow. It could be that Michael has always longed to be more educated, more introspective, and Janet may be just what he needs to develop these qualities. Of course, this works best if Michael is also helping Janet to develop some of the characteristics she has always wanted to strengthen— her sense of humor, her flexibility, for example.

2. *If the qualities that Michael doesn't fulfill for Janet are not as important as the qualities he does express.* Let's say you make a Compatibility List and test your present partner, and you come up with a 60 percent compatibile verdict. Before you panic, take a close look at the missing 40 percent. In some cases, the qualities on the 40 percent list could be minor enough to not make much of a difference in your ultimate compatibility. For instance, Stuart makes a Compatibility List and rates his girlfriend Shari. Shari comes out with a score of 60 percent. Stuart notices that the majority of the qualities Shari is "missing" have to to with physical fitness, outdoor activities, and health. These are all important parts of Stuart's life. If Stuart and Shari's relationship is strong enough in other areas, however, they may be able to have a very fulfilling relationship, and Stuart may learn to enjoy pursuing these activities by himself or with friends. However, if a very large part of Stuart's life is devoted to fitness and health, Stuart and Shari may be incompatible. The only way for them to find out is to communicate and tell the truth to themselves about how they feel and what they want.

▶ Tips for Meeting Your Ideal Mate

Are you single and looking for a partner? If so, here's a suggestion for you: Carry your Compatibility List in your wallet so that it goes everywhere you go. Read it often. Share it with your friends. Add qualities when you think of them. I like to think that *the list acts*

*like a magnet, attracting that special person into your
life.* How does it do this?

1. Your list will *help you avoid "dead-end"* relationships by reminding you of what you really
   want.
2. Your list will help you become as wonderful a
   person as the one you seek by reminding you of
   the qualities you admire.

▼

SECRET:
   *You will look for those qualities in a partner that you
   want to develop in yourself.*

▲

If you don't believe me, read your list again. You will
probably find that it describes not only your ideal
partner but your ideal picture of *you!* So you can use
your list as a reminder of the qualities you want to
work on developing.

One comment about how to meet the ideal mate:

>>>*Become the kind of person you want to attract in
your life.*

Don't expect someone to want to be with you if you
aren't living the same qualities you expect him or her to
have!

Once you do meet someone who you think might
be "right" for you, you can get a good idea of what
kind of person he is by talking to him about the things
on your list. For instance, if you want someone who is
very affectionate, romantic, loves to work on helping
relationships to grow, is introspective, and is open to
new ideas, then bring these subjects up when you are
on a date. Ask him his philosophy about love and
relationships; ask him what went wrong in his past
relationships; ask him what he is looking for. Most
couples don't talk about these things until they already
have gotten involved, and by then the attraction is too

strong and it is too late to be as objective about compatibility as they should be. *They are turned on to one another, but they are not compatible.* Have you ever met someone and known from the beginning that you weren't compatible, but you ignored that little voice inside and went ahead with the relationship, only to have it turn out exactly as you feared it would?

I have counseled thousands of people who have told me they knew from the beginning that they probably weren't compatible with their partner, but they were lonely or desperate or intrigued, and got involved against their better judgment. Weeks, months, or sometimes years later, those same major differences were responsible for breaking the couple up. All that pain could have been avoided if they had been honest with themselves right at the start. So use your list!

Remember however, that you are not looking for perfection—you are looking for someone who already is becoming the person you want to be with, someone who is interested in growing in that direction. Perhaps you meet Steven, and he hasn't been very involved with learning how to talk about feelings before. Does that mean he isn't right for you, if talking about feelings is on your list? Not necessarily. If Steven is interested in learning to talk about his feelings, if he is open to becoming that kind of person, then he rates a "yes" for that quality. He is developing that quality.

The Meeting of Two Compatibility Lists

Amanda had been involved with several men who were definitely not right for her. We worked together to make her Compatibility List, and I instructed Amanda to read it every day, share it with friends, work on becoming that person herself, and carry the list with her in her wallet. Two months passed.

One day I got a phone call from a breathless Amanda. "You'll never believe what happened!" she exclaimed. "I met a wonderful man at a lecture. He invited me out for a snack after the lecture, and we talked for hours. He seemed so right for me, it was hard to believe. Finally, I couldn't stand it anymore. I took the list out of my wallet and read it to him. And guess what! He took out his wallet, and there was *his* Compatibility List! He had heard you talk about it on TV and had made his own. Our lists were very similar."

Even if you don't meet someone who already has a Compatibility List, it's a good idea to ask him to make one and to sit together and talk about both lists. It's a great way to get to know someone.

▶ Incompatibility: To Break Up or Not to Break Up?

If you are in a troubled relationship and have gone over your Compatibility List and found evidence that you and your partner are not very compatible, you have two choices:

1. You can try to change your partner or yourself to fit the other's picture.
2. You can end the relationship, freeing yourself and your partner to find people more suitable for each of you.

In my work with couples, I rarely find a couple who can make their relationship work *without* basic compatibility. They may spend years struggling to stay together, but they never achieve the harmony and peace that a truly compatible relationship should provide.

Remember Janet and Michael? Michael wasn't sophisticated and intellectual enough for Janet, and she wasn't satisfied in the relationship. Once Janet understood what she wanted in a partner and talked to Michael about it, it became clear that love was not the issue over which they were breaking up. Janet loved Michael very much, but she wasn't happy because their lack of compatibility created tremendous tension between them. Michael loved Janet also, but wasn't willing to become the person she wanted him to be. He was happy being Michael, and he didn't want to be an intellectual.

I pointed out to Michael not only that he was not what Janet wanted but that Janet wasn't what *he* wanted, either. He admitted it was true. He wanted and deserved a woman who could accept and love him completely.

▼

SECRET:
If your partner isn't what you want, then you aren't what he/she wants, either.

▲

Compatibility is a two-way street. There is no such thing as Janet being perfect for Michael but Michael not being perfect for Janet. If you end a relationship due to incompatibility, don't let your partner walk away feeling like a victim because you are perfect for him, yet you are leaving him. Sit down with your partner and have him make a list of all the qualities you are missing that he seeks. Support him in recognizing that you are not all that he wants, either.

Each of us deserves to spend our lives with someone who thinks we are the most wonderful person in the world. I believe there is someone out there who is the ideal mate for every one of us.

Freeing your partner to find someone who will truly love and accept him just the way he is is an act of love.

Staying with someone because you don't want to hurt him is not an act of love. It takes tremendous selflessness and honesty to let go of a partner when you know you can't love him the way he deserves to be loved. This is truly loving someone: releasing him to find a mate who will give him the love and acceptance you cannot.

18 | Letting Go With Love

I experienced letting go with love in my own life when I decided to end my marriage. I loved my husband very much, and we were growing in the same direction, but as I "grew up" and came to know myself and what I needed, I realized how incompatible we were. Our love was so strong that it carried our relationship for a while, but as time passed, I became more and more critical of him for just being him. I felt it was time for us to end our marriage, believing strongly that there was someone out there who was compatible with the "new" me, just as there was someone out there who would love my husband just as he was.

The hardest thing I ever had to do in my life was to release my husband and all the love he had for me, to set him free to find the love and acceptance I couldn't give him. I knew he deserved more, and so did I.

Many months of pain and tears and healing passed. I felt tremendous guilt—I felt I had abandoned my husband. Yet I knew deep in my heart that this was the most loving act I could offer him. I loved him enough to know I wasn't giving him enough, and never could, and so I had to let him go. We remained very close, talked often, and I kept telling myself I had done the right thing.

Several months later, I received some wonderful news—my former husband had gone to visit a former girlfriend of his, had fallen in love all over again, and had decided to get married. When I heard this news, I cried tears of joy and relief. I knew the woman he was talking about, and I knew she had loved him very much. As I listened to him on the phone, telling me how perfect she was for him, my heart filled with gratitude to her for loving him in the way I never could. Today they are happily married and have a child, and my former husband thanks me for ending our relationship as I did, because it released him to find the love that was waiting for him.

Breakup Reason Three: You and your partner aren't growing in the same direction at approximately the same speed.

A truly successful relationship has more than love and compatibility as its foundation—it has direction. Having a direction in your relationship allows it to grow, and allows you to grow. It is the difference between just *being* together and *becoming* together. It transforms a relationship into an exciting process of change and discovery.

The kind of direction your relationship takes is up to you and what your interests are:

The direction your relationship takes is an expression of your compatibility.

For instance, you and your partner may be moving in the direction of *creative excellence:* both striving to express your full potential as writers, artists, or musicians. You may be moving in the direction of *social contribution:* both desiring to improve society with your talents, your time, and your career choice. You may be moving in the direction of *spiritual fulfillment:* seeking to find a deep connection with spirit through your involvement with religious groups or your own personal spiritual or meditative practice. You may be moving in the direction of *physical mastery:* both dedicated to creating perfect health and fitness in yourselves and your family through the way you eat, exercise, and help others do the same. Your direction may be that of *creating peace on the planet:* contributing to the peace and harmony of your family, your friends, and improving the quality of life around you. Or your direction may be a blend of some or even all of these.

When your relationship has a direction, it takes on a new dimension. Imagine two people relating to each other, and their only purpose in being together is to have a partner. Their relationship looks like this:

Him ◄————————————————► Her

Now imagine two people in a relationship which also has as its purpose a direction in which the couple is moving together. Their relationship looks like this:

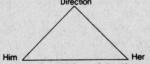

The energy in a relationship with direction moves outward and then back to the couple. The couple's mutual goal acts as a constant inspiration for growth and movement.

▶ The Problems That Develop When a Partner "Changes"

If you are growing and learning as you should be, you will not be the same person at thirty that you were at eighteen; you will not be the same person at forty-five that you were at thirty, and so on. The more you have dedicated yourself to self-discovery and self-knowledge, the more different these sequential "yous" will be. You may want different friends, different challenges in your work—and perhaps a different kind of relationship.

Here is where the trouble arises: Suppose you got married at twenty-two and, at the time, you were perfectly compatible with your husband. You wanted the same kind of life and had a similar direction: You both had goals of having a family and living a comfortable life. Now twenty-three years have passed. You are forty-five, and you have gone through a radical personal transformation. Your interests have shifted drastically from a more simple homelife to social contribution—suddenly, you have a new direction. This is your next step in personal development. There is only one problem: Your husband has little or no interest in this area. He is content to be doing what he is doing.

Millions of couples are faced with this dilemma at some time in their lives. The solution for many of them is the same: Ignore the fact that they are going in different directions, and just lead lives more separate from one another. In this case, the woman would begin to get involved with projects, career, or organizations in tune with her new direction, spending much of her time with people also moving in her direction. Her husband would become compartmentalized in a portion of her life marked "home and marriage." They would grow further and further apart. Perhaps she would eventually meet someone who was also involved in her new direction and be tempted to begin a relationship with him.

This marriage has turned into one of convenience. The partners are not growing in the same direction at approximately the same speed. Of course, it's unrealistic to expect your partner to share all your interests and grow at exactly the same pace you do. Differences can add dimension to a partnership. Only you can determine whether the new direction your growth or interests are taking is contributing to the relationship or creating distance and separation.

If you want a relationship that fulfills you on every level, however, you cannot ignore these life changes. The only solution is to sit down with your partner and talk honestly about what is happening. Tell him or her what direction you want to move in and ask what direction he wants to move in. You may find that your directions are close enough to blend together. Or you may find you are growing apart.

If you discover that you and a partner are moving in very different directions, you have a big decision to make:

1. You can choose to go in your direction *alone,* stay in the relationship, and accept that *just a part of you* can participate in being with your partner.
2. You can choose to end the relationship and find a new partner with whom you can travel in your direction *together.*

Problems With Decision One

Your partner may have a difficult time supporting your direction when it doesn't include him, thus taking you away from him. For example, your partner may resent your going to lectures, conferences, and weekend seminars on spirituality, complaining that you are never home and feeling threatened by your new friends. You will have a hard time resisting the temptation to try to convince your partner to "change" and travel with you, and he may end up feeling judged and pressured.

On the other hand, let's say you attempt to take your partner with you to conferences, lectures, and events. You try to engage him in conversation about your new interests, and the more disinterest he shows, the more upset and resentful you become. In this case, you don't feel fully loved and accepted by your partner because you cannot share all of yourself with him. Human beings have the compelling desire to merge completely with someone they love, to share all parts of themselves and have those parts be adored. This is impossible to do when you are moving in a direction completely different from one your partner is comfortable with.

The Divided Path

It's not easy to love and care very much for someone, and yet realize that your time together is up. You have traveled together on the same path happily and shared many wonderful moments. Suddenly, the single path divides into two, each going in a different direction. *For either of you to take the other's path would be a detour from your own destiny.*

This is the hardest kind of good-bye, because you are not separating from lack of love. You are separating because you are destined to travel in different directions.

I have arrived at the Divided Path several times in my life. I know the pain of having to leave behind someone I loved, and I know the pain of being left behind as I watched someone I loved take a new path that led away from me. Each time I suffered. Each time I grew. And each time my new path brought me greater happiness, wisdom, and love than I had ever known before. Through my journeys I have learned to trust my own path and its changes, for it has always led me to more and more of myself.

If you are on the Divided Path at this time in your life, either planning to go on or being left behind by someone, know that love will not abandon you. There is so much more waiting for you at the end of your own special path! Follow your heart in the direction it is leading you, and you will find everything you seek. And I know that along the way, you will bump into a fellow traveler going in your direction, who will be your perfect loving partner.

When You and Your Partner Are Traveling at Different Speeds

Naturally, you will never find a partner who is moving exactly at the same pace as you all the time, even if you are both growing in the same direction. We all have our own personal cycles of growth, rest, and integration. However:

If you and your partner are growing at very different speeds, it will create tremendous tension in the relationship.

Growing at very different speeds in the same direction is almost like growing in different directions or like not being compatible. *True compatibility includes not only the direction you are moving in but how quickly or slowly you choose to travel.*

Paula and Samuel had been married for ten years when they realized that they were traveling at very different speeds and that it was damaging their relationship. Both of them were very dedicated to personal growth. In college, where they met, Paula and Samuel took many of the same classes and spent hours discussing psychological theory. After they married and had a child, they occasionally attended a relationships seminar together, and still spent time talking once in a while about their relationship.

When Samuel turned thirty-five, he began to re-evaluate his life. He decided he was tired of working as an engineer and really wanted to devote himself to helping people. He began studying for a counseling degree, attending night school, personal growth semi-

nars, lectures, and weekend retreats. At first, Paula
was excited about Samuel's new interest and attended
one or two seminars with him. But when he announced
that he was quitting his job to devote all his time to
counseling, Paula became upset. "This isn't what we
had planned," she complained to Samuel. "You are
doing so well with your engineering, and now you want
to start all over again. I'm tired of you spending so
much time at these seminars."

"But I want you to be there with me," Samuel
pleaded. "I thought you really cared about growing and
communicating and helping people."

"I do care about it," Paula replied, "but not as
deeply as you do. I'm happy to read a book about it
once in a while. I want to grow, but the way you're
doing it is too intense for me."

*Paula and Samuel were traveling on the same
path, but suddenly they were going at very different
speeds.* Samuel had accelerated into high gear, and
Paula felt very uncomfortable with this. Samuel felt
unsupported by Paula, and Paula felt abandoned by
Samuel.

Who do you think is right? Of course, *the answer is
that they are both right:* Paula deserves a husband who
is happy to grow at her speed and doesn't push her to
make personal growth her mission in life. And Samuel
deserves a woman who is as dedicated to self-discovery as he is.

Some couples in this situation can compromise
without sacrificing their integrity. In Paula and Samuel's case, however, the tension produced by their differences overshadowed their love and closeness. They
weren't fulfilling each other's needs anymore.

Paula and Samuel's story had a happy ending,
though perhaps not a traditional one. They decided to
end their relationship, and Samuel went on to become
a therapist and consultant. Several years later he met a
woman who worked as an art therapist, and they mar-

ried. Paula went to school and got her real estate license and began doing very well selling real estate. Soon after, she met a man who owned his own business, and they married. Each found partners who were going in the same direction at the same speed.

▶ How to Tell When Your Relationship Is Over

Here are five steps to help you determine whether or not you should continue in a relationship you suspect may be over:

STEP ONE: Ask yourself *if you feel you are getting enough love from your partner.* Turn back to the first part of Chapter 17 and review the five reasons why you may be feeling unloved. Remember: If you feel unloved because (1) Your partner doesn't know how to show his love, (2) you are an expert at pushing love away, or (3) you and your partner are emotionally shut down due to the buildup of tension, then you have a chance of saving the relationship by using the tools in this book.

STEP TWO: Take time to think about *how compatible you and your partner are.* Make a Compatibility List and check your partner against it as I described earlier.

STEP THREE: Ask yourself *if you and your partner are going in the same direction at approximately the same speed.*

STEP FOUR: Sit down with your partner and *discuss Steps One, Two, and Three.* Only you *and* your partner can take an honest look at what is happening in the relationship. Make an agreement to keep talking until you have a clear idea of where your relationship stands.

STEP FIVE: *Seek professional help* to assist you in making your decision. Find a caring marriage counselor or therapist and share what you have learned from your own evaluation of the relationship. Sometimes it takes a third party to help you see things clearly.

▶ Beware of Tempting Reasons to Stay Together

In deciding whether or not it's time to end a relationship, you may find yourself "torn" for the following reasons. *Don't let them confuse you.*

1. You may be very compatible in one area, but not in another. You may find that you feel very loved and you are very compatible with your partner, but you are growing at different speeds. You may find that you are going in the same direction and are compatible, but that your partner can't give you the love you need. You may find that your partner loves you very much and wants to grow in the same direction, but that his or her personality just isn't compatible with yours anymore. I never said it would be easy.

Don't be fooled by how good one part of your relationship is. Remember: It takes *all three components* discussed in the previous chapter to make a relationship that will grow and last.

Some people will tell you, "Hey, you can't have everything." My answer to that is: "I am going to try to have everything, and I believe I can have everything I want in a relationship if I work hard enough on it with the right partner." I don't expect my partner to be perfect. But I *do* expect those three basic elements to be present *most* of the time.

2. You may still love your partner very much. If you haven't buried your love under suppressed anger and hurt, then *of course you will still love your partner, even if you are considering ending the relationship.* Love never dies. That special connection between yourself and another person will always be there on some level.

If you wait until you stop loving someone to end a troubled relationship, you may have to wait forever.

I have never stopped loving those I truly loved. I am no longer "in love" with them—which means I no longer invest time and energy in loving them. But in my heart I still feel love and appreciation for them.

------------------------▼------------------------

SECRET:
Love is not enough.

------------------------▲------------------------

Loving someone is not a good enough reason to be in a relationship with him. *Love alone will not make a relationship work*—you need the other two elements: compatibility and common direction. Many of us have been in relationships that ended even though we still loved our partners deeply, but we learned that love was not enough.

3. *You don't want to hurt the children.* This is a painful and difficult issue to consider when thinking of ending a marriage. No parent wants to be a source of unhappiness to their children, and the guilt that accompanies discussions about breaking up can be devastating.

I want you to know something I have discovered in all my work with children and adults:

Your personal unhappiness has a much more damaging effect on your children than your divorce ever could.

Children want to see their parents happy. They feel responsible for making their parents happy. If you stay in an unhappy marriage for the sake of the children, you will be causing them more emotional harm than if you divorce and find happiness elsewhere.

I have counseled thousands of grown-up "children" in my seminars and private practice and I have found this to be true: The children whose parents found love and happiness, either alone or with new partners, grow up feeling good about themselves and about their parents. *They have a healthy attitude toward love and relationships because they had positive role models for loving themselves and making love work.*

In contrast, some of the most unhappy people I work with are grown-up "children" whose parents stayed together in passionless, dead relationships, colored with suppressed anger and resentment. *These children develop a mistrust of love and relationships and an inability to express love or feel worthy of receiving it—all because they had negative role models for making love work.*

If your children see you being well loved, they will feel lovable. If your children see you being unloved, they will feel unlovable.

My parents stayed together for many years before finally divorcing when I was eleven. In my emotional healing work with myself, I have the most pain *not* from the actual divorce or the years that followed, but from the eleven years prior to that when I lived with two unhappy people. I felt responsible for not being able to make them happy.

When my mother remarried, and I saw her being loved, I was learning that I, too, deserved to have a man love me that much. Seeing both of my parents happy and well loved was more important to me than having all of us live together.

Divorce is not easy on children, and obviously, the

ideal is for children to grow up with the same mother and father in a happy home. However, if your relationship is not happy, your children are suffering from it. When you do what is best for the two of you, it will be the best for your children as well.

> Andy, age seven: "Mom and Dad used to scream a lot. Now Dad lives in another house and doesn't scream anymore. I miss him sometimes. But they both seem nicer now. Especially Mom, since she is seeing Phil. I like Phil, because Mom laughs a lot when she is with him."
>
> Jessica, age eleven: "My folks thought they were keeping their problems a secret for those years before the divorce, but my brother and I knew something was wrong. I cried when they finally told me. But things have gotten better. For one thing, my mom doesn't cry all the time anymore. I hated that. Now she takes better care of herself and I feel better about her."
>
> Amanda, age nine (when asked why she had been misbehaving so much): "If I am really bad, maybe Dad will leave. I know he wants to. But I heard him say he'd never leave because of me. But he always looks so sad. He never hugs Mommy anymore. I don't want him to be sad because he has to stay here with me."

▶ Some Important Do's and Don'ts About Breaking Up

Don'ts

1. *Don't complicate an already difficult situation by having an affair.* It is hard enough to figure out how you really feel about a partner without complicating it by bringing in a third party.

Never leave a relationship for another person— leave because the relationship isn't working.

Having an affair only masks the real problem: You aren't getting what you want from your partner. Resist the temptation, and use your desire as a warning signal that your relationship is in trouble. Use your energies either to heal or to complete the relationship with your partner.

2. *Don't wait until you feel nothing for your partner before you leave.* If you know your relationship isn't going to work, but you don't leave because you still feel a lot of love for your partner, here is what happens: The more time you spend together not getting what you want, the more resentment builds. At some point, you feel so resentful that you will become numb to your partner. Then it is easy to leave without hurting so much, and although waiting to leave until you feel nothing for your partner will help you avoid the pain of loss, it will have a negative effect on you and your partner in the long run:

A. You will do permanent damage to your relationship with your partner and to any friendship you might have after breaking up.
B. You will have numbed yourself emotionally and will carry this numbness into your next relationship.

3. *Don't try to avoid hurting your partner by leading him or her on.* One mistake I see couples make when in the process of ending a relationship is trying to "soften the blow" by leading their partners into thinking that things aren't so bad as they are, or that there is still hope, when they know deep inside that there isn't. If you know a relationship is over, don't take a month to tell your partner by leaking out bits and pieces of information. Tell the Complete Truth as soon as you are aware of it. It hurts less in the long run when you are honest than when you give your partner false hope. You are showing much more love and respect for your partner by being honest.

4. *Don't be influenced by the advice or criticism of well-meaning friends.* When you ask your friends for their opinion on whether or not you and your partner should break up, be prepared for their reactions. Your friends will advise you based on their own emotional circumstances. For instance, if you ask a woman who is likewise in a troubled relationship but isn't telling herself the truth about it, she will advise you to stay in your relationship and might even criticize you for being "picky." On the other hand, if you ask a woman who is single and bitterly jealous of any couple, she may advise you to leave based on her own envy.

The best adviser is that little voice inside your own heart.

5. *Don't wait until you feel 100 percent certain before making a decision.* One of the worst mistakes you can make is to stay stuck in a relationship until you feel completely certain and good about breaking up. No one ever feels good about breaking up, even when he *knows* it is right. You have a history with this person—emotional attachments and a strong sense of familiarity. It will never feel good to let go of that while you are doing it. There will always be that little voice of fear whispering in your head even as you say good-bye, "What if you never find anyone else? What if you are making a mistake?"

These fears are normal. Don't wait for them to disappear completely before deciding what to do, or you may wait forever. Once you have explored all your feelings and know in your mind that the relationship is over, you may have to ignore that fear long enough to do what you now need to do.

Do's for Breaking Up

1. *Do discuss all of your thoughts and feelings about your relationship as they come up with your partner, and not just with your friends.* Your partner

has a right to know if and when you are doubting the relationship and considering breaking up. The more you share with him or her, the better chance you have either of working through the problems and staying together, or of ending the relationship amicably. Don't wait until you have it "all figured out" from talking with a friend, and then dump it on your partner. Share your feelings and thoughts as they arise.

2. *Do let your children know what is going on.* If you don't discuss your feelings with your children, they will sense them anyway and blame themselves for the tension they are feeling in the house. Children are more frightened of what they don't know than of the facts, no matter how painful. Let them know that "Mommy and Daddy aren't getting along and are discussing what to do so that everyone is happy." You'd be surprised how much love and support your children can give you when you need it. When they feel included, they will be less hurt if you do break up.

3. *Do reach out for help.* We often find it difficult to share our heartaches with others, wanting only to show them our strong, happy side. During a breakup, it is important for you to reach out to others for love and support. Don't hide what is happening from friends and family. You may not want their advice, but their caring will help make this difficult time easier. A marriage counselor, therapist, or support group can also be very helpful.

Letting go is never easy. But letting go with love will help you and your partner to heal your hearts more quickly so you can go on and find the love you both deserve.

19

Breaking Up Without Breaking Down: The Four Stages of Recovery

Working with thousands of people and remembering my own personal experience has led me to the conclusion that breaking up involves four inevitable stages of recovery. These stages take approximately one to two years to complete, although, of course, this can vary. And the interesting thing is that these stages are unavoidable. You can put off breaking up and try to escape the inevitable recovery, but you won't succeed. The sooner you decide to end the relationship and start the recovery process, the sooner you will be free of pain.

Stage One: The Tearing Apart
Duration: two weeks to two months

When you love another person, you merge your hopes, your dreams, your energies, and your heart with that person's. When you end the relationship, you go through a process I call the Tearing Apart, because that is how it feels—like a part of you is being torn away. Even if you *want* that familiar person out of your life, you will still experience the Tearing Apart. *The longer you have been together, the longer the Tearing Apart will last.*

Characteristics of the Tearing Apart

> You feel lost and alone.
> You cry a lot.
> You feel hopeless.
> You may lose your appetite.
> You feel a constant pain or ache in your heart.
> You are swamped with painful memories and nostalgia.
> You have a hard time imagining a happy future.
> You are tempted to return to your ex-partner.
> You have a difficult time just getting through each day.
> You feel very sorry for yourself.

The Tearing Apart is the hardest part of breaking up. It feels as though it will never end—but it will.

Tips for Getting Through Stage One

1. *Let yourself cry and mourn as much as possible.* Don't hold it in, or it will take longer to pass.

2. *Keep busy and spend time with friends and family.* Schedule yourself way in advance to avoid those melancholy weekends when you sit home doing nothing and feeling miserable.

3. *Take good care of your body.* The more you rest, eat well, and exercise, the better you will feel physically, and this will help you to feel psychologically stable. *Avoid drugs, alcohol, and heavy doses of sugar,* all of which will be tempting, but will just add to your sensitivity and depression.

4. *Avoid spending a lot of time seeing or talking with your ex-partner.* You will be tempted to call or see

your ex-partner when you are feeling alone or frightened. *Don't do it!* Give each other the space to feel who you are separate from one another. The more you stay connected, the longer Stage One takes. Later you will have time to re-form your relationship under different terms.

Stage Two: The Adjustment
Duration: two to six months

You know you have entered Stage Two when you actually start feeling good for a few days at a time. *The most intense pain of Tearing Apart is over. Now it is time to adjust to your new life without your partner.* You begin to re-form your personality and identity as a single person. You get your life back in order; you start to bond with other people. You begin looking ahead to the future.

Characteristics of the Adjustment

You begin making plans for the future.

You notice yourself having fun again.

You can talk or think about your partner without feeling you will fall apart or get angry.

You no longer feel as much like a victim.

You begin noticing attractive people you'd like to meet.

You cry or feel intensely melancholy less frequently—maybe once or twice a week.

You begin settling things legally and materially with your partner.

You have a clearer perspective on what went wrong.

Stage Three: Healing
Duration: six months to one year

Stage Three sees your life becoming normal again. You no longer feel as if you are in transition—you are recovering from the painful time and feeling better every day. You may be involved in a new relationship or interested in beginning one. You will have much of your business with your partner settled or on the way to being settled. *You have survived!* Now you are healing the wounds and becoming whole again.

Characteristics of Healing

You are in or interested in a new relationship.

You feel and look better than you have in a while.

You can talk with your partner without getting upset.

You feel positive about the rightness of what has happened.

You feel enthusiastic about what is ahead.

You feel sad or nostalgic less often—maybe once a week or every two weeks.

You work to understand what went wrong and what you want to make happen in future relationships.

Stage Four: Recovery
Duration: one to two years

Stage Four is a transitional stage in which you clear out any remaining pain from the relationship you have ended, and firmly establish yourself in your new life. You no longer think of yourself as having just ended a relationship. By now, you have a new social structure around you—new friends, new love interests, new directions in your life. You and your ex-partner have settled into a new kind of relationship with each other which should feel fairly comfortable most of the time. *Your new life has begun. Enjoy it!*

Characteristics of Recovery

> You have adopted new habits and ways of behaving as a result of the mistakes you made in the previous relationship.
> People no longer ask you how you are doing all the time.
> You are ready to love and be loved again.
> You occasionally think of your former partner and perhaps feel nostalgic a few times a month.
> You feel happy in your new life.

Going through these four stages can take one year, or it can take five. It all depends on how willing you are to let go of the past, work through your feelings, and use the tools in this book to heal your hurt and disappointment about your relationship not lasting. It still won't be easy, but it won't last forever, and before you know it, you *will* be loved again.

▶ Healing Your Relationship With Your Partner

Part of the process of recovering from a relationship involves healing with your partner.

> *If you don't heal your negative feelings toward your former partner, you will carry those feelings into your next relationship.*

You know you haven't healed with your partner when:

1. You still *blame* him/her for what happened.
2. You say *negative things* about him/her to friends.
3. You feel like a *victim*.

4. You want *revenge,* or to see him/her unhappy.
5. You feel what happened wasn't *fair.*
6. You are *angry at all men or all women* because of what your partner did.
7. You feel as though you *wasted your time in the relationship.*

How to Heal Your Relationship With Your Former Partner

1. Write Love Letters to him from you, and Love Letters to yourself from him, until you have *released the negative feelings and feel the love and understanding again.* (See Chapter 9.)

2. Think and talk about what happened with friends, a therapist, or your partner (if possible) until you fully understand how *you were equally responsible* for how the relationship turned out.

3. Write yourself a Love Letter about all the mistakes *you* made in the relationship, until you *forgive yourself fully.*

4. Write or speak with your partner and *ask him to forgive you* for any way in which you weren't truthful, loving, or supportive.

5. Work with all the tools you have, with a therapist, or with your partner to *understand his behavior, and forgive him* for not giving you what you wanted.

The sooner you truly forgive yourself and your partner, the sooner you will attract a new loving relationship into your life.

Remember: Forgiveness doesn't mean pushing down all the negative feelings and just saying "It's okay—I forgive you." It means working through the anger, hurt, fear, and guilt until you find your love and caring for this other human being. *Don't be in a hurry to heal.* Do what you need to do to come to a state of true understanding and forgiveness.

Some people confuse forgiveness with approval: "I forgive you for cheating on me—it's okay that you did that." Forgiveness does *not* mean that you approve of what someone did. It simply means that you can understand what motivated him, can see how you allowed yourself to be a part of what happened, and can wish him well and hope he will grow into a better, more loving person from the experience.

When you forgive others for their imperfections, you forgive yourself for your own.

Healing a relationship with a former partner doesn't necessarily mean that you will be good friends afterwards—just that *you have released and resolved the negative feelings and come to a place of understanding and forgiveness.*

In my own life I have gone through two major relationship breakups. In the first one my former partner wasn't willing to stay in communication with me after our initial split. I decided to do a lot of healing on my own, and wrote many letters to my partner, telling him of my realizations, forgiving him and asking his forgiveness. Several years passed, and I never got any response to the letters. I was determined to keep reaching out until I felt understood and forgiven.

Last year I received a Christmas card at my office addressed in a handwriting that looked familiar. Suddenly, I realized it was a card from my former husband. I tore the envelope open and read the message that I had waited to hear for so long: "All is forgiven and forgotten. I wish you only love, joy, and peace in your life."

Reading those words, I felt as if a ton of bricks had been lifted from my heart, and in that moment I realized again how essential it is for us to heal our past relationships, no matter how long it takes.

In the second big breakup of my life I was more fortunate—my partner and I both worked very hard to heal our relationship, and came to a place of forgiving ourselves and one another. Today we are close friends.

You are the winner when you work on healing your past relationships.

20

How to Avoid Relationship Burnout

Each time you end a relationship, *it is important to understand what went wrong and what mistakes you made*. If you don't, you may become a victim of "Relationship Burnout."

Here are the symptoms of Relationship Burnout:
- You feel that relationships are too much trouble.
- You feel that you can't trust anyone.
- You feel cynical when hearing how happy other couples are.
- You convince yourself that you enjoy being alone more than being in a relationship.
- You feel your past relationships were a waste of time.
- You feel all men or women are "the same" and will disappoint you in the same ways.
- Your idea of companionship is owning a dog or some other pet.

As we've seen throughout this book, relationships don't just "go bad"—*it is you who are responsible for choosing an incompatible partner or not knowing how to make love work.* This is why it's essential to evaluate yourself after ending a relationship so you can learn from your mistakes.

I suggest you *make a list of all of the mistakes you made in the relationship* and think of ways you can avoid making them the next time.

Robert came to see me because he felt depressed and lonely. "I got divorced last year," he began, "and I feel so disillusioned with love and relationships that I can't seem to get excited about seeing anyone." Robert was suffering from Relationship Burnout—he didn't understand what had gone wrong, and so he blamed it on relationships.

I asked Robert to make a Relationship Mistake List, starting from his first date with his wife:

1. I got a charge out of being impressive during our first dates rather than finding out more about her.
2. I liked feeling smarter than she was.
3. I ignored the fact that we talked only about superficial things.
4. I ignored the fact that she never talked about her family or her feelings.
5. I was overly impressed with her looks.
6. I suppressed my resentment of her disinterest in reading and learning.
7. I ignored her lack of independence and told myself it was nice to have someone to need me so much.
8. I carried most of our conversations.
9. I ignored the fact that she was sexually passive.
10. I ignored the fact that my friends didn't wholly respect and admire her.

11. I didn't tell her the truth about my feelings of resentment.
12. I tried to convince myself that I couldn't find a woman who was beautiful *and* intelligent, and that I should be happy with what I had.

When Robert read his Mistake List, it was obvious to him why the marriage hadn't worked. *The same problems that sprang up later in the relationship had been apparent on their first few dates, but Robert had ignored them.* Now Robert had a good idea of what his weaknesses were in relating to women. The next time he has a relationship, he can pay attention to these areas and avoid making the same mistakes he made before. Robert felt much more positive about starting a new relationship after making his Mistake List, because he realized that he didn't have to repeat his old patterns if he didn't want to. He learned that *he*, and not the relationship, dictates what happens, so there was no reason to blame or avoid relationships in the future.

If you are suffering from Relationship Burnout, try the following:

1. Make a Relationship Mistake List for every relationship you've been in.
2. Make a Relationship Rule Book for yourself based on the first list.
3. Read the second list before and after every date to review your behavior.

Here is an excerpt from Robert's Relationship Rule Book.

1. Never talk more than your date.
2. Find out how intelligent your date is by asking her questions about politics, philosophy, etc.
3. Ask your date about her family and past relationships. *Don't go out with anyone who dislikes her parents.*

4. Make sure your date is interested in reading and learning.
5. Make sure you feel comfortable being with your date and your friends—be sure that she fits in.
6. Tell the truth about your feelings from the beginning.
7. If your date makes you feel like a big strong man who is protecting her, run fast in the other direction.

I know you will have fun making your own Mistake List and your Relationship Rule Book, and I hope these tools help you to recover from Relationship Burnout.

▶ Finding Your Dreams Again

You've read this chapter, you've checked your relationship for compatibility, feeling loved, and direction, and you've decided to end it. You are going through the four recovery stages; you've made your Mistake List and your Rule Book. But somehow you still feel hollow. What is missing?

You have lost your dreams of love and need to find them again.

Often when a relationship dies, our dream of love dies with it. We offer all our hopes and fantasies to the person with whom we fall in love, and when we admit to ourselves that the relationship cannot work, we leave not only the person but our dreams as well. We forget to take our dreams back. It is not your dreams that have failed you—*it is your relationship.*

Imagine owning a beautiful guitar and dreaming that one day you will hear someone play that guitar and make heavenly music echo from its strings while you sing along. The years pass; you meet different people, and when you hand them the guitar, they either don't know how to play it or they play melodies that sound terrible. Each time a new musician picks up that guitar, your hope of hearing its lovely sounds becomes dimmer and dimmer, until one day you decide that the guitar must be no good, and you don't even bother retrieving it from the musician who most recently attempted to play it. Nothing is wrong with the guitar—the musicians you chose just weren't suited for that instrument.

Similarly, nothing is wrong with your dreams of love and a lasting relationship—it's your choice of inappropriate partners and your lack of knowledge about how to make love work that has caused your dreams to seem so unattainable.

Don't leave your dreams of love buried in the disappointment of past relationships. *Take your dreams back.* Brush them off, and, strengthened by your new knowledge, start on your search again. This time you have a much clearer idea of whom you are looking for and of what to do when you find him. It *is* possible to make love work. You don't deserve anything less. And somewhere out there is another wandering musician, carrying his own battered but beautiful dream, searching for you. Together, you can make beautiful music. Corny? Well, a little. But all dreams sound corny—until they come true.

PART FIVE

▼▼▼▼▼▼▼▼▼▼▼▼▼▼▼▼▼▼▼▼▼▼▼▼▼▼▼▼▼▼▼▼

Secrets for Making Love All the Time

▲▲▲▲▲▲▲▲▲▲▲▲▲▲▲▲▲▲▲▲▲▲▲▲▲▲▲▲▲▲

21

Living in Love: The Ultimate Relationship

Love bridges the gap between yourself and the universe around you. *When you are living in love, you no longer live in a world of a million separations, but of a million connections.* You are in a loving relationship with everything.

A loving, growing relationship is the ideal "teacher" to develop you into a person who is truly *living in love*. You have learned to find the love beneath anger, hurt, and fear; you are reaching from behind your walls of pride to extend your heart to the person you love. Most of all, you are committed to creating love and harmony where there appears to be none.

Your relationship with your intimate partner becomes a microcosm for your relationship to the rest of the world. And the purpose of your relationship with the world becomes the same as the purpose of your relationship with your partner: to bring out the goodness in that which you love, and, through your loving it, raise it to the greatest expression of its own magnificence.

Experiencing your relationship to the whole of life brings you tremendous spiritual peace. You no longer are living in a separate bubble, but feel an important and inseparable part of the universe. This sense of connection is the truth of life—it is the unity of all things that spiritual teachers have talked about.

▶ My Story's Happy Ending

When I was a child, I had very powerful dreams of a world in which everyone lived in peace and love. Instead, I saw a world full of violence, bigotry, and ignorance. Instead of the loving, caring people I longed to find, I saw angry, frightened, and emotionally shut-down grown-ups. As I grew older, I became very cynical and told myself I didn't care about anything; that nothing real mattered.

Then one day I had a powerful revelation. I realized that *I had the power to change the world around me by how I decided to live my life. I was the solution,* just as each of you is. I decided to dedicate my life to creating peace on our planet. I became a therapist and a teacher, and eventually created Making Love Work: Personal Growth Seminars. Each weekend I would help a hundred people struggle through the maze of their emotions until they found the tremendous source of love inside themselves once again. I'd see couples find their passion for each other underneath the numbness; I'd witness parents and children listening to each other for the first time. I'd see people find the courage to tell themselves the truth, and regain their powers of love and integrity. And each weekend I would feel fulfilled to know that the world had one hundred fewer problems, and one hundred more solutions! They were becoming peacemakers by learning that peace begins at home.

As the years passed, I began to notice a powerful transformation in my own awareness. I used to feel quite a contrast between being with my seminar participants on a Sunday evening after the course was over—all feeling so much in love—and interacting with the rest of the world on Monday. Slowly, however, I began to experience that same blissful feeling of connection wherever I was, and with whomever I spent time. I saw the love inside of people longing to come out. Their walls of protection and fear appeared transparent to me. And somehow they felt this when we were together, and their hearts would begin to open.

I was beginning to live in love, and what a joy it is! It took me many travels down dark roads and many heartaches to get here, but the journey was worth it. I am making love all the time in my life, and I feel privileged to be helping so many of you to do the same.

▶ Your Story's Happy Ending

You may be thinking to yourself, "This all sounds wonderful, but I'll never achieve this loving state." I want you to know that *you have already started*. You have taken the first step by reading this book and being willing to make love work a little better in your life. The next step is to practice the principles and techniques in this book. When you do, you will begin to notice that it becomes easier and easier to live in love and increasingly unacceptable to live any other way. Thousands of people already have used this knowledge to transform their lives, and I know you can, too.

Living in love means:

- Seeing the love in all people, even when they can't see it themselves
- Seeing through the walls of anger, hurt, and fear in others, and understanding their source
- Helping to connect others to the love inside of them
- Having the courage to be an example of loving

presence, and to keep trying until you get through to someone's heart

When you are in a relationship with the world, your joys are multiplied a thousandfold. The world becomes a wonderful mirror, reflecting your own loving spirit back to you. Life turns into an exciting adventure dedicated to discovering love in everyone and in every situation.

▶ The Miracle of Love

Imagine for a moment that you have come to the end of your life. You find yourself in a large white room, waiting to be interviewed by God to determine whether or not you will be accepted into Heaven.

God enters and asks you to sit down at a white desk. He hands you a piece of paper with one question on it and asks you to answer it. Based on your response, He will make His decision regarding the future of your soul.

What do you think that question would be? Think about it for a moment. Do you think God would ask, "How much did you net after taxes in 1986?" or "How much money did you spend on yourself and your children?" or "How many times were you right in an argument?" or "How fashionable was your wardrobe?" No . . . I think the question on that piece of paper would be: "How well did you love?"

How well did you love? How many people's lives did you touch for the better? How many times did you bring happiness to someone's heart? When people were around you, did they feel uplifted, or upset? *Were you part of the problem or part of the solution?*

If each of us asked ourselves this question every day, and made a commitment to be a living example of the peace and love we so desperately want for the rest of the planet, our world would be transformed.

Life is truly a miracle.

And the ability to love is the greatest gift you have been given.

Celebrate the miracle of life by cherishing every moment of it.

Celebrate the gift of love by living *in* love and living *as* love.

And then you will become the miracle . . .

And the earth will be blessed with peace . . .

Index

SEMINARS WITH
BARBARA De ANGELIS, Ph.D.

© Matthew Rolstor

All of Barbara De Angelis's books have been inspired by the experiences of thousands of people who have undergone a powerful transformation after attending her workshops and seminars. Barbara is highly sought after for lectures, conferences and speaking engagements throughout the world, and in her own unique, dynamic and entertaining style, uplifts and motivates audiences on the topics of love, relationships and personal growth.

If you would like to receive a schedule of Barbara's seminars in your area, or contact her to set up an event, please call or write: